The Art of
Dance in
Education

The Art of Dance in Education

Second edition

Jacqueline M. Smith-Autard

BLOOMSBURY

LONDON • NEW DELHI • NEW YORK • SYDNEY

Bloomsbury Methuen Drama
An imprint of Bloomsbury Publishing Plc

50 Bedford Square	1385 Broadway
London	New York
WC1B 3DP	NY 10018
UK	USA

www.bloomsbury.com

First edition published 1994
Second edition 2002
Reprinted 2009, 2010 (twice), 2011, 2013

British Library Cataloguing-in-Publication Data
A catalogue record for this book is available from the British Library.

ISBN: PB:	978-0-7136-6175-0
ePDF:	978-1-4081-1688-3
ePub:	978-1-4081-0318-0

Library of Congress Cataloging-in-Publication Data
A catalog record for this book is available from the Library of Congress.

Typeset 10/12 pt Palatino
Printed and bound in Great Britain

Contents

Acknowledgements

I am indebted to Jim Schofield, my partner in Bedford Interactive Research. His brilliant insight and creativity in inventing new multimedia techniques to support my ideas for the delivery of the art of dance in education has led to publication of the world-leading CD-i/CD ROM resource pack – *Wild Child* (1999/2001). Twelve years of research and several projects undertaken with funding gratefully received from the Foundation for Sport and the Arts and the Arts Council of England in particular, have permitted me to put into practice the theory related to resource-based teaching and learning that was presented in the first edition of this book. In fact, this understates the developments made in my own pedagogy, because there is no doubt that working with Jim in finding ways to use multimedia to expose the intricacies in dance aided by multimedia has deepened and enhanced my own teaching.

Evidence of this has been gained in many different venues and working with children and students in primary, secondary and tertiary education. To this end, I am grateful to the teachers and students in the schools, colleges and universities that have invited me to demonstrate the use of *Wild Child* in practical and/or theory dance lessons. These lessons in the UK, Ireland, Sweden, Finland, Australia, Canada and the USA have confirmed that visual analysis of a professional dance resource leads students to quickly produce creative work that shows understanding of the concepts and principles learned. For example, a one-hour lesson delivered to year 9 students in many different schools has resulted in them understanding the concepts of abstraction, symbolism, motif, repetition, development and transition. These lessons have also witnessed students' improvement in performance qualities through learning how to aesthetically perceive the dance exemplar on the multimedia resource.

Knowledge gained from the above research and experiences in the use of technology to greatly benefit teaching and learning has, I believe, expanded the ideas presented in this book. Certainly, the sections on resource-based teaching/learning provide many more practical examples to support the theoretical bases. In this regard, use of the Ludus Dance Company's *Wild Child*, choreographed by Jane Scott-Barrett and produced as a CD-i/CD ROM Resource Pack by Bedford Interactive Productions Ltd, is also gratefully acknowledged.

Preface

The aim of this book is to present a theoretical basis for the art of dance in education and to demonstrate how it applies to current practice. To date, there is no one text that provides a theoretical framework to support dance education practice. This text fills the gap in offering teachers a thoroughly-argued rationale and a means of developing a clearer understanding of what and how to teach the art of dance in education. It is *not* concerned with other types of dance, e.g. social or folk dance, and their role in education.

The focus in this book is on schools, colleges and universities (state or private) which offer full-time education and form part of the national provision for compulsory education between the ages of five to sixteen, or for further and higher education for those wishing to continue. (The book is also relevant to adult education where this provides the content offered in full-time education.)

There is no attempt to discuss the part-time opportunities for dance experiences offered by dance schools, clubs, youth groups or even by extra-curricular dance activities at the above-mentioned schools and colleges. Vocational schools are also excluded, even those offering full-time education, because they do not normally offer the *curriculum* art of dance experience that is under scrutiny here. The focus is, therefore, on schools, colleges and universities, and what occurs in the name of dance within curriculum time.

The first edition of this book was in process for a number of years prior to publication in 1994. The foundational premise that the art of dance in education is best considered as a *midway* model combining the best practices of two opposing models was first proposed in my master's dissertation (1977). This work developed out of an initial exploration of the concept of dance as art discussed in *Dance Composition* (1976), in which the three-stranded process of creating, performing and appreciating dances was identified. In this new edition of *The Art of Dance in Education*, in subsequent editions of *Dance Composition* (1992, 1996 and 2000), in articles and reports of conference preceedings, these ideas have been developed and extended – much informed by practical experience in teaching dance across the sectors: primary, secondary and tertiary education.

In providing a theoretical basis and a detailed exposé of contents and methods of teaching the midway art of dance in education model, the second edition of this book is now even more relevant for teachers and lecturers. At school level, particularly in the UK, the marginalisation of dance within physical education has reduced the content in the National Curriculum to a seemingly very poor level of provision, both quantitively and qualitatively. Although schools and teachers can interpret and extend the broad-outline syllabus statements more or less how they wish, the overloaded curriculum is unlikely to permit more provision than the minimal statutory requirements. However, all recent texts other than the National Curriculum Orders, place importance on the dance experience in schools being inclusive in its delivery of the art of dance as defined in this book. This is endorsed in a report produced by Her Majesty's Inspectors for schools, *The Arts Inspected – Good Teaching in Art, Dance, Drama and Music* (1998: 29):

> Dance is a discipline that requires pupils to compose and to explore ideas, improvise solutions to problems, select the most appropriate actions and shape movements into dance phrases and motifs, and practise and refine their work. This is preparation for controlled performance which combines technical competence and appropriately rehearsed interpretation of a theme. Being able to comment critically on a finished dance or work in progress requires observation and analytical skills, knowledge of appropriate criteria, and understanding of the different styles and forms of dance.
>
> Gordon Clay HMI

Clearly, the three-stranded process of creating, performing and appreciating dances is confirmed here, and further government or government-sponsored publications[1] reinforce these organising principles as central in the art of dance in education.

---

[1]Department for Education and Employment, *All our Futures: Creativity, Culture and Education* (1999) National Foundation for Educational Research, The Arts Council for England and the Royal Society for the Arts, *Arts Education in Secondary Schools: Effects and Effectiveness*, 2000.

This edition's greater emphasis on the use of information technology to deliver primary, secondary and tertiary dance education through a resource-based teaching and learning methodology, is also endorsed as 'good practice' for all teachers by the Teacher Training Agency for England and Wales[2].

At the tertiary education level there is continued consensus of agreement that study of the art of dance includes the practical creation and presentation of dance combined with a range of related theoretical study. The various combinations of practice and theory are too extensive to mention here, but suffice it to say that application of the theoretical implications of the *midway* art of dance model is as important now as it was in 1994. The Quality Assurance Agency for Higher Education has produced benchmarking statements that support this claim[3].

It is clear, therefore, that the content and teaching methods discussed in this book will remain relevant for teachers in the UK and abroad for many years to come.

[2]Teacher Training Agency, *Using information technology to meet teaching objectives in physical education initial teacher training*, 1999.
[3]See http://www.qaa.ac.uk   Click on current work then Benchmarking. The final Benchmarking Standards for Dance, Drama and Performance in Higher Education are due to be published in March 2002.

Introduction

Dance is a broad term which covers many varied activities and dance is performed for many reasons. The need here is to make clear what the term the *art of dance* has come to mean in dance education parlance over the past thirty-five years. This period has seen significant changes in dance in education. An outline of these changes has been written elsewhere[1] and chapter 1 summarises the essential details for the purpose of this text.

The term *art* is also much debated in philosophical treatises. Here the concern is not with the meaning of art as a concept but with the meaning that the word has when it prefaces or follows the term *dance*. In education, the *art of dance* or, perhaps more commonly, *dance as art* has been a label used to distinguish content and approaches which are different from those associated with former terms such as *modern educational dance, creative dance* or *expressive dance*.

Changes in recent years have made it helpful to use the qualifying noun of *art* with *dance*. Dance as art shares the characteristics of other forms of art such as painting, poetry, music and drama. It puts dance alongside other arts in the production of objects for aesthetic enjoyment. This is, of course, not the only function of art works but it is an important and distinguishing one. It also brings into focus the processes of creating, performing and appreciating. Indeed, in education these processes are key factors in determining teaching and learning programmes. Even the youngest pupils can engage in creating, performing and appreciating dances. Dance art works are not only publicly acknowledged professional performances but also the dances that children make for themselves.

In education, then, the art of dance is centrally concerned with the creating, performing and appreciating of art works that cannot be

---

[1] *Dance Composition*, fourth edition, Jacqueline Smith-Autard, 2000.

produced in a vacuum. As in other arts, reference is made to publicly recognised examples of dance works of which pupils must become aware. This requires some contact with the professional world of dance which was ignored in former school or college dance practice.

Chapter 1 defines and analyses the *midway* art of dance in education model, examining the features that it has retained from other models and those that are new and distinctive. This analysis exposes the underlying theory of the art of dance in education.

Chapters 2 and 3 apply the theoretical framework to teaching and learning dance in primary and secondary education. In both these chapters one example dance outcome is scrutinised in relation to the *midway* art of dance model, as well as proposed syllabuses for dance that can be delivered in stages 1–4 for the five to sixteen age range and syllabuses for dance examinations for the sixteen to nineteen age range.

Chapter 4 applies to tertiary education the theoretical framework underpinning the *midway* art of dance model. In this context, dance modules typically offered as part of modular degree courses are examined. Since a number of modules are discussed in this chapter, no further examples are included in the appendix.

The appendix contains further examples of work suitable for the primary and secondary age range and includes reference to the use of multimedia resources in delivery of the *midway* art of dance model.

1

The Art of Dance in Education – A Theoretical Basis

Models for teaching should always be dynamic and constantly changing, so to define and promote any one model for teaching may seem over-prescriptive.

Processes of change, however, often occur in practice well before any model can be defined, and indeed, new practice has to develop before it is possible to reflect on its nature. When the new practice has been tried and tested by teachers and students it becomes necessary to define and promulgate the practice and theories which underpin it in order that it becomes known and developed as a valued model for teaching. The model then becomes reinforced through initial teacher training, in-service courses and texts for teachers, so disseminating and developing its aims, contents, methodologies and processes of assessment.

The dominant and most advocated model for dance education today has been labelled the *dance as art* model (in this book it is called the *art of dance* model). This is the model which I proposed in 1976 in my book *Dance Composition* and which was strongly advocated in the subsequent Calouste Gulbenkian Foundation report *Dance Education and Training in Britain* (1980). It is also the model implicit in the UK National Curriculum (2000), GCSE, AS and A level syllabuses (2001–2) for schools and in current degree courses in universities. The *art of dance* model seems thus to have been confirmed as a model of 'good practice'.

As we have seen, the art of dance model did not emerge suddenly – it has taken at least twenty years to develop. One of the first dance theoreticians to propose it was Betty Redfern (1972), but the content and methods of teaching emerged gradually and have been the main focus of my work since 1965. The theoretical basis of the art of dance model presented below is the result of my reflection on the

3

nature of current practice in dance education and is grounded in much experience and trial of different approaches. Although it has new and unique features of its own, it has retained elements of the two models which preceded it. For this reason, although the old elements are reoriented, it can be called a *midway* model.

Predecessors of the art of dance model

The somewhat 'free', 'open' and 'child-centred' approach which has been variously labelled *modern educational dance, creative dance,* and the like, was derived from Rudolf Laban's ideas in the late 1940s and lasted as the consensus practice until the early 1970s. The essential characteristic of his 'educational' model was its emphasis on the *process of dancing and its affective/experiential contribution to the participant's overall development as a moving/feeling being.* The benefits of feeling personal expressive significance in movement outcomes derived from various stimuli were considered important contributions to the all-round development of the personality. Here, emphasis was laid equally on the physical, emotional and social dimensions of the personality, the development of which might be fostered in dance movement situations in which spontaneous individual responses were complemented by group work where interaction through movement was the aim. In particular, the stress was on a meaningful *process* rather than on the outcome or *product* that might emerge.

The opposing model which influenced much of what was going on in dance education in secondary schools, further and higher education colleges in the 1960s and 1970s, could be called the *professional* model, in that the main aim was to produce highly skilled dancers and theatrically defined dance products for presentation to audiences. Such dance outcomes would be considered as vehicles through which the range of dance skills constituting any one style could be exhibited. The content of such courses was an already-defined set of dance skills in the style of dance being studied, e.g. Graham, Cunningham, ballet or jazz. If time allowed, the prescribed formulae for choreography as laid down by American contemporary dance teachers such as Humphrey and H'Doubler were also included. This very particular approach was apparent until the late 1970s in *some* quarters of dance education (though the majority of school teachers, especially primary teachers, still held to the Laban *educational* model). Of course, there was much criticism of those who adopted the *professional* training model, especially since the prescribed techniques needed time spent on body training leaving no time for creative work in the short periods of dance allowed in secondary schools. This *product-based* model is that which is used fully and expertly by our professional dance training schools and colleges where the aim is to produce dancers as performers. Such a form of dance education is surely not suited to the majority.

A MIDWAY MODEL

Today's *midway* model amalgamates some of the elements of the *educational* and *professional* models, yet includes new ideas, too. Its distinctiveness lies in the concept of the art of dance in education contributing towards artistic education, aesthetic education and cultural education. It identifies the three strands of creating, performing and appreciating dances as the conceptual basis underlying dance experiences for pupils. The need for balance between creating, performing and viewing dances, on the one hand, and an overall concern, on the other, that pupils come to appreciate dances (their own and those produced professionally) as art works, became the central organising principle of dance education in the 1980s and beyond.

In order that we understand, why, for me, the model is labelled the *midway* model, a list of features which, to a lesser or greater degree, it retains from its predecessors is presented on page 6. This is followed by discussion of each of them and the modification or reorientation that has occurred because of the changes in the conceptual basis for the art of dance in education. Central themes of each of the past models have been listed and the ensuing discussion demonstrates how the art of dance model has laid equal emphasis on these previously opposing concepts.

Process versus product

Emphasis on process

The *educational* dance model was often regarded as an instrumental means of permitting the expression of the individual's personality in the process of dancing. Attention was paid to the subjective experience of creating and expressing during the act of dancing rather than to the object created. The object, if there was one as outcome of the dance experience, was judged more in terms of personal gains: for example, sense of satisfaction, release of emotions, feelings of joy. Laban's emphasis on process as an important feature of dance

Table of features retained from the **educational** *and* **professional** *models.*

EDUCATIONAL MODEL	PROFESSIONAL MODEL
Emphasis on the process	Emphasis on the product
Emphasis on development of creativity, imagination and individuality	Emphasis on knowledge of theatre dance as the model towards which to aspire
Emphasis on feelings – subjectivity of experience	Emphasis on objective ends – e.g. trained bodies for performance of dances
Emphasis on a set of principles as a source of content	Emphasis on stylistically defined dance techniques as content
Emphasis on a problem-solving approach to teaching – teacher as guide, pupil as agent in own learning	Emphasis on directed teaching – teacher as expert, pupil as apprentice

education encompasses elements of a romantic ideology, with dance as a means through which the individual may become aware of him/ herself, develop creative/expressive abilities and social skills in group work. This makes the process of creating and performing dance totally subjective and, as Best (1985) states, 'impossible to assess and educate'. Best goes on to argue that mental processes involved in creative work which cannot be seen and cannot be judged except through the end products. Similarly, in the context of performance, no matter how wonderful the process feels to the performer, there is surely concern for what is produced in terms of aesthetic and artistic appeal.

The view that it is process alone which counts and that the product is immaterial cannot be considered viable, especially in the current educational climate which emphasises evaluation, assessment of attainment and teacher accountability. Indeed, to place importance on an intangible and immeasurable process would have put dance into a vulnerable position within the school, college and university syllabuses in the 1980s and beyond, in which measured achievement in terms of skills, knowledge and understanding is paramount.

The quality of the process then should be reflected in the quality of the product. This means that the process skills of creativity, for example, can only be judged as indicative of originality, flexibility, flair or inventiveness, if the product has signs of these qualities. Such a judgement is to be made in relation to other products generated by the individual, by peers or by artists of recognised status in the public world, whichever is the most appropriate.

Similarly, the process skills of performance such as focus, character-isation, projection of meaning and artistry cannot be assessed without reference to shared knowledge of such criteria.

Emphasis on product

As indicated above, the central idea underlying the use of the *professional* model in secondary schools and colleges in the 1960s and 1970s, was that adolescents and young adults were ready and had a need for the development of technical skills. Teachers in Britain adopted this model primarily because the *educational* model had no identifiable skill repertoire. Their aims, it appeared, were to secure motivation and enjoyment of dance through the professional aura of technical classes, students identifying such work with theatrical dance, which was becoming more and more accessible through television, theatre and visits of artists in schools. It was believed that by this means the dance experience would become more relevant because the ends, even if unattainable for most, were identifiable.

To achieve a theatrically-styled and skilled performance level was the emphasised product of the *professional* model. This was the main aim even if other goals, such as development of imaginative and creative responses, were not met. The emphasis on skilled bodily performance in most cases required concentration on one technique only in the time available. This meant that if, for example, the Graham technique was the medium, the students might become very skilled and knowledgeable in this small part but would remain ignorant of dance as a richly diversified whole. This constituted a very narrow dance experience which could hardly be called dance education. In this way, the *professional* model, especially in the hands of inexperi-enced teachers, became devoid of process in that pupils only received and practised prescribed skills and dances. No good dance teacher would limit pupils to this form of training. Such indoctrination became taboo even in examination programmes in which pre-set dances had to be learned and performed. Rather, the view promoted here is that personally textured and artistic rendering of such examination pieces, like music, is much the favoured presentation.

Equal emphasis on process and on product

Clearly then, the art of dance in education model should emphasise neither process nor product in the ways in which the preceding *educational* and *professional* models seemed to advocate. Rather, there should be equal emphasis on both quality of process and quality of product. The means towards this will be discussed in depth later in the book, but suffice it to say that, in creating dances for example, the process of exploration, selection, and final refinement can be as rich and as personalised as the teacher deems suitable for the experience of the pupils and their abilities to handle the dance tasks given. First, however, there must be some clear objectives on the nature of the product to be devised and, again in the words of Best (1985), 'in order to produce it one needs to have learned the requisite discipline of the medium of expression'.

Moreover, in performing dances or dance studies, the process of coming to know the nuances of expression and meaning intrinsic to the content and form of the piece is vitally important if the performance is to have 'life' and feeling in presentation. Too often, as a GCSE or A level examiner one is confronted with a mechanically sound but lifeless rendition of a technical dance study. Usually this indicates the way in which it has been taught. If the technique involved has been mastered by the student then, as with an actor who has learned his words, much more is required in the performance of the product. In the art of dance model, there is much to be learned through the process and about the product in creating and performing dances.

Creativity, imagination and individuality versus acquisition of knowledge of theatre dance

Emphasis on creativity, imagination and individuality

In the words of Haynes in Abbs (1987: 149), it appears that Laban:

> viewed the dancer as creator… and placed strong emphasis on personal expression; on spontaneous improvisation and experimentation; on creative activity as a means of evolving a style of dance which was 'true' to the individual personality. One of the fundamental aims of his work was embodied in the belief that a training in the 'art of movement' facilitated harmonisation of the individual and helped lead towards self realisation (towards what Jung called the process of individualisation).

Hence, development of creativity, imagination and individuality through making personal responses to the given tasks in dance were the stated concerns of the *educational* model. However, recent writings of eminent philosophers such as Best (1985 and 1992) demonstrate just how misconceived were these notions. They dispute that such development could occur in the context of exploring and experiencing movement for oneself and that creativity and imagination are inborn facilities which need not be educated. As Best (1985: 78–9) says:

> To be creative requires a grasp of the criteria of validity and value in the activity in question. Originality is given its sense only against a background of the traditional ... imagination is imagination only in so far as it operates within limits.

What are these criteria of validity? What is the background of the traditional in dance education? What are the limits placed upon the imagination?

The answers must lie in the fact that the art of dance, like other arts, is a public phenomenon which is removed from the everyday into the 'art world'. It is, therefore, subject to the influence of public conventions, styles and meanings; pupils learning to 'create' in dance (including those at primary stage) need to learn how to portray or discern meaning in dance movement and at the same time become aware of and use the shared public references. The means to this end will be discussed later, but here it is important to acknowledge that creating in dance is not going to advance beyond the cathartic release of personal feelings through unstructured and self-expressive movement responses unless teachers understand how creativity and imagination *can* be educated. This recognition does not prevent the individual's feelings and ideas from entering the expressive form. Although it is not easy to say how this happens, it is often the case that pupils who have studied dance choreography within the theatre as part of their GCSE course, for example, nevertheless produce dances that are fresh, original and obviously derived from their own experiences.

Clearly then, dance in education should no longer be a rarefied, exclusive and differentiated activity. Rather, as indicated previously, creating and imagining in the dance context *depend* upon extending from the givens towards something new. As in other arts, there is need for constant reference to and interaction with the art of dance as it exists in the public world.

The Department for Education and Employment's Report *All Our Futures: Creativity, Culture and Education* (1999: 29) reiterates the above by offering the following definition of creativity:

> Imaginative activity fashioned so as to produce outcomes that are both original and of value.

Clearly, this lays emphasis on both process and product. It also points to the importance of there being an interrelationship between the originality of the individual and the criteria of the public art world. This is reinforced in the ensuing discussion by stating that:

> Creative insights often occur when existing ideas are combined or reinterpreted in unexpected ways or when they are applied in areas with which they are not normally associated. (1999: 29)

What then, are the 'existing ideas or criteria' that need to be learned in dance if the outcomes of creativity, imagination and individuality are to be valued?

Emphasis on knowledge of theatre dance

From the above, it would appear that the *professional* model holds the answer for the art of dance in education in that there is constant reference to the public theatrical art model. However, to adopt the same content and procedures normally associated with training performers and choreographers in the professional context is not recommended either. Such training requires full-time courses containing daily classes in techniques which require certain mastery levels prior to the learning and practising of repertoire. Some courses also study the art of choreography based mostly on prescribed formulae to be learned and employed. This sort of programme (though much modified and developed) will be discussed in the context of further and higher education later in the book but, at school level, there is no time to give to this intensive and professionally-oriented training. As suggested earlier, for those who adopted this model, there was a tendency to restrict the content to a study and practice of the technique aspect of the theatre dance model. Dance in education must be more embracing and less predetermined in terms of its outcomes than the making of professional dancers and choreographers.

The main emphasis must be placed on developing the students' knowledge of the many dimensions of the art of dance. Thus the type and range of study differs from those outlined in the *professional* model with its dominant focus on technique as a prerequisite to artistic participation. Its essential differences lie in the equality of emphasis put on the three strands (creating, performing and viewing dances) even for beginners and on the concept of the art of dance as a publicly-derived phenomenon.

In the study of creating dances, for example, pupils should become aware of the styles and choreographic conventions that characterise the range of works available to them in the theatre repertory. These, like musical compositions, are historically and socially derived and extend from those termed classical ballet to those of 'new dance' catagorisation. Knowledge of this variety, which should grow slowly through the school years, provides students with a rich source of ideas for creating dances; it also extends the boundaries of the concept of dance as art and offers a frame of reference within which the student can organise perceptions of dance works. This is part of Best's 'background' cited on page 9.

Similarly, in the context of performing dances, by making reference to theatre dance examples students can become acquainted with the public notion of what constitutes skilfully-executed dance movements through experience of dances performed by professionals. Here, in mainstream theatre dance at least, attributes of good dance posture and body alignments, grace, ease of movement, extra stretch, resilience, pliancy and the full use of body parts or the whole body in numerous dance co-ordinations, dynamically and spatially differentiated, offer exemplary performance targets towards which students can strive. This also is part of Best's 'background'.

Equal emphasis on creativity, imagination, individuality and acquisition of knowledge of theatre dance

With the above reorientations clearly defined, the *midway* art of dance in education model demands knowledge of theatre dance as a prerequisite for creativity, imagination and individuality of expression. To quote Best (1985: 89) again:

> A necessary condition for being creative is to have mastered at least to some extent the discipline, techniques and criteria of a subject or activity.

Feelings and subjectivity versus training and objectivity

Emphasis on feelings

In Ruth Foster's book *Knowing in my Bones* (1976) we find a plea for retaining an emphasis on the personal and subjectively unique experience of the creative act. This must have been the result of the over-emphasis on the *professional* model which she saw in secondary schools and colleges at the time of writing. She states, for example, that:

> The arts are concerned primarily … with the springs of feeling and its manifestation in various media. (1976: 4)

and that:

> In dance, movement takes on very closely the shape of sensation and in turn shapes it. The experience of the dancer is an intimately personal one in which action may be said to be the very fabric of feeling itself. (1976: 6)

How exactly movement 'takes on very closely the shape of sensation', or is even associated with sensations in the mind of the composer, is not clear. A weakness of the argument rests on the assumption that, along with the memory of feelings, there is a stored-up vocabulary of associated movements. In other words, if the composer recalls the feeling, a ready recipe of movements comes to mind and these are 'the very fabric of feeling itself'. Conversely, certain movements could be found to induce a recall of feelings. This reminds one of Laban's (1948) idea 'that varying emotions can be induced through [the performer's] actions'.

The stress upon the psychological impact of dance on the individual puts Foster (1976) in a clearly supportive position for the *educational* model. It is also evident that she is strongly influenced by Robert Witkin's ideas concerning *The Intelligence of Feeling* (1974). Witkin sees the arts as the creative expression of subjective feeling. He makes a distinction between the public and the private worlds and suggests that, in the school curriculum, the arts are the only means of entering into the latter. This is concerned with sensations and feelings and is removed from the object world and factual knowledge. It is also clear, however, that as noted by Foster (1976), Witkin (1974) does not consider a spontaneous outpouring and simple discharging of feelings to be expressive action. This he describes as reactive behaviour. Rather, it is reflexive action he advocates as that which arts teachers should encourage. By this he means that the pupils should be helped to look inside themselves, respond to their feelings in a reflexive manner and express them in the art medium without reference to the external world or techniques imposed by the teacher. The critics of this view hold that if the artist wants to communicate feelings, some account has to be taken of public conventions and shared meanings. As Redfern (1973: 82) says:

> What can be expressed is partly, and perhaps largely deter-mined not only by what others have 'said' but also on how they have 'said it'.

This is not new, of course. Langer wrote that:

> Art is a public possession because the formulation of felt-life is the heart of any culture and moulds the objective world for the people. It is their school of feeling and their defence against outer and inner chaos. (1953: 409)

For Witkin in 1974, however, the product is not accountable in the public world. His thesis, reiterated by Foster for dance education, lays emphasis once more on the participatory benefits of art on the individual coming to grips with problems and feelings. For example, in discussion on dance composition, Foster almost exclusively concentrates attention on inspirational moments, especially at the start of the creative act, when intuition seems subconsciously to direct the work. She admits that 'a full description of the whole process of composition' is not given. She certainly ignores the cognitive aspects of the creative process.

A more valid view of intuition is provided by Louis Arnaud Reid (1981: 80):

> This intuition … is not without conceptualisation. Whatever we apprehend directly is, inescapably apprehended in terms of concepts, infused with, has assimilated an indefinitely large body of knowledge about things, knowledge-that.

Since feelings/intuitions and knowledge are so inextricably linked we can say that we are gaining knowledge through experience of feelings in dance. An interchange of thought and feeling occurs when the pupil interacts with the art work in the making. This interaction will not occur unless pupils become aware of movement and form structure as complexities of meaning. Pupils should be led to explore movements, and at the same time be encouraged to learn their mean-ing associations according to their 'colour', 'texture' and feeling conno-tations. The initial process in creating a dance expressing a certain feeling then, after research or reflection on the feeling to be expressed, is to select from improvisation of new movements and from the learned repertoire of movements associated with that feeling. From the moment that something is made, however, there should be interaction between the pupil's intuition or feeling and knowledge. This is a feeling response to the emerging creative form, not the initial feeling which is being expressed. The feeling that emanates from the process of creating itself – the feeling of 'rightness' – acts as motivation to drive the creative act on. It is not easy to say from where this derives or to disassociate it from knowledge. Maybe, as Reid implies, it is merely old knowledge/experience which has been forgotten but somehow emerges as if from subconscious depths as an inspirational answer to the creative problem in hand. As Reid (1983) says:

> What is needed is absorption of discursively reflective thinking and study, an assimilation of it, a conscious forgetting of it, and a return to illuminated intuition.

The two kinds of feelings discussed above – those being expressed as the theme of the dance and those which direct the creative process – provide the subjective and individual elements in the composition. However, taking account of Reid's views, we have to conclude that these subjective feelings are cognitive and that feeling and knowing occur simultaneously. To concentrate on the one without the other makes no sense. We should also acknowledge that expression in art emerges as a mix of subjective experience with culturally derived objective knowledge. Pupils need to learn how to objectify their subjective experiences through the artistic medium.

The above proposes that the subjective feelings and intuitions which enter into creative art-making processes are not instinctive or without thought. Yet, the 1999 Report cited on page 9 shows that there remains some ambiguity about this, since it states that:

> Creative activity involves a complex combination of controlled and non-controlled elements, unconscious as well as conscious mental processes, non-directed as well as directed thought, intuitive as well as rational calculation. (1999: 32)

This statement sits uncomfortably in a section which also states that:

> Creative abilities are developed through practical application: by being engaged in the processes of creative thought production: making music, writing stories, conducting experiments

and so on. A key task for teachers is to help young people to understand these processes and to gain control of them. These are particular techniques and skills which are specific to different disciplines and forms of work. (1999: 31)

The message in the latter quotation counteracts the former. However, for the most part, the Report is consistent in reinforcing the views expressed in this book with support of Reid (1981 and 1983) and Best (1985). These can be summed up by Best (1992):

It is a serious *distortion* to regard the emotions and artistic feelings as non-rational, non-cognitive experiences... To summarise, we need to reject the long-held subjectivist dogmas by which arts educators continue to damage their own case... We need to reject subjectivism, and to insist that artistic feeling is itself *cognitive* and open to objective justification. (1992: 5–15)

So what techniques and skills should we teach to provide the means of attaining such objectivity as a corollary? If the *educational* model for dance emphasises the subjective, perhaps the *professional* training model should be considered for its objectivity.

Emphasis on training

It has already been established that the *professional* model for dance in schools is largely that which in America is termed Modern Dance, and in Britain is called Contemporary Dance. Its form, style and conventions, demanding as much discipline and time in training as Classical Ballet, have become established through several generations of practising artists and teachers. One of the most influential of founders, Martha Graham, has been quoted many times in saying that 'it takes ten years to build a dancer. The body must be tempered by hard, definite technique' (1935).

It was this aspect of American Contemporary Dance which came to be promoted in secondary schools and colleges in the late 1960s and early 1970s. Teachers who adopted this model held that the body, as an instrument, needs to be refined and fashioned for the purpose of art. There was the notion that if pupils created for themselves, using natural movement of the body (as in Laban's Modern Educational Dance lessons), the movement would not be good enough, not technically refined or advanced enough to be acceptable on an 'art' level.

The teachers therefore adopted a technique, such as Graham's, which through strict discipline imposed a vocabulary of refined movement skills on pupils. Although status and recognition were thus gained in the professional world, teachers soon found that in order to do this successfully it is necessary for pupils to have and maintain what Glasstone (1986: 214) calls 'facility':

> ...a well-proportioned body, with easy joint mobility; strong well-shaped, flexible feet; a spine that is both straight and flexible ... attributes ... essential for a dancer to be able to function satisfactorily at a purely mechanical level, enabling him or her to perform the required movements accurately and without physical injury.

Not only is it necessary to have all the physical attributes prescribed, but pupils need also to be able to adjust to the discipline and demands of training to achieve the heights of correct technical and artistic mastery. It is exceptionally difficult to adhere to the traditional practices, slowly building bodily expertise, and retain individual flair even though prescriptions for success insist that this should be the aim. Because it takes so long to shape and train the body – and it is hard work to achieve a standard sufficiently good for artistic performance for an audience in an ordinary once-a-week school situation – there would be many participants who would never experience this as an end product of their labours. They unfortunately would go no further than perceiving dance as the class exercises or basic training schedules for dancers which they fail to master.

On the other hand, in the spirit of today's education which places much greater emphasis on objectives and achievable ends, there is, as the Calouste Gulbenkian Foundation report on *Dance Education and Training in Britain* stated as long ago as 1980:

> widespread agreement that for older children a higher level of skill acquisition is desirable and that a more structured approach will not kill spontaneity but will increase the power of expression by widening the vocabulary of movement. (1980: 49)

However, later the report continues:

> By technique we do not mean here the mastery of skill and accuracy in a particular vocabulary of steps and exercises in a particular style. Such a concept of technique is too narrow...

Rather we mean by technique the discipline of the art, some-thing a child might acquire in three concurrent stages – personal development through movement; the acquisition of skill in movement; the bringing together of skill and personal qualities for an artistic purpose expressed through dance. (1980: 50)

Clearly, the views expressed here reiterate what has been said above in respect of the narrow overspecialisation of training the body in one technique. The shift from an obvious acknowledgement of the *educational* model for the primary stage, to an unidentifiable means of the child becoming skilful in movement and a nebulous bringing together of these experiences does not help the teacher to under-stand how to develop performance skills as part of the art of dance in education. Further on in the report, there is mention of how specialist help in ballet, etc. may be made available for the talented few and how dance artists might function in demystifying the art form. There is some reference to training teachers so that they have knowledge of techniques, but no conception of what kind of technical training is appropriate for schools is offered in the report.

Since the report was published, however, dance examinations – GCSE, AS and A level in the UK, for example – have found ways of objectively testing technical skills by means of pupils performing set technical studies in an assessment context. This innovation is largely one to which I can lay claim and much more detailed discussion of the underlying theory behind it will be presented in the ensuing sections.

Skilful dance performance is not the only aspect of the art of dance in education model which can be assessed objectively. In the GCSE examination, for example, students present dances to be assessed in choreographic skills and their dance appreciation is examined through coursework packages and examination scripts. Hence all three strands of the art of dance model – creating, performing and appreciating – offer potential for objective testing. Examples of assessment will be discussed later in the book, but it is certainly not easy to define criteria that will be appropriate and sufficiently flexible to be applicable to all artistic and aesthetic achievements. Herein lies the problem of overdoing objectivity in the arts.

It could be said then that the *professional* theatre dance model has shown the way towards greater accountability as an antidote to the over-indulgent subjectivity upheld by those perpetuating the *educa-tional* model. But, as shown above, there is need of a much broader definition of the predecessor *professional* model than that taken up by dance educators initially with the central interest in technique *per se*. The broader view of the *professional* model derives from the shift in the conceptual basis towards the art of dance model. Here the whole of the professional artistic world of dance is in focus. The dancers, the dance works – how they are created, rehearsed, interpreted and notated – the choreographers, design, music, lighting, theatrical setting, cultural, historical and social contexts constitute the range of dance study. Knowledge, understanding and skills can be developed and assessment criteria need to be formulated to determine what the pupils know, understand, and can do in the dance art context.

Equal emphasis on feelings and on training

The clearer account of feeling/intuition offered above (as opposed to the view that sensations and feelings are the private domain of the individual into which it is not possible or desirable to intrude), together with broader objectives in stating what can be learned in all three strands – performing, creating and appreciating – provide a degree of balance to the art of dance in education model. This is the most difficult aspect of the conceptual basis to discuss, but it is important that teachers and lecturers are constantly aware of the tenuous interplay between feeling and knowing and the dangers of overplaying one at the expense of the other. Keeping such a balance is a persistent theme throughout this book.

Movement principles versus stylised techniques:

Emphasis on movement principles

A particular characteristic of the *educational* model is that the dance experience is based upon a set of principles or concepts rather than systematised or graded groups of exercises and skills which consti-tute a *professional* model. Laban formulated his principles through observation of *movement* in varying situations. They are general principles of movement, therefore, and not specific to dance. In other words, Laban's system is not codified into set patterns of movement which need to be fed to pupils according to age, ability and expertise. Rather, though there are progressive stages inherent in the use of the principles which Laban organised into sixteen movement themes, the teacher interprets them in his or her own way. It is 'without a preconceived or dictated style and the whole range of the elements of movement is experienced and practised' (Laban, 1948).

Although Laban's principles of movement are often referred to as an analysis, in that movement is broken down into various components, he does this only in a descriptive way. It serves the teacher well who wishes to use a free exploratory approach, because movement is classified into broad concepts, each of which suggests a range that may be explored in different ways by individual pupils.

Fundamentally, Laban put forward the view that movement can be described under four headings: action, effort (now more often called dynamics or qualities of movement), space and relationships. The following questions may give a clue to the meaning of these terms. What action is being done, and with what body parts is it being performed? How do the actions use time and force (quick – strong – slow – delicate) and are they continuous or intermittent? Where in space do the actions begin, move and end? In which ways are the actions related to objects and/or other people? The basic premise is simply that characteristics of body actions alter in varying situations. In dance, every action that the body can perform, according to its expressive purpose, may be variously coloured by how it uses time, energy, flow space and relationship factors. For example, travelling steps may be light, quick, freely going, upward and forward to express joy or conversely, heavy, withheld, slow and downward to express sadness.

The benefits of using the principles of movement as a source of content are that the whole range is available, and the choice of movement in dance compositions is likely to be dependent upon the meaning to be conveyed rather than upon a range of already-learned dance movements. The latter are ready-made 'wholes' with specified use of the components of action, dynamics, and space and have defined stylistic properties. Laban's principles, on the other hand, are more valuable for varied expressive purposes because they expose components only and it is up to the dance choreographer to make up the 'wholes' and ascribe a style according to the dance idea. In this respect, the principles can be likened to a paint palette.

Not surprisingly, criticisms of the principles as content highlight the lack of technical skill required of pupils. Because they are free to explore their own natural movement range in response to movement tasks, they may have no concepts of how to refine movements beyond the everyday into dance. Hence there is probably no extra extension, no projection of focus, no polish in co-ordinations of movements and certainly no particular style. Indeed, the movement outcomes were often criticised as self-indulgent wallowing in improvised undifferentiated movement which could be performed by anyone. The artistic and aesthetic concerns for what it looked like were sacrificed for what it felt like for the performer. But really this is not so much a criticism of the principles but how they were employed and the romantic theories attached to them. It is contended here, in the same way as in my book *Dance Composition*[1] (2000), that the principles themselves remain a very useful tool for the art of dance in education model, and it will become evident that they can be beneficially employed in teaching all three of the activities – creating, performing and appreciating dances.

Emphasis on stylised techniques

In the above text the word *technique* is used when discussing the acquisition of physical skill. However, in dance, the term is also used in discussing style. Detailed discussion of the relationship between techniques and styles can be found in the second and subsequent editions of my book *Dance Composition* (1992, 1996, 2000).

In the context of the *professional* model, study of a defined technique as content of dance education would entail participation in technique classes in order to learn a particular range of movement and perfect performance of it with attention given to its particular style. Most often technique classes in the professional dance world are in named techniques – in the contemporary dance context, for example – Graham, Cunningham, Limon and Hawkins techniques, to name but a few. Students taking a Graham class will learn the technique and acquire the style through participation in floorwork exercises, standing centre exercises for legs and feet, *barre* work, centre practice including stepping, falling, tilting and balancing, and exercises travelling across the floor including jumps. In most techniques there is a division between performing exercises and dancing sequences or parts of repertoire. Through the former the dancer is gaining physical attributes such as strength, flexibility, balance, posture, alignment, co-ordination and stamina, and in the latter is learning how to present and give expression to the movement by attending to qualities of (for example) rhythm, phrasing, dynamics, spatial patterning and style. Of course, the best technique teachers concentrate on such qualities at all times even whilst the pupils are performing the most mundane of exercises. In fact, some

[1]This is the fourth edition. Laban's principles of movement are proposed as appropriate content for dance composition in all editions of this book, first published in 1976.

techniques require this *performance* approach. The Graham technique, for example, gains such an acclaim from De Mille (1960: 55):

> One reason the Graham technique has such wide-spread appeal is that the exercises... induce dancing while strengthening and limbering. Each exercise is a fragment of movement exquisitely devised... [students] learn phrasing, dynamics and form whilst working on tendons and breath. The work-out is in reality a collection of tiny dances, all lovely, all shaped providing transition to the next group... so even... start[ing] the first contractions, the student is... absorbing performance, technique and what is more subtle, dance form.

It must be clear to all who have experienced such classes, however, that it is necessary to have considerable facility for dance movement (as pointed out by Glasstone (1986) above), and considerable time given to practising the technique before even the most basic of standards is reached. This kind of dance training may be appropriate for intensive dance courses in further or higher education but it certainly is not appropriate for secondary school pupils.

Even at college level, however, study of only one dance technique – such as the Graham technique, with its most distinctive style – limits students to the kinds of expression that this particular technique can articulate. Although few students study the Graham technique now, and more generalised mixes of contemporary techniques are experienced under headings such as 'release' or 'contact' techniques, the same can be said for all techniques because each contains its own strong stylistic character and implicit expressive capacities. Hence, a comprehensive art of dance curriculum should expose students to a range of techniques and styles so that they can select the right combinations for their compositions or consider their own performance with a knowledge of the technical and stylistic characteristics pertinent to the piece they are practising, whatever its technique/style.

As stated above, in the past ten years or so, it has become common to study a more generalised technique rather than a prescribed or named technique such as the Graham technique. A contemporary dance class, for example, includes movements emphasising the torso, feet in parallel, and movements of isolated parts of the body as well as the whole body. It puts emphasis on the pelvic region and centre initiating and arresting momentum, on floorwork and on extensive variations of dynamics. Phrases of travelling, leaping, tipping, and falling emphasise movements into, across and off the floor. Such stylistic flavourings give a mainstream contemporary feel to the class. A different range of movement characteristics and vocabulary would emerge from jazz, classical ballet or Indian classes. Whatever the technique, whether specifically named or a generalised essence of many, the students would be learning a vocabulary of set movements and the style of the technique. Perhaps, as indicated above, the best art of dance education should include experience of many of these techniques/styles so that, as in the case of a music student, the art form is studied as a multifarious and richly varied phenomenon.

Equal emphasis on movement principles and on stylised techniques

Clearly then, rather than the teacher/lecturer in the art of dance in education context settling on one technique, students need to be equipped with a repertoire of techniques which offer a range of stylistic and expressive possibilities. How such a programme can be considered in the limited time available for dance will be discussed in more detail later, but some hints may be appropriate here in that important aspects of the conceptual bases include theatre-based exemplars and pre-choreographed dance studies to teach students about techniques and styles. In developing an ability to perform jazz-like pieces, for example, through learning a jazz-based dance study students could be exposed to the essential features of a jazz vocabulary – movements initiated and isolated to specific parts of the body such as the hips and shoulders, syncopated rhythms, downward-stressed grounded movements with sharp changes of direction and focus – and then, through the study of professional jazz dancers on video or CD ROM perhaps, dramatically advance their learning. The sensation of moving in a jazz-like way seems to be transmitted through seeing it well done into doing it well oneself. Indeed, because it is possible to employ all the jazz-like characteristics in a non-jazz style such as disco, it is essential that the nuances of the style are illustrated through a physical demonstration so that pupils recognise the distinctive textures of jazz dance as opposed to anything else. The importance of visual resources, together with experience of ready-made dance studies/snippets of repertoire for students of secondary age and above, cannot be over-stressed. However, even young children can extend their range and colour their dance movements with stylistic properties through the use of visual resources such as videos or dance artists in school. Basic characteristics of Indian dance styles, for example, have been successfully transmitted to six and seven year olds in this manner with much supplementary material in the form of pictures, music, costume and stories. Such a dance education substantiates the cultural world in which children live and they come to know more about that world through the experience of dance.

It will also become clear to the reader that the art of dance in education model advocated here puts equal emphasis on developing knowledge and understanding of dance techniques and styles along with principles of movement. The guidelines offered by Laban in the form of a descriptive analysis form the language and concepts shared by all who are participating in the dance experiences. Thus, instead of learning special names of movements such as *arabesque, jeté*, spiral and suchlike, students and teachers/ lecturers describe the actions with common terms such as balance, jump and twist, and then distinguish dynamic and spatial character- istics of each of these actions with words such as continuous, quick, sharp, upward and forward. Indeed, the use of this everyday language permits a greater degree of clarity and depth in observing and describing the details of the movements. Just to say *arabesque*, for example, describes only the type of movement, for there are hundreds of ways in which an *arabesque* can be performed. Laban's principles provide the means of detailed description.

Another important use of the principles, especially for the teacher, is in providing frameworks within which pupils explore. Dance composition can be guided by the teacher in that the overall structure and range of content for the dance can be set before the class takes place. A *Happy Dance*, for example, could include a section within which the young pupils make a phrase of bouncy jumps from two feet to two feet. This concept could be thoroughly explored and then, with the idea of *Happiness* uppermost in their imaginations, pupils would be led to select and link their jumping movements to create a suitable phrase within a certain length of music. With older students, too, the principles are very useful in dance-making contexts. If a motif has been created it might well be developed and repeated: the level in space can be changed, dynamics or spatial focus altered or the action content increased. The flexibility of this set of principles as a creative tool for the dance composer (discussed in detail in *Dance Composition* 2000), together with a knowledge of stylistic conven- tions, provides the balance which will eventually lead towards pupils/students gaining greater autonomy, not only in making dances but in performing and appreciating them, too.

Problem-solving versus directed teaching methodologies

Emphasis on problem-solving

In the *educational* model, stress on the private and psychological effects of dance upon the dancer has implications for methodology. Such ends can only be achieved through an open, discovery approach in which the individual directs his or her own learning. Discovery learning is effected by the teacher who presents a problem-solving situation which delineates an area for exploration by the pupil. For example, a task such as 'move quickly, turn, rise and fall' can lead the student into many varieties of quick movement, ways of turning and so on, some of which may be original discoveries for the individual. Members of the class, therefore, would not all be performing the same movement, but would be working inventively within the confines of the task or dance idea and their abilities, both physical and imaginative. The teacher's role in this situation is a difficult one:

> The dance teacher not only sets up the situation and suggests the material to be explored, but through suggestion and questions opens up a world of possibilities to be experienced by the child...The teacher therefore acts as guide rather than director.   (Russell 1974: 289)

Whilst pupils work individually or in groups in order to find their movement answers to movement tasks, the teacher draws attention to variety and/or quality of content from what is observed and aims to improve responses in these terms by means of suggestions, practices and demonstrations. As Foster (1977) states, 'it is not easy to become a catalyst in the creative process' but, essentially, this was the role of the teacher in the *educational* model. However, as Foster goes on to say, this methodology poses problems for evaluation. First, in respect of the problems set: how does the teacher assess what is good and what is trivial? Also, how may progression be ensured for each pupil?

What seemed to be missing in the *educational* model were standards, levels and publicly acceptable frames of reference. Even in the context of creating dance movement there was a difficulty in that, in the main, publicly acknowledged aesthetic criteria for art criticism were not a part of the teacher's know-how. Guidance of the creative act, therefore, remained an insular private event between each teacher/lecturer and a group. Decisions as to what was good were made without reference to relevant theatre models or examples on video or film. So it would appear that it was not so much the dominance of open-ended teaching styles that caused problems but the overall lack of knowing what ends these methods were achieving. As Foster (1977: 140) says, unless clear ends are identified, there is danger that this method:

> leads to children not approaching creative heights, but settling for an inadequate destination. Neither is the goal of merely approaching. It should contain an element of achieving as well.

Nevertheless, there is a clear relationship between the philosophical bases of the *educational* model and approaches to teaching which lead pupils to become agents in their own learning. Although texts supporting this model advocate a range of teaching strategies, their authors definitely urge teachers away from didactic methods or intrusion and aim to persuade the teacher to take on the role of stimulator and catalyst rather than knowledgeable expert.

The emphasis on creativity advocated in the DfEE *All Our Futures: Creativity, Culture and Education* Report, 1999, would appear to imply that a return to the progressive teaching ideas of the 1960s is also suggested. No, they say, this is not the case. Rather:

> We are advocating a new balance between learning knowledge and skills and having the freedom to innovate and experiment. (1999: 13)

Emphasis on directed teaching

De Mille (1960) said that 'the best way of learning is still apprenticeship under a professional' and, to date in the 2000s, in professional training contexts in all the performing arts, this seems still to be the case. In teaching the named techniques, for example, the teacher needs to be an expert in the sense of knowing and thoroughly understanding the range of exercises and patterns of movement which have evolved as the content of the dance style. It is also necessary to know how best to instruct so that learning is effected in the most economical way. The teacher as an instructor enforces what is to be done, how it is to be done, for how long the practice will take place and the standard it reaches. The learner must be disciplined, succumb to teacher control and work towards optimum physical performance. This is teacher-centred education.

Equal emphasis on problem-solving and on directed teaching

It will become evident in the following chapters that the successful teacher needs to be able to employ both these kinds of teaching strategies and many combinations of them.

The open-ended problem-solving approach is most readily associated with creative dance-composing situations as illustrated above, but it is also important for pupils to learn how to improve their own and others' dance performances through, for example, writing a checklist of things to look for in good performance and using this to comment critically upon their individual performances on video or those of peers in the live situation. The teacher here acts as catalyst, guide and consultant, rather than instructor. For the appreciation of professional dance works it is also very important that teachers/ lecturers frequently employ an open-ended non-instructive method of teaching. Here, students' perceptions need to be guided rather than directed because they must interpret the meanings/feelings in the works in their own way. There are many different ways in which such guidance can be effected through setting the students to research in books, to study critics' opinions and to write their own in response to questions about the work seen, to discuss or to write about certain aspects of it, and so on. In all of these activities students are required to think for themselves and are not *given* information. The aim is that they come to know the works for themselves and can back up their own views about them with clearly argued reasons. More on this later.

The closed instructive approach should also be used at appropriate times in the art of dance in education model. This is especially the case where acquisition of skills or initiation into new ways of thinking is concerned. Pring, as far back as 1976 for example, states that:

> learning ... should be seen much more as a kind of apprentice-ship than it normally is – learning how to do something along-side the successful practitioner, by imitating, by subjecting oneself to correction and to direction. (1976: 27)

This didactic approach has become fashionable again in an environment in which achievement of standards is reported at prescribed intervals in each child's education. Certainly, in the art of dance in education model it has its place, but the implication is that the teacher should be a good dancer with training and experience in performing and also with an ability to demonstrate clearly, explain carefully, and to observe quickly and correctly.

Moreover, the teacher should also have been a choreographer of some note if the role of expert in this context is to be assumed. Perhaps this is where dance artists can play an important role in imparting high-level technical training and teaching repertoire in 'master class' experiences for students. Certainly, artists most often use a directed teaching method and, if properly prepared, the students' learning can progress dramatically under such expert guidance.

FEATURES OF THE *MIDWAY* MODEL

The following table demonstrates how, in my view, elements of the *educational* and *professional* models have been absorbed, albeit in much altered form, into a new model for teaching dance in education. The *midway* model, however, as stated previously, has distinctive features of its own.

Table to demonstrate features of the art of dance in education model

EDUCATIONAL	MIDWAY	PROFESSIONAL
Process	Process + Product	Product
Creativity Imagination Individuality	Creativity Knowledge Imagination + of public artistic Individuality conventions	Knowledge of theatre dance repertoire
Feelings Subjectivity	Feelings + Skill Subjectivity + Objectivity	Skill acquired Objectivity
Principles	Principles + Techniques	Techniques
Open methods	Open + Closed	Closed methods
	THREE STRANDS	
Creating	Composition Performance Appreciation	Performing
	OF DANCES leading to ARTISTIC EDUCATION AESTHETIC EDUCATION CULTURAL EDUCATION	

The three strands: creating, performing, appreciating

These three processes constitute the conceptual basis of the *art of dance in education* model. Most of the current literature reinforces this. It is my view, however, that the term 'appreciating' should not be used to describe the third process involved in dance education. Its meaning is more all-embracing than this. Appreciation in an art context can be defined as an ability to perceive and value the qualities in an object. Full appreciation of the features in the art work – its expression, form and style, together with admiration of the cleverness, precision and originality with which it has been wrought – can produce a sense of enjoyment, sometimes even elation.

> The enjoyment and emotion, however, are not identical with what the use of the terms in ordinary discourse and everyday experiences denotes although they could not exist or develop without roots in that experience.   (Broudy 1972)

The key to this enjoyable appreciation resides in the object itself and in the depth of feelings and understanding the perceiver brings to the experience of it. Hence, 'appreciation' is the term to use when the perceiver comes to value an art work for the artistic, aesthetic and/or cultural qualities and meanings it has for him or her. In the art of dance in education context, such an appreciation will emerge as a result of much experience in creating, performing and viewing dances.

The conceptual basis of the art of dance model, for me then, might be illustrated thus.

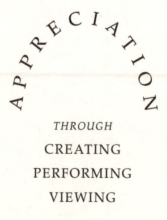

APPRECIATION

THROUGH

CREATING

PERFORMING

VIEWING

The *processes* involved in the art of dance in education – creating, performing and viewing dances – describe what the pupils/students do in their dance lessons/lectures.

The *products* – dance compositions, dance performances and dance appreciation – are the outcomes of their learning and it is these products that can be assessed.

The dance syllabuses in schools delineate what it is expected that pupils will achieve in each stage. Dance examinations such as GCSE, AS and A level and degree courses in dance also assess or examine through dance compositions, dance performances and dance appreciation. The last is most often assessed through written work, though there are other ways in which appreciation can be evaluated. Perhaps the most obvious way to arrive at the outcome of in-depth appreciation of dance works is through learning how to compose and perform dances oneself. The knowledge, understanding and artistic sensitivity gained from composing and performing dances underpins and augments knowledge and understanding gained from viewing dances. That is why the diagram above shows appreciation as an 'umbrella' concept, an ultimate aim, for dance education which results from qualitative experiences of the processes of performing, creating and viewing dances.

In my view, the conceptual basis for the art of dance in education has been defined and explained in many texts incorrectly in that the three strands have been called 'creating', 'performing' and 'appreciating'. These are verbs to describe the processes involved in dance education. But appreciating is not a process, it is an outcome. Hence, as the diagram above demonstrates, appreciation is constantly being developed through all three activities – performing, creating and viewing.

The logical conclusion of this argument is to be clear as to whether it is the process or the product that is being described. As stated above, whilst it is certainly possible to arrive at a product of a dance composition through the process of creating, and a product of dance performance through the process of performing, the product of appreciation is not gained through viewing alone. Appreciation is an overall outcome.

Nonetheless, even though the above definition of appreciation clearly indicates a more complex meaning, it has become common parlance in dance education to use the word as a third strand. Other art forms use different terms. For example, music in the National Curriculum of England and Wales refers to 'listening' and 'appraising'. In the context of dance education, however, appreciating has become linked with processes of viewing, responding, describing, analysing, interpreting and evaluating dances and learning about dance and its history. In adherence to this common practice in dance education, therefore, the term *appreciating* is used throughout this book. Rather than change it for the sake of accuracy, readers are asked to keep in mind the broader definition of appreciation as an outcome of the three processes – creating, performing and viewing dances – whenever the term is used.

Artistic education

The processes of creating, performing and viewing dances and the overall appreciation gained from these experiences can be defined as artistic education in that the learner is coming to know more about the art form itself. So far in this text the concepts of artistic and aesthetic education have been coupled. Indeed, it is difficult to disentangle artistic from aesthetic education, since in all dance art experiences they are interdependent; but, for the purposes of clarity, it is suggested here that the artistic aspects of a dance education tend to be those which are learned in an objective way, those which relate to the discipline of dance.

A discipline-based education in the art of dance is concerned with developing the students' skills, knowledge and understanding. Physical dance skills are developed in performance. Choreographic skills are developed through creating one's own dances and learning from dances created by others. Appreciation skills are developed through learning how to view dances, describe, interpret and evaluate them. Of course, these skills cannot develop without knowledge and understanding of the concepts involved in creating, performing and appreciating dances. Skills, knowledge and understanding cannot be separated and developed in a linear manner. Rather they develop simultaneously in a balanced art of dance education.

In order to distinguish the nature of artistic education, however, we need to consider the range of concepts involved in creating, performing and appreciating dances.

The central requirement is that an understanding of the nature of a dance develops throughout the experience of dance education. The concept of a dance will constantly change. For the younger pupils it may simply be thought of as a collection of movements, patterned in time and space to create a form with a beginning, middle and end. This is suggested in most dance education syllabuses for pupils between five and seven years of age. For the university student it is impossible to produce any one definition, since the concept of what a dance is differs considerably in historical/cultural context and artistic *milieu*. Nonetheless, understanding of dances as artefacts each with distinguishing features is an essential aspect of artistic education. The art object or product, usually intended for an audience, is the main focus.

Most of the concepts and skills developed through the processes of creating, performing and viewing dances can be labelled artistic. The following lists are not intended to be comprehensive but are useful in determining what is meant by the term *artistic education*.

Artistic learning, at the level appropriate to the learner's experience/age, through:

Creating dances

- understanding of and interpretation of themes/ideas
- translation of themes/ideas in dance terms, i.e. into symbolic action
- making decisions about the type of dance, e.g. dramatic, pure, comic, abstract; and about the style, e.g. contemporary, balletic, jazzy
- exploration of movement ideas, discovering actions, qualities, rhythmic and spatial features to express the theme in the type and style of dance planned
- exploring and making decisions about numbers of dancers and relationship possibilities to express the idea, e.g. positioning, group shapes, orchestration
- understanding of how the music or accompaniment can be used
- selecting and linking movements to make motifs and phrases
- stylising content appropriately
- deciding the order of movements and refining motifs and phrases
- structuring motifs and phrases in time and space, and the relationship between dancers
- developing the phrases, perhaps repeating them in time, space and relationship configurations
- understanding the use of formal devices: repetition, development, contrast, transition, progression, unity or alternative construction processes such as chance
- creating sections or parts of the dance and combining them to make a whole dance

- considering staging aspects of dances: lighting, design, costume, make-up, use of accompanying visual/audio materials, etc.
- presenting dances in conventional/alternative spaces with consideration of the role of the audience: programme notes, etc.

Performing dances

- acquiring physical skills: actions combined with dynamic, rhythmic and spatial patterning or stylistically defined skills from specific techniques
- performing the above with co-ordination, accuracy, fluency, control, balance, poise and confidence
- practising co-ordination in movements to link phrases, sections and dances
- performing the content concentrating on qualitative expression through variation of dynamic, spatial and relationship features
- performing dances and parts of dances with understanding of the formal qualities, e.g. pauses, highlights, contrasts
- presenting the theme through dancing expressively
- practising dance to music or other forms of accompaniment alone or with others in unison and canon
- developing performance qualities such as extension, projection and focus in order to express meaning
- concentrating on line, body shape, clarity of design, positioning
- showing clarity and unity of style

Viewing dances

- observing, describing, analysing and evaluating all the aspects involved in creating and performing (such viewing by students of their own and professional choreography should take place throughout dance education)

These three processes – creating, performing and viewing dances – will develop the ability to appreciate artistic features of dances.

Appreciation of artistic aspects of dance

- students will learn to discern with increasing accuracy and sensitivity a range of qualities in choreography and performance. Through analogy with their own experiences in choreography and performance, and through learning how to employ description,

interpretation and evaluation, they will be able to perceive distinctive artistic features: style, form, expression, techniques and production
- in order to further appreciation, students will learn to employ a range of resources to discover background information and specific details about dances, choreographers, performers, designers and musicians

Aesthetic education

Aesthetic perception, though probably something with which we are all endowed, needs, like other kinds of perception, to be nurtured and developed. The individual learns to use sense modalities in increasingly differentiated ways and to organise the vastly complex sensory world by use of several frames of reference. However, it is not through a simple process of maturing that we are able to use an aesthetic frame of reference. We need to learn to attend to contained qualities in dance rather than the mere physicalities of bodies in action. What these qualities in art may be and how they may be related is, in essence, what aesthetic education in dance is about.

Aesthetic education is essentially an education of feeling. In the aesthetic qualities of a work of art we receive an experience of the feelings embodied. For example, we often attribute human feelings/ meanings to music we hear (sad music perhaps) and the dances we see (an angry dance, maybe). Through appreciation of their various dynamic, temporal and spatial 'textures', students of dance should become aware of the expressive power of movements and their juxtaposition. Movements kinesthetically felt can become increasingly differentiated in tone and texture if the students become sensitive to the elements and combinations of elements which yield insights into human feeling. Furthermore, thinking about symbolic meaning in movement and learning about its components and significance should occur alongside feeling it.

How then do we guide and develop this education of feeling? As indicated above, an aesthetic frame of reference might be useful here for teachers. But is there such a thing? It is certainly difficult to accommodate these two seemingly conflicting notions: first, that each piece of art has its own meanings, and second that general principles or categories of aesthetic judgement exist within a single frame of reference. It is naive to suppose that the essences of all works of art, throughout time, can be distilled and appraised by one single uniform method. Moreover, art works are viewed subjectively by individuals in distinctive ways. Nevertheless, as Reid (1969) says, description and evaluation 'need to be held together in some general framework (even if is a flexible one); if not it will tend to degenerate into loose talk about personal impressions'. What is needed, then, is a general framework which allows for individual subjectivity of feeling yet classifies aesthetic qualities in works of art in general terms so that discussion of them may be shared.

Osborne (1970) classifies aesthetic qualities under the headings of sensory qualities, expressive qualities and formal qualities. The sensory qualities which pertain to movement are infinite and a problem of language is immediately encountered when asked to detail the qualities perceived in a dance. Not only are there never adequate words, but there is a tendency not to notice that for which we have no language. Where there are no words, training is needed to enable the perceiver to see. This is a skill which needs to be developed if the ability to appreciate is to be attained.

In dance there is always the danger that perceived movements become named (e.g. *arabesque* in ballet and 'contraction' in contemporary dance). It is, therefore, important that teachers extend their pupils' understanding of movements in sensory terms so that, for example, the qualities of an *arabesque* could be described as linear, balanced, flowing, angular, curving, smooth, arrested or lingering according to how it is performed. Just to name a movement is not enough because the same action can be performed with various qualities which in turn create different aesthetic feelings in the onlooker. The teacher, then, should help students to notice and attend to sensory qualities, which may be called the superstructure of the overall aesthetic.

Expressive qualities are emergent features of sensory qualities and again language for naming them is crude. A further problem is that there is no special language to describe expressive qualities of works of art as distinct from human emotions and expressions. Hence, human sadness is attributed to a dance which appears sad. Of course it is not possible to attribute particular expressive qualities to particular movements, because their meanings become different in different contexts and juxtapositions. However, there are some general pointers – for example, that curves in space can denote gentleness; that one person high and upright with several at his feet might denote power and submission. Care should always be taken not to *fix* correlating ideas and movements, since their expressiveness depends upon their role in each individual dance.

The aesthetic qualities which are called formal are denoted by such terms as unity, balance, integration, harmony, texture, proportion, contrast, etc. Here, older students could be guided to follow motifs consciously and to appreciate the intricacies of development, variation, combination, deconstruction and reconstruction that they go through in order to create the unified form. They could also consider how sections of dances are proportioned and balanced in relationship to each other, how the rhythmic 'time picture' is presented in terms of quiet moments, activity, transition, climax, and how spatial patterning is rhythmic, asymmetric, formal, intricate, for example.

If the teacher can develop devices for presenting the aesthetic aspects of dance, students may gradually come to view dance with deep and creative contemplation. Furthermore, concentration on sensory, expressive and formal aesthetic qualities in art works directs attention away from evaluations which bear no reference to the art work itself.

In aesthetic education, then, we have a situation in which as Gibson (in Abbs 1989: 58) says:

> feelings show us the limits of our language. They bring home to us that language is not omnicompetent; for we know far more than we can say. It is when we try to put into words our feelings, when we attend to explore our inner states (states that vividly and significantly exist, have reality and are of profound consequences for action) that the gap between language and experience is starkly exposed. It is at such moments we must turn to poets and artists, not scientists, for genuine illumination. Those understandings are rarely or never fully recoverable in written or spoken language, but it is common experience that they are nonetheless both grasped and valid.

Aesthetic education, the education of feeling, is an intangible and immeasurable aspect of dance education. As Gibson goes on to say:

> Feelings have puzzling relationships with time. They are processes not products: they have, in their intense here-and-now sense, a fleetingness and fugitiveness in their experience and expression. They are grasped and intuited only in their moments of experiencing... Such experiences are of the present to be enjoyed at the time. They are not future-oriented and not rewarded with grades or certificates. It is with this

present, shared, experienced, nature of emotions in mind that
we return to the question of the education of feeling. (1989: 58)

The education of feeling may not be measurable, yet it is very
important that it is not lost or put aside in favour of what can be
assessed. Those teaching the art of dance need to keep in mind a
framework such as that of Osborne described on page 34, in order
that it underpins dance experiences.

Cultural education

According to Reid (1986), the first approach to an art work cannot be
'intellectual' or 'conceptual':

> We cannot come to know and understand works of art first
> from the top of the head, and then downwards. Experience,
> feeling, direct, particular, concrete, comes first; intellectual
> analysis, perhaps later.
>
> (1986: 127)

This puts emphasis on aesthetic education above other kinds of education. However, through the art of dance, it is also important to
encourage understanding of culture amongst the young. Art is an
important aspect of culture, and should therefore be valued not only for
its aesthetic and artistic character but as a teacher of and about culture.

Western culture is, of course, the predominant focus of the art of
dance model, the roots of which are in Western theatre dance. The
form, style and expression of a theatre dance work reflect Western
traditions and ideologies and can therefore be analysed as a semiotic
picture of Western culture. Such a study of theatre dance as a
complex sign system is perhaps the province of higher education,
yet, from an early age children should learn that Western theatre
dance is distinct from other cultural forms. Whilst it is possible to
'read' universal messages in some dance movements, there are
particular meaning connotations attached to dance vocabulary, too.
An *arabesque* in ballet and a 'contraction' in contemporary dance
have in-built Western meanings. Moreover, contemporary dance
choreographers often employ everyday gestures with their
culturally defined meanings to form the basis of expression. Pupils
therefore need to be able to apply their understanding of non-verbal
communication in Western culture to dance works of this type. In

the Western world for example, we understand that the hitch hiker's thumb jerk calls for a lift, but the same action has very different meanings in other contexts! Increasingly then, pupils should become appreciative of the cultural meanings, artistic traditions, style and presentation of choreography in the theatre and of how such meanings, traditions and styles have developed.

Understanding the history of the art form as part of Western society is therefore an essential aspect of cultural education. Through such study pupils will become aware of the meanings of terms such as *contemporary dance*, *classical*, *neo-classical*, *romantic ballet* and *post-modern dance*, and appreciate the ways in which the art works themselves signify changes and developments in the practices of the art of dance. Knowledge of the history of the art of dance needs to be supported by study of the political, social and philosophical ideas at the times and places from which the dance works emerge. In this way students will appreciate them as ever-changing cultural phenomena.

Although Western culture is rich in artistic achievement and there is much to learn about the traditions and practices that underpin all the various kinds of theatre dance, there are other dance cultures to be learned about. As stated in *Dance in Schools*:

> We live in a multicultural society. Dance is a prime expression of culture, of heritage, identity and achievement. The richer the diversity of cultures within a given community, the richer the dance can be. Pupils can share their various dance heritages through traditional dances and they may bring into school a rich movement vocabulary and different understanding of dance.
>
> (Arts Council 1993: 10)

This suggests that a typical group in any sector of education will have pupils of different cultural backgrounds working together, and that teachers should make sure that a range of dance forms is experienced.

The art of dance model puts an emphasis on Western dance forms but it can be appropriate (as professional choreographers demonstrate) to integrate dance forms from other cultures into Western dance works. An example of this in contemporary dance is Jiri Kylian's *Stamping Ground* (1982) which derived from a close study of aboriginal dance and an integration of some attributes of this form with that of contemporary dance. This practice of mixing different dance forms creates new and interesting outcomes, reflecting the cultural richness of a community in art works. Students at school and college should be able to bring their own dance vocabularies, including social dance vocabularies, into the creative processes of creating dances. The greater the range of movement content and the more cultural influences entering the dance experience, the better it reflects our multicultural society.

A comprehensive experience in the art of dance will not only include the use of different ethnic and social dance forms; it will give some attention to different groups in society that participate in the art of dance. For example, it is becoming more accepted that disabled people can perform as dance artists in the same ways as able-bodied dancers. *Candoco* is a prime example of success in this context. Also, community dance workers demonstrate that the art of dance does not have to take place in the theatre with trained dancers. There are more and more groups performing in non-conventional places and including audience/non-dance participants in the outcome.

An important way in which the art of dance can contribute to cultural education is through the use of a range of themes for dance composition that explore differing values, beliefs, ideologies and social behaviours. Such themes might range from the experience of refugees in cultural settings strange to them to differences of expectation between generations. Young people can and do explore issues and concerns that affect their lives through the dances they create, and in so doing perhaps come to understand their own and others' attitudes and values relating to such issues. The complexities of conflicting messages from the media, from home, school, peers and from street culture can be dealt with in working with others to imaginatively explore and express in dance various points of view. For example, greed and ambition as opposed to compassion could be explored through a dance based on Lady Macbeth or on Scrooge. Through the use of such themes in creating dances themselves, or through interpreting issue-based dance works of professional choreographers (e.g. Pina Bausch and DV8), young people can become clearer about their own opinions, attitudes and feelings.

Cultural education in the art of dance, then, takes account of all of the above concerns and, as stated in the DfEE Report *All Our Futures: Creativity, Culture and Education* (1999: 48), aims:

a. To enable young people to recognise, explore and understand their own cultural assumptions and values.

b. To enable young people to embrace and understand cultural diversity by bringing them into contact with the attitudes, values and traditions of other cultures.
c. To encourage an historical perspective by relating contemporary values to the processes and events that have changed them.
d. To enable young people to understand the evolutionary nature of culture and the processes and potential for change.

RESOURCE-BASED TEACHING

The *midway* art of dance model demands a resource-based teaching methodology as the central and most important approach. Clearly, as indicated in the preceding text, this is because of the focus on the public dance art works as references for teaching and learning in dance education. The aspects of the *professional* dance model which have been retained and reoriented in the art of dance model (*see* the table on page 27) give professional dance works a new importance as essential resources for dance in education. In discussion of each of these aspects, there has been illustration of ways in which professional dance exemplars may be employed to develop the pupils' performing, creating and appreciation skills in the art of dance.

An analysis of the theory underpinning resource-based teaching of dance composition can be found in my book *Dance Composition* (2000). To avoid repetition, the following text provides a rationale for the approach and explains briefly how a professional dance resource may be employed in primary, secondary and higher education.

A good professional example demonstrates artistic and aesthetic quality in its composition and its performance. It also has implicit cultural and historical significance. Although a dance cannot be frozen in time for the purposes of study, technologies such as video, CD ROM and DVD permit repeated viewings of sections or the whole work in order to study it as an example of creative, original and qualitative choreography/performance and/or a token of a particular time and place.

It has been witnessed many times in my own practice across the sectors – from primary to higher education – that in-depth study of a work, even a small part of it, enhances, reinforces, consolidates, extends and inspires the students' own work. A dance work employed for these reasons is much more than a stimulus. Like a classic novel in the study of English literature, it becomes a starting point for the student's own creativity, a means of learning more about the discipline *per se*: style, form, expression, stage/costume/lighting design and performance. As suggested above, studying a choreographer's interpretation of a theme may extend the student's understanding and awareness of such issues. A dance work can also be studied as an example of choreographic traditions or trends and of the cultural context from which the art work and the choreographer emerge.

Consequently, all the entries under the heading of artistic learning on pages 31–33 can be augmented through the appropriate use of dance works in resource-based teaching/learning activities.

Moreover, if the engagement with an art work is 'feelingful' in the sense that the individual's own feelings and emotions can enter the processes, then it can be labelled an aesthetic experience. In my view, aesthetic interaction between students and art works is an important aim for resource-based teaching/learning; teachers/lecturers should ensure that their students' perceptions of sensory, expressive and formal qualities in art works are awakened and developed through the tasks they are given.

Resource-based teaching will work well if the resources selected are appropriate to the objectives of the lessons/lectures, rich in artistic, aesthetic and cultural features and used in balance with other activities within a total programme. In most instances at school level, dance works should not be studied in their every detail (perhaps A level study is the exception) nor analysed with infinite precision. This kind of scrutiny kills the artistic and aesthetic dimensions of the work and makes the study into a pseudo-scientific chore. It serves no purpose unless the intention is to reconstruct the work. If this is the case, the detailed analysis is a means to an end: a reconstructed section or whole dance *re-interpreted* in the students' own way. Hence, as in music, analysis of a professional performance of a work serves only as a qualitative example. It cannot and should not be copied exactly; rather it acts as a detailed reference text against which the students place their own interpretations. In other words, a dance ready-made is a resource to be employed in support of the students' own learning. It is not a set formula to be learned by rote and copied exactly. Neither is it a supply of content for the students' own choreography. This amounts to choreographic plagiarism! Rather, in my experience, the movement vocabulary and choreographic techniques in a dance work resource should become part of a bank or repertoire of ideas for the students from which they select and develop in their own ways. Making the movements or choreographic principles your own is a very important principle to maintain in resource-based learning. The

Wild Child Resource Pack for Dance Education (1999 and 2001)[2] puts this theory into practice in an exemplary manner. Demonstration of ways in which this multimedia pack and future such packs can extend and enhance artistic, aesthetic and cultural learning in dance will be included in later chapters.

The above makes clear the rationale for a resource-based teaching/learning approach in the art of dance in education model. It should not be the only approach, though. Students and, more particularly, children need to derive their ideas and inspirations for choreography from their own imaginations, from other stimuli such as poetry, etc., and from dance experience itself. They should also learn much from the teacher/lecturer and from their peers. Moreover, dance works *per se* are not the only resources applicable to dance education. Films such as *Singing in the Rain* (an example used in the section on primary education), *West Side Story* and *Fantasia* are appropriate resources, too. In these examples, the dance movement and choreography itself is used as a means of teaching/learning something more about dance. Films on natural phenomena such as volcanoes, the sea, animals and insects are better described as very good stimuli for dance and are therefore not of the same order as the former resources for resource-based teaching/learning programmes.

However, in order to learn from complex and highly developed examples of dance works, pupils need to be guided through structured tasks which are sufficiently open for them to make their own responses to the art work, yet structured enough to aid progression and constructive learning. The following methods may help achieve these objectives.

Viewing tasks

Watching dance is difficult. Movements are transient, illusive and complex. The view of dancers on video is two-dimensional, though, of course, the movement itself is three-dimensional. The spatial canvas of dance is never visible – it has to be imagined by the viewer. A simple example of this non-visible and abstract nature of spatial patterning is a dancer travelling on a circular pathway – the circle is not there, it is constructed by the viewer while the dancer

[2]This pack was first published by Bedford Interactive Productions in a CD-i format in 1999. It was published in CD ROM format in 2001. Jacqueline Smith-Autard and Jim Schofield authored these world-leading products to provide teachers and lecturers with quality resource-based pedagogy enhanced through the use of modern technology.

travels. For these and other reasons, the teacher/lecturer needs to help learners to see the dance as it passes through time.

In order to do this without telling the students what to see, however, it necessary to provide frameworks or leading questions to guide perception. It would be quite wrong in an artistic/aesthetic context to determine exactly what they should notice by directive means. Hence, a student-centred approach is beneficial for most of the viewing tasks.

Methods might include use of teacher-prepared questions (which may be presented in discussion or on worksheets) requiring students to observe, make comparisons, describe, interpret and make evaluative comment on what they see. For example, in relation to the initial 'ghosts' dance in Christopher Bruce's *Ghost Dances* (1981), they might be asked to observe and describe the movement of the ghosts' heads in relation to their bodies and suggest why Bruce selected such actions. This requires observation, description and interpretation. The next task might require the students to note how these head movements are repeated and developed throughout the section and then they might be asked to make evaluative comments on the ways in which the choreographed head movements enhanced the meaning/feeling and at the same time produced form in the ghost section of the dance work. Such questions lead rather than direct the students in their viewing but they also leave a broad scope for possible interpretations.

Alternatively, a multiple choice type of question on screen or on a worksheet could offer a range of possible words to describe the qualities in a phrase of movements, asking the students to select the most appropriate and perhaps to add their own to the given list. This helps the students to develop language to describe what is seen and also subtly opens their eyes to the range of qualities in the movements studied. Younger pupils may be asked for words to describe these qualities and the teacher could write them on the board. Children and students alike should be encouraged to use analogies and metaphors to make clear their perceptions of sensory and expressive qualities.

On almost every occasion of viewing a work, students should have opportunity to reflect on or talk about the feelings that the work evokes in them. These feelings could be positive or negative, but should be backed by reasoned comments. Articulating feelings, even if only for the students' own benefit, is important if the art of dance is to contribute effectively to aesthetic education.

Viewing tasks are often necessary precursors of performing and creating tasks since the dance work resource is the starting point for such work in resource-based teaching/learning.

Performing tasks

A most beneficial way of 'getting inside' a dance work, especially for older students, is to dance the whole or parts of the work. In order to learn a section, for example, the teacher or, occasionally, a dance artist might employ a directed teaching approach so that the students replicate as accurately as possible the choreographed movements. Access to notation scores and slow-motion video – or better still, to quality multimedia discs to allow instant repeats of short phrases, stills, frame-by-frame advancing through touch-button control to demonstrate the qualitative aspects of the professional dancers' performance – enhances the learning process. However, once the piece is learned, this instructive approach should end because students need to colour the movements in their own ways to express the perceived choreographic intention.

This kind of experience is a very valuable way of coming to know a work. To be able to dance a piece of professional choreography, it is necessary to learn how to perform the actions and the rhythmic, dynamic, spatial and relationship patterning in order to understand how the choreographer expresses the idea. Without altering the style and content of the work, the students then have to make their performances their own so that they show understanding of the 'text' through their presentation. The resource, then, constitutes a professional and expert example with which the students can compare and check their own work.

Methods of using the video resource have already been mentioned above. There is need of resource packs based on the works of established choreographers. Use of technology now allows the user access to a bank of computer-authored data (front and back view video, notation, stills, graphics of floor pattern and body shape for example, close-ups from different angles). To date, there is but one such pack: the *Wild Child CD Resource Pack* already mentioned. Until more such packs become available, teachers and lecturers need to design their own ways of teaching dance performance with the aid of videos. A good VHS recorder that holds the picture still enough to discuss the positioning of the limbs, head and shoulders, for example, and that can be moved frame by frame, helps the analysis of the movement – and of course, notation confirms the detail. Unfortunately, however, there is little access to notated scores and most teachers/lecturers have insufficient skill in reading notation. In my view, literacy in dance notation will grow when there are enough resources containing scores!

To date, then, teachers/lecturers should develop their own ways of teaching performance in a resource-based context. Many viewing tasks need to be integrated with performing tasks. For instance, a group might be asked to observe and make a graphic representation of the time-force-accent content of a phrase before attempting to dance it. The students would then learn the sequence having first gained understanding of its qualitative content. Learning becomes much faster and better consolidated if performance grows hand in hand with understanding of the 'text'.

Teachers/lecturers may also create a dance study based upon aspects of the dance work, thus providing a means of working on some of its 'essences' at the students' own level. This 'technical study' approach will be discussed in greater detail in the sections on the art of dance in secondary and tertiary education, but perhaps it is important to say here that an adaptation or 'watered down' version of the real thing might be a better way of getting something like the feeling of the work through performance into the students' experience, than attempting to perform movements which are technically beyond their capabilities. As with music, simplified adaptations of parts of dance works taught to students might prove to be a helpful way of 'getting inside' them through learning and performing them.

Creating tasks

It will become evident to the reader of the sections in ensuing chapters relating to resource-based teaching/learning in primary, secondary and tertiary dance education that there are many ways in which a dance ready-made can be employed as a basis for creative work. Suffice it to say here, that young children may be asked to recall one or two movements and talk about them and then to create their own versions of them. Older pupils may learn a part of a phrase and then end it in their own way, building on and perhaps developing the material. Secondary students, for example, may view a section noting the kinds of leaning and counter-balance actions the pairs of dancers are using and extract them to use in their own choreography. University students may study the style of movement or choreographic devices used and extract the essence of the style and/or the principles behind the choreographic devices for use in their own work.

Numerous examples could be given here, but the above are perhaps sufficient to indicate to the reader the advantages of resource-based teaching in developing the students' creative abilities in choreography. Learning from 'givens', i.e. choreographically rich examples (as discussed in the text above on creativity and imagi-nation), and working on these bases towards something new, individual and of creative value depends upon a student's coming to know and understand the discipline/techniques of the art form through in-depth study of its art works. Moreover, carefully formulated tasks which guide the students' perceptions of the way in which the dance work has been choreographed will teach them as much, if not more, about the processes than practical choreography experiences themselves. Thus artistic and aesthetic appreciation of the choreographer's skill and originality should be a primary objective in all resource-based teaching/learning creating tasks.

Cultural/historical context tasks

This kind of study is important for older students in that in order to understand a dance work they need to put it into a context of place and time. As indicated above, a study of dance works as historical phenomena provides students with knowledge of the practices, trends, styles and genres evident at any one time and of changes that have occurred over time. A study of dance works as cultural products provides students with an understanding of characteristic features of the works and their place in history. Looking inwards at the art work itself, and looking outwards at the society from which it emerged, provides a problem-solving means of study whereby students interpret evidence in dance works in the light of their research about the choreographers and the cultures in which the works were created.

Multiple resources are needed in this context. Through reading about works, watching them and making critical comparisons and contrasts, the students gradually become aware of classifications of genre and style and also recognise that some works do not fit easily into such classifications. The students should be led to support their study of a dance resource with research into books, programmes, choreographers' writings or interviews, critics' writings and tele-vision documentaries, photographs, and any published views of the dancers. Any opportunities to work with the choreographers or dancers themselves would be very beneficial. Such a mixture of primary and secondary sources should offer multiple means of looking *into* the dance works. At the same time, however, such study should be complemented with study of external influences – politi-cal, social, economic and cultural – which affect and are reflected in the choreographers' works. Characteristics of the works can then be better understood and explained.

Resource packs

The above approach indicates a need for resource packs containing a variety of materials, in addition to a video performance of the dance work studied, preferably on digital discs. Surprisingly, since the first edition of this book was published in 1994, very few dance education resource packs have been published, and none bar the *Wild Child Pack* mentioned above are on CD discs. Videos of works are available (especially those studied for examinations) and some have accompanying teachers' notes, but these notes are frequently brief and do not provide in-depth analyses or use of the dance works as bases for the students' own creating and performing activities. Rather, they give information to inform the teacher/students about the 'set' works so that students may answer appreciation questions presented in examinations.

If resource-based teaching is to be fully effective, the pack should offer creating, performing and appreciating tasks to be presented by the teacher or undertaken by the students working independently or in groups. The tasks should be derived from the dance work featured in the resource, and need to engage the students in problem-solving activities if they are to gain artistic, aesthetic or cultural understanding of the dance work through use of the resource. Hence, resource packs will build up students' knowledge of the professional dance work/s featured. However, at the same time they should contain a range of activities, emanating from the dance work, that promote the students' own practical and theoretical study of dance. For example, worksheets could direct them to study the form of an excerpt and then to answer questions to demonstrate their understanding of the relationship of motifs, repetitions and developments to the overall structure of the dance work.

The content of resource packs will differ according to their purposes. The emphasis above has been on professional dance works as content, but it is also appropriate that packs contain study material such as specific dance techniques or be based on development of dance composition and performance skills through making visual the theory currently contained in text books[3].

---

[3]A new CD ROM pack entitled *Motif and Variations* is to be produced by Bedford Interactive Productions. In addition to teaching dance performance, this resource will provide visual exemplification of all the concepts explained in text in *Dance Composition* (2000).

A description of the content contained in *Wild Child*, the world-leading CD-i/CD ROM resource pack, will demonstrate the depth and range of content that, in my view, should be available to aid development of the students' knowledge and understanding of a dance work and to extend their own abilities to create, perform and appreciate dances.

Wild Child – A CD Resource Pack

[4]The Ludus Dance Company's production of *Wild Child* – made into an interactive CD Resource Pack published by Bedford Interactive Productions – is an excellent visual exemplification of dance concepts for dance education at all levels. The pack contains two interactive CD discs, an audio CD disc and a book. The latter is a resource book, not just a manual. The interactive CD discs and the book have been created to augment and complement each other.

This resource pack is unique in that it is generic in demonstrating a new resource-based teaching/learning pedagogy that can be applied to other resources. The *Wild Child* pack has a huge range of teaching materials. Through a number of worksheet activities it teaches *principles*, *concepts* and *methods* of working in dance composition, performance and appreciation. It therefore has an extensive shelf life and adds to, extends and enhances the use of other resource packs and dance texts.

Unlike many CD ROM discs, the *Wild Child* discs are not dense with text. There are three main reasons for this. First, because there is very little room for readable text on screen alongside reasonably sized movies. Second, because multimedia technology is wasted if it merely replaces paper. Third, and most important, because the book is designed to work in conjunction with – and to reinforce, extend, and supplement – the information contained on the interactive CD discs.

Hence, the open book can be glanced at while studying dynamic, full-screen moving images. Quick reference to the book can be made while simply pausing the images on screen, rather than going to another level within the disc. It is important to stress, therefore, that this availability of the supporting written materials makes for a coherent and uninterrupted access to a topic of study.

[4]Text describing the content of the *Wild Child CD Resource Pack* was first published in *Dance Composition* (2000).

Additionally, of course, the CDs are *interactive*. This in itself implies constant user interaction with the resource. Moreover, since it is a *resource* – not a self-contained, programmed learning pack – interaction requires the user to make the decision on which aspects to employ, and how to use them as a means of furthering or supplementing the dance work in hand. As a resource and a source for a variety of dance purposes, each aspect of the visual material can be employed in different ways. It is the book itself that suggests variable usage of the CDs according to perceived differing needs. A full range of such different approaches is best presented on paper so that work for specific groups of users is contained in separate sections.

The content of the pack is summarised below.

CD RESOURCE DISC 1: full performance by the Ludus Dance Company of *Wild Child* – choreography by Jane Scott Barrett, and music and artistic direction by James Mackie on full-screen digital video

a. **Film view** of 56-minute video – *Wild Child* – a dance piece depicting the plight of a 19th century child, abandoned in the forest at a young age, captured as an adolescent and 'civilised' through socialisation into play, love, work and attendance at social events.

b. **Access and Control** screen to provide access to six main scenes and 31 sub-sections of *Wild Child*. Throughout, the digital video has controls to single shot, stop/go, go back, slow motion and exit.

c. **'Viewing and Doing'** study linked to the **Resource Book**. This study of the whole work is presented under the following headings:
   - Themes
   - Dance Content
   - Dance Form
   - Music and Sound
   - Costumes and Set

CD RESOURCE DISC 2: Creative Dancework – excerpts of *Wild Child* on full-screen digital video

a. **Composition** includes further study of:
   - Dance Content – contact/partner work
   - Dance Form – detailed analysis through macro and micro analysis charts
   - Orchestration – analysis of dancers in time and space

b. **Performance** study includes:
- Technique – contact work – beginnings to advanced sequences
- Repertoire – teaching of two items from *Wild Child*
- Performance Qualities – study/practice of artistic qualities to improve performance

c. **Appreciation** study includes:
- Aesthetic Qualities – perception of sensory, expressive and formal qualities

RESOURCE BOOK
As mentioned above, a distinctive feature of this resource is the strong interrelationship between the CD discs, the book, the teacher and the learners while working interactively. To this end, the Resource Book is inextricably linked to the content of the discs. Furthermore, *the approach used lays emphasis on requiring responses to questions or tasks based upon the use of* Wild Child *as a resource and source for teaching and learning in dance performance, composition and appreciation.*

- **Section 1** describes the *Wild Child* resource pack and interactive CD as a medium.
- **Section 2** describes resource-based teaching and learning and provides 80+ worksheets to advance dance knowledge and practical expertise in performance and composition. These worksheets are based on the contents of both CD discs.
- **Section 3A** explores use of the *Wild Child* resource pack for primary teachers through increasing their own knowledge of dance and their understanding of how to teach dance.
- **Section 3B** explores use of the *Wild Child* resource pack for non-specialist secondary teachers through increasing their own knowledge of dance and their understanding of how to teach dance.
- **Section 3C** explores use of the *Wild Child* resource pack for secondary (specialist teachers) and tertiary dance education.

Though most appropriate to and comprehensive in its objectives, content and methods of delivery for the art of dance *midway* model, the above resource pack is somewhat unique. It is predicted that further such multimedia packs will be authored but, because of the costs involved, that not many will emerge in the foreseeable future. On the other hand, linear video-based resource packs are still emerging. Some of these will be referred to in subsequent chapters so that teachers appreciate that the principles and methods underpinning resource-based teaching/learning in the art of dance in education can still be applied in circumstances that are limited to the use of 'low technology' linear video. These examples will show that teachers can supplement use of video resources with use of the Internet, books, newspapers, radio or TV documentaries, pictures, notation scores and programmes for research of dance topics. A bank of such resources should be available to aid students' study of professional dance works. However, a source of qualitative dance work may also be captured by videoing the students' own work. Former dance students' compositions could be very informative for ensuing groups but, in common with all other resources, these created and performed dances should be used in conjunction with worksheets or tasks that require users to analyse and actively learn from them rather than passively view them. In such ways, resource-based teaching can take place to the benefit of students' practical and theoretical learning in the art of dance in education.

Conclusion

The preceding text has presented a theoretical basis for the art of dance in education. The *midway* model which derives from and combines the best features of both the *educational* and *professional* models has been shown to have distinctive features of its own. Its three strands – creating, performing, and viewing dances – culminate in appreciation of the art of dance. It also confirms the kinds of education towards which the art of dance strives to contribute, i.e. artistic, aesthetic and cultural education. Resource-based teaching/learning has been presented as an approach which focuses on the study of established dance works at the core of its rationale.

The art of dance in education model has developed over a period of time. However, like all teaching/learning models, it is not static. Teachers should reflect on and develop their own practice so that dance teaching is always dynamic and responsive to change.

The following chapters give some suggestions as to how the theoretical basis described above underpins practice in teaching the art of dance in primary and secondary and in tertiary education. Because the central concern of this book is to provide teachers with a theoretical basis for their work, the headings used in chapter 1 provide the structure for each of the following chapters. The practical examples, however, should further elucidate the theory, a reciprocal relationship between theory and practice being the ideal outcome.

2

The Art of Dance in Primary Schools

Dance in the primary curriculum – the background

Young children love to move to music, and when they perform movements expressing qualities or moods in the music we often say that they are dancing. Indeed, we say this when watching birds courting, insects around a light or dolphins performing rhythmic skims and twirls. In these contexts, dancing is a word used as an analogy to describe movement performed for its own sake, especially that which emulates a known dance form such as the turning in a waltz, or the forward and back meeting and parting in a folk dance. There is a difference, however, in this use of the word and in its use to describe the purposeful act of dancing a dance.

Similarly, a child's natural spontaneous joy of expressive movement is dancing in an analogous sense only. It is not the art of dance but it certainly forms the basis of it. Just as children need to learn how to write stories and poems, how to create music, and how to paint pictures, they also need to learn how to create, perform and appreciate dances.

In one form or another, dance is an established part of education in many primary schools. The Department for Education and Employment with the Qualifications and Curriculum Authority (2000) continues to include dance as a statutory part of the Physical Education National Curriculum for England. As in the 1992 Order and subsequent amendments, although not explicitly stated, the curriculum content advocates an *art of dance* experience for primary education in that it requires that pupils 'use movement imaginatively' and 'create and perform dances' to 'express and communicate ideas and feelings'. However, the new National Curriculum for

England (DfEE, QCA 2000) also prescribes that, throughout the primary years, children should learn about and be able to perform 'dances from different times and places'. While the latter requirement is an attempt to attend to the cultural education of pupils, in the context of dance as a mere fraction of the Physical Education programme, it is unlikely that sufficient time can be allotted to this range of dance experience to deliver anything more than very superficial coverage. It also puts an impossible burden on teachers in that their knowledge and teaching expertise has to be extended to embrace traditional, folk and social dance forms in addition to the art of dance. This is totally unrealistic, given the very limited training time allocated in teacher education courses for Physical Education as a subject including games, gymnastics, swimming, athletics and outdoor and adventurous activities as well as dance.

A further concern, especially in relation to delivery of the art of dance for primary pupils, is the dilution and distortion of the conceptual basis. The content described for dance in the National Curriculum for England in 2000 is no longer definable in the terms used in the 1994 publication of this book. Here, it was reported that from a background strongly influenced by the *educational* model described in chapter 1:

> ...there has been a gradual shift towards the art of dance model. In recent years, it has become good practice for pupils in primary schools to experience dance both through creating and performing their own dances and through viewing dances: their own, their peers' and dance works of professional choreographers. Although the terms are different, this three-stranded approach is embodied in the programme of study for dance in the Statutory Order for physical education in the National Curriculum.   (Smith-Autard 1994: 47)

The new curriculum for 2000 reflects little of the three-stranded approach. Indeed, with the inclusion of an alternative type of dance experience (the traditional and social dance forms), together with an emphasis on performance through an acquisition of physical skills and fitness (appropriate, perhaps, for physical education), there appears to be little room for a comprehensive art of dance experience in primary schools. This concern is expressed by Veronica Jobbins, Chair of the National Dance Teachers' Association:

A major concern for the dance community is whether or not the artistic and creative aspects of dance have been lost within the physical education framework. (Jobbins 2000: 2)

Later in the same report, and in the context of commenting on the bias towards exercise and fitness in the syllabus, she states that:

This has to be to the detriment of the essential aspects of arts education, the development of critical and appreciative understanding. None of the bullet points within the programmes of study highlight this aspect. (Jobbins 2000: 2)

In fact, the absence of reference to appreciation makes it difficult to understand how the requirements that pupils learn how to 'use movements imaginatively' to 'create and perform dances' that 'express and communicate ideas and feelings' (DfEE, QCA 2000) can be attributed to the art of dance model that has been prescribed as 'good practice' for primary education for at least the past ten years.

However, adherence to a list of content within a syllabus does not stop the teacher from adding to it. Nor does it affect the teacher's choice on how to deliver the dance content. Indeed, the 'Top Dance' resource cards and handbook – subject content for in-service courses that have been provided for primary teachers under the auspices of the Youth Sport Trust and Sport England (2000) – include all three activities: composing, performing and appreciating/evaluating in all lessons. Clearly, the experienced dance educators who have written these resources and are delivering the much-needed in-service training for primary teachers are not compromising the art of dance model. Other texts such as *Setting the Scene – The Arts and Young People* (Department of National Heritage 1996) and *The Arts Inspected* (Office for Standards in Education 1998) fully endorse the ideas encapsulated in the art of dance model. Both these reports refer to the development of appreciation as an important aspect of arts education. Indeed, these texts contain a good deal of reference to pupils' viewing their own and professional dance works and to occasionally working with dance artists in live situations to inform their own creative and performance work.

In line with the above texts' confirmation of the art of dance model as 'best practice' for primary schools, the second edition of this book makes no changes to the model defined and presented in the first edition. However, the references made to the National Curriculum content for dance in the first edition have been removed from this edition. Rather, opportunity is taken to consider the art of dance model as a generic approach for the teaching of dance in primary schools across the world. The concepts and principles underlying the *midway* art of dance in education model that have been proposed in chapter 1 are therefore comprehensively applied to the ensuing recommendations for primary dance pedagogy.

A dance syllabus for primary schools

The following text outlines possible content for the art of dance for primary pupils. It is taken and adapted from the guidelines for content presented in the appendix of the first edition of this book. This content was derived from my interpretations of the 1992 National Curriculum syllabus for dance. These interpretations emerged from study of syllabuses that have been delivered in 'best practice' primary schools. The content is re-presented here because it is still considered appropriate for all primary teachers who wish to deliver the art of dance model where there is equal emphasis placed on pupils learning to create, perform and appreciate dances and a concern that dance contribute to the pupils' artistic, aesthetic and cultural education. The latter, in compliance with definitions offered in chapter 1, is embedded in experience of the art of dance and, therefore, does not demand study of social and traditional dance forms in isolation.

A summary chart on the opposite page is followed by a detailed syllabus for each stage of the primary curriculum.

SYLLABUS FOR THE ART OF DANCE IN PRIMARY SCHOOLS

STAGE 1: pupils aged 5–7

Individually, in pairs and small groups experience of:

A) Dance Content – Actions
control, co-ordination, balance, poise and elevation in basic body actions including travelling, jumping, turning, gesture and stillness

B) Dance Content – Qualities, Space, Relationships
contrasts of speed, tension, continuity, rhythm, shape, size, direction and level in simple spatial relationships using unison and canon

C) Dance Themes and Stimuli
moods and feelings through spontaneous responses and through structured tasks; a range and variety of contrasting stimuli, including music

D) Dance Form – Making Dances
making dances with clear beginnings, middles and ends

STAGE 2: pupils aged 7–11

Individually, in pairs, small and larger groups experience of:

A) Dance Content – Actions
increasing the range and complexity of body actions, including step patterns and use of body parts

B) Dance Content – Qualities, Space, Relationships
enriching their movements by varying speed, tension, continuity, rhythm, shape, size, direction and level in varying spatial and numerical relationships using unison and canon

C) Dance Themes and Stimuli
expressing feelings, moods and ideas and creating simple characters and narratives in movements; a range and variety of contrasting stimuli, including music

D) Dance Form – Making Dances
making dances with clear beginnings, middles and ends involving improvising, exploring, selecting and refining content, and sometimes incorporating work from other aspects of the curriculum, in particular music, art and drama

Syllabus statement

Individually and when ready in pairs and in small groups, with or without accompaniment and through different DANCES pupils should:

- *experience and develop control, co-ordination, balance, poise and elevation in basic body actions including travelling, jumping, turning, gesture and stillness*

Interpretations of the above statement to define: *DANCE CONTENT – ACTIONS*

LEARNING ACTIVITIES

- movements of the whole body – stretch, curl, twist and different body parts – head, trunk, legs, arms, shoulders, elbows, wrists, hands, fingers, hips, knees, ankles, feet, toes – moving independently, taking weight or leading
- travelling actions – walk, run, skip, crawl, stagger, slide, creep, rush, stride, march, prance, prowl, jog, dodge, trot, gallop
- jumping actions – jumping from two feet to two feet, one to the same (hop), one to the other (spring or leap)
- turning actions – spin, whirl, spiral, roll
- gestures – movements of free body parts, e.g. arms, legs, shoulders (includes everyday non-verbal communication like waving and shrugging; work actions like digging and sweeping; and symbolic dance gestures like stretched arms high to express elation or arm punch with closed fist to indicate anger)
- stillness – stop, freeze, balance, hold, hesitate, pause, settle

LEARNING OUTCOMES

CREATING – pupils should be led to:

- respond spontaneously and to improvise to stimuli and/or accompaniment, emphasising particular body parts or actions or showing a variety of actions according to the task
- explore, discover, select and refine dance actions suitable for the dances they experience
- create their own actions and action phrases and remember and repeat them in the dances they experience

PERFORMING – pupils should be led to:

- isolate and use all body parts separately and in simple co-ordinations (e.g. arms swinging with legs marching)
- be able to control their bodies in balances, elevations and in moving in the space
- stand/sit well with poise and move with ease to change body shapes/positions
- be able to perform the actions listed above separately and in simple sequences (e.g. travel into jump and hold still)
- practise and improve the clarity of and quality in actions (e.g. extension in jumping and resilience in landing) and dance them with confidence and co-ordination

APPRECIATING – pupils should be led to:

- name all body parts and describe the movements they do with them
- name and describe the actions they and other dancers perform
- suggest meanings implicit in actions they experience in dance (e.g. dragging feet for sad, miserable feeling)

STAGE 1: *pupils aged 5–7*

Syllabus statement

Individually and when ready in pairs and in small groups, with or without accompaniment and through different DANCES pupils should:

- *explore contrasts of speed, tension, continuity, rhythm, shape, size, direction and level in simple spatial relationships using unison and canon, and describe what they have done or seen*

Interpretations of the above statement to define: *DANCE CONTENT – QUALITIES, SPACE and RELATIONSHIPS*

LEARNING ACTIVITIES

- vary actions through contrasts of speed – slow, fast, sudden, enduring
- vary actions with degrees of tension – strong, light, forceful, gentle
- vary actions with differences in continuity – flowing freely, hesitant, ongoing/continuous or stopping with ease
- use body shape and size – round, twisted, narrow, wide, small
- use space around them and room space, directions – forward, backwards, sideways, up and down, levels (high, medium, low)
- use pathways on the floor – curved or straight, squares, circles, zig-zags; use pathways and shapes in the air – curved or straight – circles, squares, alphabet letters, numbers, etc.
- combine elements to create rhythmic patterns – accent, phrases, simple divisions of time (e.g. skipping, running, marching)
- use simple spatial relationships (e.g. side-by-side, follow-my-leader, under, over, around, etc.)
- work with a partner in unison and canon

LEARNING OUTCOMES

CREATING – pupils should be led to:

- respond spontaneously and improvise with a variety of stimuli (music, sound, poetry, objects, etc.) using contrasts of speed, tension and continuity relevant to the task/idea
- differentiate and select the above qualities appropriately in creating dance movements/phrases to express ideas, feelings/moods (e.g. sharp, strong, quick movements to depict lightning)
- vary the actions they select by changing direction, level, size and shape using their own and the general room space effectively
- create floor and air patterns in response to tasks, e.g. travel in a circle and then draw a circle around your body
- respond spontaneously and accurately to different rhythms and create movements showing awareness of them
- improvise and make sequences using simple relationship variations (e.g. dancing side-by-side in unison)

PERFORMING – pupils should be led to:

- perform actions with different qualities – speed, tension, continuity – and to contrast these qualities, e.g. change from slow to fast, strong to light
- practise and improve the qualities in their movements and show understanding of them as expressive features in dance
- perform actions in different directions, levels and pathways showing awareness of size, shape and space around the body, in the room and in relation to others
- dance rhythmically to a variety of music/stimuli showing awareness of accent, phrasing and simple time changes
- demonstrate ability to relate to others in space and time

APPRECIATING – pupils should be led to:

- describe the qualities, rhythms and the spatial and relationship patterning in the actions they see
- interpret the kinds of meanings/feelings that such content conveys (e.g. fast, light, ongoing and large actions, on zig-zag pathways – for excitement)
- evaluate the expressive features in their own and others' dance performances

STAGE 1: pupils aged 5–7

Syllabus statement
Individually and when ready in pairs and in small groups, with or without accompaniment and through different DANCES pupils should:

- *be given opportunities to explore moods and feelings through spontaneous responses and through structured tasks*
- *experience working with a range and variety of contrasting stimuli, including music*

Interpretations of the above statement to define: *DANCE THEMES and STIMULI*

LEARNING ACTIVITIES

- use of a range and variety of stimuli – stories, colours, patterns, sculptures, poems, pictures, natural phenomena, objects, shapes, etc.
- experience of a range of music as both stimuli and accompaniments – different in type (classical, folk, percussion, electronic, etc.), in rhythm, style, mood and instruments used
- exploration of moods (happy, sad, calm, angry, etc.) of feelings/ emotions (caring, proud, greedy, scared, etc.) in response to various stimuli (e.g. music) spontaneously and/or in structured tasks

LEARNING OUTCOMES

CREATING – pupils should be led to:

- improvise and explore a range of actions, qualities and spatial features of dance in response to a variety of stimuli (e.g. cats provide a range of different actions – pouncing, creeping, arching, stretching, rolling, curling – which can be performed with varying qualities of speed, tension and continuity in different directions, levels and pathways)

- improvise and explore a range of moods and feelings and the actions, qualities and spatial features of dance which express them (e.g. sad: subdued, heavy, slow steps, head lowered and sinking movements)

- in response to the teacher's structured task, select and create actions, qualities and spatial features appropriate to the stimulus and/or feeling/mood of the dance

PERFORMING – pupils should be led to:

- use different kinds of accompaniment (music, poetry, percussion sounds) while dancing, showing an ability to listen and respond sensitively

- dance with musicality and an awareness of rhythm, tempo, beat and intensity

APPRECIATING – pupils should be led to:

- describe, simply, the elements of the stimuli (e.g. the changes in a piece of music – slow, quiet beginning, a loud fast middle section and repeat of the slow bit at the end; the colour contrasts in a picture; the movements of a cat)

- describe ways in which the stimuli suggest movements (e.g. the movement of the sea on the shore – forward and back gentle hand movements)

- interpret the expressive meanings/feelings in the stimuli they use and/or see in the dances of others

- comment on the stimuli and their feelings about them (e.g. whether they like the music or not and why)

STAGE 1: *pupils aged 5–7*

Syllabus statement

Individually, and when ready in pairs and in small groups, with or without accompaniment and through different DANCES pupils should:

- *experience and be guided towards making dances with clear beginnings, middles and ends*

Interpretations of the above statement to define: *DANCE FORM – MAKING DANCES*

LEARNING ACTIVITIES

- respond to a stimulus to find movements
- experiment and/or explore movement vocabulary – actions, qualities, spatial and relationship features to express the idea, mood or feeling
- select appropriate movements in response to structured tasks
- refine movement content and repeat it accurately within the dance
- structure the movements into dance phrases and sections within the teacher's framework, e.g. create a sequence of swinging movement to depict swings in a playground dance
- find starting and ending positions appropriate to the theme
- work alone, with a partner or in a small group to respond creatively to tasks set, e.g. having been led to explore turning actions with a partner, they could make a sequence to depict roundabouts for the playground dance
- match movement to accompaniment
- perform the dances they make (normally based on the teacher's framework) showing an understanding of beginnings, middles and ends
- with the teacher, plan frameworks for whole dances and (occasionally towards the end of the key stage) make short dances of their own – choosing theme, music/accompaniment and movements by themselves

LEARNING OUTCOMES

CREATING – pupils should be led to:

- employ the above processes – exploring, selecting, refining, revising and repeating movements and sequences to make dances based on the teacher's frameworks
- solve problems and make decisions on the appropriateness of movement in response to tasks
- make individual and group responses to creative tasks using their own ideas
- develop concepts of form through considering how the parts of the dances – beginnings, middles and ends – relate to make whole dances

PERFORMING – pupils should be led to:

- remember the order of parts of dances
- show clarity in starting and ending positions
- dance expressively to show understanding of meaning
- practise and improve whole dance performances to accompaniments (if used)
- perform dances with awareness of other pupils in pairs or groups, taking turns or working in unison

APPRECIATING – pupils should be led to:

- describe in simple terms the content, accompaniment and structure of the dances they experience
- interpret the meanings in dances they make or see
- comment on the dances they make or see looking for beginnings, middles and ends
- begin to discern different types of dances, e.g. dramatic or lyrical, and styles of dance, e.g. folk and social

STAGE 2: pupils aged 7–11

Syllabus statement
Individually, in pairs, in small groups and (with teacher guidance) in larger groups, with or without accompaniment and through different DANCES pupils should:

- *be given opportunities to increase the range and complexity of body actions, including step patterns and use of body parts*

Interpretations of the above statement to define: *DANCE CONTENT – ACTIONS*

LEARNING ACTIVITIES

- combine and isolate two or three moving parts of the body in simple co-ordinations, e.g. head, arm and leg movements (robot dance)

- discover different ways of performing each body action, e.g. extending the vocabulary of jumps to include one foot to two feet and two feet to one foot, travelling on different body parts, turning part of the body (twist), turning in different amounts (half, quarter, two) and in a variety of ways (spiralling, hopping, stepping)

- combine actions, e.g. travel and gesture, turning jumps, travelling turns (rolls), travelling turning jumps

- perform step patterns, e.g. four walks, four skips, eight gallops

- combine step patterns with other body actions, e.g. in a dance about making friends, the above travelling step pattern could be performed twice to find a partner (chorus) then together the children could perform a jumping sequence (verse); the step pattern could then be repeated to find a new partner and a turning sequence could be performed

LEARNING OUTCOMES

CREATING – pupils should be led to:

- improvise and explore actions to create a range of appropriate vocabulary for each of the dances they experience
- explore and discover ways in which actions can be linked and combined to create action phrases and step patterns
- select appropriate actions and use of body parts in relation to the themes of dances and accompaniment used

PERFORMING – pupils should be led to:

- perform sequences of actions with control, co-ordination, balance, poise and elevation
- practise and improve precision, clarity and quality in the use of body parts in combination and in performance of actions separately and/or in combination
- perform actions rhythmically and expressively in relation to dance themes and accompaniment
- perform actions in relationship with other dancers in unison and canon with appropriate timing and spacing

APPRECIATING – pupils should be led to:

- describe and comment on appropriateness, range, variety, originality of body actions and use of body parts in dances they create and perform and/or dances they see (e.g. videos of professional dances)
- observe, describe (sometimes in writing) accurately and evaluate sequences of actions performed by themselves or others
- appreciate the meanings implicit in dance actions

STAGE 2: pupils aged 7–11

Syllabus statement

Individually, in pairs, in small groups and (with teacher guidance) in larger groups, with or without accompaniment and through different DANCES pupils should:

- *be guided to enrich their movements by varying speed, tension, continuity, rhythm, shape, size, direction and level in varying spatial, numerical relationships using unison and canon*

Interpretations of the above statement to define: *DANCE CONTENT – QUALITIES, SPACE and RELATIONSHIPS*

LEARNING ACTIVITIES

- combine separate qualities – e.g. strong and fast or gentle and slow – with a range of actions
- make gradual or sudden changes of speed, tension and continuity using a range of actions
- develop greater sensitivity to rhythm and rhythmic changes
- show clarity of shape, direction, level, and size in performing different actions
- understand and use qualitative and spatial elements as expressive features of dance
- work in pairs and small groups using spatial and numerical relationship variations in unison and canon
- develop awareness of others in dance relationships, including simple contact work

LEARNING OUTCOMES

CREATING – pupils should be led to:

- improvise, explore and select from separate and combined qualities – speed, tension and continuity to colour their actions and to express feelings/moods/ideas
- pattern their movements in space paying attention to size, level, direction, shape and pathway according to the

expressive intentions (e.g. large, high, stretched movements travelling forward on a straight pathway to convey aggression)

- use a range of different stimuli – music, poetry, pictures, etc. – to discover how the qualitative and spatial features they contain stimulate dance expression (e.g. strong, gushing, sweeping music with changes in pitch up and down might be appropriate for a windy day dance; a Lowry painting might stimulate different rhythmic working actions and group walking patterns in hunched-up body shapes)
- use a range of spatial relationship variations (e.g. in front, behind, beside, under, etc.) in simple group shapes (e.g. circles, lines, huddled, scattered) and unison and canon
- explore simple contact work with a partner to express ideas

PERFORMING – pupils should be led to:

- practise and improve actions with contrasting qualities (e.g. fast then slow), combining qualities (e.g. fast and strong), and gradually changing qualities (e.g. accelerate/decelerate)
- show clarity in body shape, size, level, direction and pathway of movement
- enrich their expressive performances paying attention to the above qualities and spatial features
- further develop their ability to dance using more complex rhythms and variations of phrasing (e.g. Vivaldi's *Les Quatre Saisons*)
- practise and improve dancing with others, paying attention to relationships in space and time
- show sensitivity and control in working with others, with or without contact

APPRECIATING – pupils should be led to:

- describe changes in qualities of speed, tension and continuity, and in rhythmic, spatial and relationship patterning in the dances they perform and see
- interpret the qualitative, spatial and relationship features of dance to suggest expressive meanings
- evaluate the qualities, spatial and relationship features in their own and others' performances

STAGE 2: pupils aged 7–11

Syllabus statement

Individually, in pairs, in small groups and (with teacher guidance) in larger groups, with or without accompaniment and through different DANCES pupils should:

- *in response to a range of stimuli, express feelings, moods and ideas and create simple characters and narratives in movement*

Interpretations of the above statement to define: *DANCE THEMES and STIMULI*

LEARNING ACTIVITIES

- extend the range of stimuli used as a basis for dance and developing responses to more mature/complex ideas sometimes linked to other aspects of the curriculum (e.g. ideas might include electricity, magnetism, war, green issues such as deforestation, football, etc.)

- give more detailed attention to music – its qualities (e.g. crescendo/ diminuendo – getting louder/getting softer; staccato/legato – sharp, clipped and separated/smooth continuous and linked), its style (e.g. full and romantic; precise, symmetric and classical; rhythmic, fluid and folky; rhythmic, beaty and jazzy), form (e.g. repeated passages, build-ups and climaxes; verse and chorus; ABA) and its rhythmic patterns (accented sounds; phrases with 'commas' and 'full stops'; time signature and tempo)

- experience further creating and performing dances based on moods and feelings, taking more responsibility in choice of actions, qualities, spatial and relationship features to express them

- study character and dramatic action between characters and ways of expressing these in dance (e.g. Scrooge-like mean and greedy actions would include grabbing, gathering towards oneself, and pushing away movements which could cause cowering reactions from Bob Cratchit)

LEARNING OUTCOMES

CREATING – pupils should be led to:

• improvise and explore a range of movements combining actions, qualities, spatial and relationship elements in response to the more complex stimuli – ideas, poems, music, pictures, natural phenomena, etc.

• through sensitive response in movement, show more understanding and knowledge of elements of music and create sequences which complement the music used

• discover and select for themselves a range of actions, qualities, spatial and relationship features which depict mood, feeling, idea (e.g. earthquake), character and dramatic events (e.g. quarrelling)

PERFORMING – pupils should be led to:

• practise and improve their dance movement so that it effectively reflects the stimulus (e.g. volcano actions need to be explosive, strong and energetic)

• perform to music with a developing awareness of its features and show this in movement (e.g. pauses, climaxes)

• perform characterisations and dramatic interaction with expressive clarity

APPRECIATING – pupils should be led to:

• interpret the meanings/feelings in the stimuli and offer their opinions as to how they might be used in dance

• use increasingly elaborated language, including metaphors, to describe the stimuli/moods/feelings/characters and narratives and the movement which depicts them

• comment on the stimuli and the dance outcomes and offer their opinion of them

STAGE 2: pupils aged 7–11

Syllabus statement
Individually, in pairs, in small groups and (with teacher guidance) in larger groups, with or without accompaniment and through different DANCES pupils should:

- *make dances with clear beginnings, middles and ends involving improvising, exploring, selecting and refining content; and sometimes, incorporating work from other aspects of the curriculum, in particular music, art and drama*

Interpretations of the above statement to define: *DANCE FORM – MAKING DANCES*

LEARNING ACTIVITIES

- improvise freely and within structured tasks
- explore and find new and different ways to answer tasks
- select appropriate answers in movement to creative problems
- refine and rehearse movements, sections and whole dances which can then be repeated
- experience further aspects of group work in dances, e.g. negotiating, planning, selecting, composing
- use other aspects of the curriculum to illustrate structural aspects of dances, e.g. rhythmic patterns, lines and verses in poetry, life-cycles in natural phenomena like a thunderstorm, volcano, day and night, musical structures, etc.
- find language, including metaphors, to describe movement, to interpret meanings and to evaluate the structure of dances they make or see

LEARNING OUTCOMES

CREATING – pupils should be led to:

- find a greater range of responses in improvising, exploring, selecting and refining movements and sequences to make dances based on the teacher's frameworks
- structure phrases and sections of dances and, with help from the teacher, plan and make whole dances
- work on tasks independently – individually, in pairs and in small groups, and, with help, in larger groups
- use aspects of partner or group work to express ideas, e.g. mirroring, leading and following, copying, contrasting, moving in unison, or in canon, making group shapes (lines, circles, clusters)

PERFORMING – pupils should be led to:

- remember, practise and perform dances they have made, sometimes over a period of time (e.g. possibly over 3–4 weeks) and perhaps building a repertoire of dances
- show greater awareness of structure of dances in their performances – beginnings, phrases, pauses, stops, sections, contrasts, climaxes and endings
- develop performance skills in presenting dances to audiences – focus, projection, expression, dancing with others and with music (if any)

APPRECIATING – pupils should be led to:

- describe and interpret the content of dances – actions, qualities, spatial and relationship aspects (what they see and what it means)
- describe and interpret the structure of dances – the phrases, the sections, beginnings, middles and endings (what happened as the dance progressed and where and why the different parts occurred)

The following text aims to help teachers to interpret the above syllabus content into lessons for primary children. It also aims to demonstrate how the theoretical basis of the art of dance model in education, described in chapter 1, can be applied to dance in primary education.

In order to do this, it is necessary to start with the end products of dance lessons – dances.

There are two reasons for this:

a. It is important to consider first what is to be achieved and learned by the children. What skills, knowledge and understanding are to be acquired through dance experiences? This question is best answered through analysis of potential outcomes of the lesson/s.

b. There is lack of literature for teachers explaining the rationale, theory and principles behind the practice of completing dance experiences with dances as outcomes in good primary dance teaching practice. Apart from a National Dance Teachers' Association video and booklet – *Teaching Dance in the Primary School* (1998) – there are several books available that describe dance content for the primary sector and provide teachers with example lesson plans and tips on how to teach these dance lessons. The latter generally outline the content starting from the beginning warm-up and give an outline of the content of the dance. These texts are good sources for ideas and at least one (*Let's Dance* by Mary Harlow and Linda Rolfe, 1992) goes some way towards demonstrating when and how the three processes of creating, performing and appreciating might occur in their example lessons. The end products – the dances the children will create, perform and appreciate – are not analysed however. Indeed, no current text examines in detail what is to be learned in dance and through dance from the lesson experiences. It is assumed that if a teacher presents a well-planned lesson out of the text, he or she will learn by example and will be able to plan future lessons.

A dance outcome

The following description of a teacher-created dance framework is intended to provide the reader with an imaginary picture of a new group of year 3 pupils performing the dance outcome at the end of maybe two lessons. A teacher-created dance framework is a composed structure for a dance denoting what kind of movement the children will be doing in each section, the order of the sections and how these relate to make a whole dance. The children fill in the detail of the movement content in their own way. Each part of the dance will be interpreted differently by each pupil, each pair, or each group. A well-made teacher-created dance framework has a clear beginning, middle and end, contains variety and contrast, develops logically and achieves coherence of form.

Lesson planning – a teacher's dance framework

Dance title *Dancing in the Rain in New Wellies*

Introduction (approximately 16 bars of walking-pace music)
Sitting on the floor – pull on to feet imaginary wellington boots. Admire them, still sitting and/or standing up. Take weight on different parts of the feet – heels, toes, outside edges and look at them. Also lift up one foot at a time to look at parts of the boots – inside the boot, outside, bottom, heels and toes, etc.

Section 1 (approximately 16 bars of skipping rhythm music)
Perform high knee movements (skips, marches, gallops, hops, etc., with knees coming up high to 'show off' boots). Do these movements anywhere in the room.

Section 2 (approximately 32 bars of lively skipping rhythm music)
Perform the actions of running through, jumping into, kicking and splashing in puddles.

Section 3 (approximately 32 bars of lively travelling and leaping music)
In pairs, using follow-my-leader and side-by-side relationship variations, perform a sequence of travelling and leaping movements in unison (over the puddles).

Section 4 (approximately 16 bars of walking rhythm music)
Individually, perform walking and spinning actions, playing at taking weight on different parts of the imaginary wellies, to arrive back on the spot where the boots were 'put on'.

Conclusion (end of last phrase of music above)
Take off wellies and finish in a position looking at them.

Resources used during the lesson/s include the music and the video snippet of Gene Kelly performing *Singing in the Rain* from the film.

Lesson planning – detailed content of lessons leading to the dance outcome above

LEARNING ACTIVITIES

(Bold text below indicates the processes involved and the aspect of the above syllabus experienced.)

1. **Exploration of dance actions** leading to identification of content for INTRODUCTION **solo** of the dance.

   a. Introduction of the idea through **discussion** with children about the idea of having a new pair of wellington boots and playing in the rain should lead to free improvisation to lively music. This would also make a good warm-up.

      - **dance actions** – running, jumping into puddles, splashing, stamping.

   b. **Discussion** of the kinds of movements that children might use to **explore** examination and admiration of their boots sitting on the floor then standing.

      - possible range of **dance actions**
        sitting: turning toes up and down – both and one at a time; lifting up one leg and looking at all angles of it – sides, back, bottom of foot inside imaginary wellie; bending legs into frog-like position to see inside leg sides; and looking at one outside edge in a side sitting position and changing to look at the other by putting both legs on the other side, etc.
        standing: lifting one foot after the other forwards, backwards or sideways high; taking weight on different parts of the feet – lifting toes from ground and leaning forward to see and reverse with heels; looking at inside edges of feet, etc.

2. **Improvise** the INTRODUCTION to the music.

3. **Performance** task for SECTION 1 of the dance: practise the **dance actions** of skipping, marching, hopping, galloping with high knee lifting movements (previously learned material) anywhere in the **space**, expressively 'showing off' wellies. Look for variety and energy, lift of legs and lightness in **quality**. **Practise** SECTION 1 two or three times to music.

4. **Exploration** task leading to identification of content for SECTION 2 of the dance:

   TASK – **explore dance actions** – *running through, jumping into, kicking and splashing in puddles.*

   Breakdown of task
   a. Set imaginary situation. 'As in the warm-up, the floor is covered with puddles and you have your new wellington boots on… show me what you would do.'

   b. Either through pupils demonstrating or through the teacher commenting with praise, take some ideas from observation of the children **improvising** in (a) and ask all the children to **practise** the **dance actions** – for example, running keeping the feet very close and almost skating over the ground; jumping onto two feet with an emphasis on making a big flat-footed splash; kicking with the inside edges of the feet; making stamping movements walking in a circle within the confines of a large puddle.

   c. **View** the video of Gene Kelly's performance of the solo dance and song *Singing in the Rain.* **Discuss** the kinds of movements seen and ask the pupils to keep one idea in mind for their own dance.

   d. **Improvise** to the music for SECTION 2 of the dance.

5. **Creating** and **performing** improved for SECTION 2 of the dance through **viewing**:

   a. **View** the whole of the dance from the moment Kelly says goodbye to the lady.

      • Questions to encourage discussion:
        – 'Why do you think he dances and sings in the rain?'
        – 'How do you know he is happy?'
        – 'Which movements do you remember best?'

   b. **View** the part of the dance between the sung sections (nearly the whole of it!) and **remember** some of the movements you really like – perhaps those which make you laugh.

- Questions to encourage discussion:
  - 'Which was your favourite movement and why have you chosen it?'
  (With one of the childrens' choices in mind)
  - 'Can we put some words on the board to describe it?' (For example, the flat-footed two to two feet jumps in the large puddle: words or phrases such as splat, splash, hit, smash, making frog-like jumps, large bounces like on a trampoline.)
  - 'Is this the biggest splashing movement he performs?'
  - 'Are there some other big movements you remember?'
  - 'Are there any small or quiet movements?'

c. **Improvise** your dance in the puddles and try to **remember** and use just one movement from the video.

6. **Perform** the dance from the beginning up to the end of SECTION 2. **Practise** all together, then **view** a few at a time. Question children about their peers' work and observe selected examples. Another **performance** all together might make a good ending for lesson 1. The next lesson could then begin with the dance so far as a warm-up and **recall and practise** activity.

7. **Create** a **partner** sequence of **dance actions** travelling and leaping for SECTION 3 of the dance:

TASK – *with your **partner**, create a sequence* **(dance form)** *of the **dance actions** of running and leaping over imaginary puddles.*

a. **Practise** and **perform dance actions** of running and leaping movements individually. The teacher should remind pupils of the different kinds of leaps they already have in their vocabulary – possibly by asking appropriate questions. The children should **select** and **practise** a range of leaps.

b. **Practise** two ways of **relating** to a partner. The teacher should set the task of children working in pairs following the leader – the follower copying the leader's run and leaping action in canon. The children should then **select** one kind of run and leap and **practise performing** it in the partner **relationships** of side by side in unison.

c. **Create** by combining the leading and following partner sequence taking turns and the unison sequence. The following structure might help:

> A runs and leaps, B follows copying – repeat with new leap
> B runs and leaps, A follows copying – repeat with new leap
> A and B run and leap together side by side with two different leaps

8. **Practise** to improve skill and **perform** these sequences possibly extracting a few of the leaps and focusing the pupils' attentions on to the use of knees and feet in taking off and landing (i.e. taking off from the whole foot and 'pushing the floor away', and landing through the foot toes first into a soft, bent knee position into travel). Also work on extension of legs and feet in the air (show Gene Kelly again perhaps), and uplifted back and head with arms used to gain height.

9. **View, discuss** and **appreciate** each others' **created** sequences and **performance** of them.

10. **View** the video dance again and note the movements used at the beginning and end of the dance, i.e. quieter and more pedestrian movements. **Appreciate** the bounce in Kelly's walks and try to get this feel in the children's **performance** of walking movements.

11. **Improvise dance actions** of walking, stepping taking weight on different parts of the feet – heels, toes, one flat one heel, one flat foot knee bent one high on toes knee straight, outside and inside edges, etc., and spinning movements to **create** SECTION 4 of the dance.

12. **Create** own ending taking off imaginary wellies.

13. **Practise** and **perform** whole dance. The teacher could identify parts that need attention and provide the necessary teaching points using language, including the use of imagery, to improve the children's work.

14. **View** each other **performing** the whole dance. Look for expression, commenting on **dance qualities**, e.g. bouncy happy walks, stretched flying leaps; **relationship** between the partners, e.g. unison, canon, leading and following; continuity and phrasing showing understanding of the **dance form** – beginning, middle

and end of the dance. If possible video the children's **performance** to enable them to **view** themselves, improve and **perform** again.

15. **Appreciate** the dance experiences in the above two lessons through writing about the dances **created** by themselves and/or Kelly's dance. This work could also include painting a picture and writing a poem, perhaps. Alternatively, if they have seen a video of themselves, the children could write an interpretation and evaluation of their work.

LEARNING OUTCOMES

By the end of two lessons, children will have:

1. **Created** improvised responses for the INTRODUCTION, SECTIONS 1, 2 and 4 and the CONCLUSION of the dance through exploration of appropriate movement content to symbolise the ideas.

2. **Created** a short sequence of travelling and leaping actions with a partner to show understanding of canon and unison and changes of relationship for SECTION 3 of the dance. The sequence should be memorised and repeated.

3. **Performed** and remembered the whole dance, demonstrating understanding of the expression and form.

4. **Performed** and practised skills in order to improve technical and expressive aspects in them.

5. **Appreciated** the appropriateness and originality of Kelly's and their peers' movements in relation to the idea for the dances.

6. **Appreciated** and made comment on their own and others' created and performed dances.

7. **Appreciated** and used artistic and aesthetic language to describe and interpret the movements and dances.

Possibilities for assessing and recording pupils' progress

Children can be assessed as **creators**, **performers** and **appreciators** by selecting and considering each child's progress under the **learning outcomes** that relate to the emphasised content for the dance experiences. For example, the above dance lessons have emphasised:

- Dance Content – Actions – use of different parts of the feet, travelling, jumping
- Dance Content – Qualities – light, bouncy, rhythmic
    Relationships – spatial (beside, following and leading) in unison
- Theme and Stimulus – imaginative portrayal of 'wellies' idea, mood of happiness
    Music – phrasing, qualities, rhythm
- Dance Form – Sense of whole dance (beginning, middle, end)
    Sections of the dance
    Sequence or motif

This implies that assessment of a child's ability to **create dance actions**, for example, could take account of the three bullet points under creating on page 65 to assess the processes of:

- responding to the theme and the music;
- improvising showing a variety of dance actions;
- exploring, selecting and refining appropriate dance actions for the idea;
- creating action sequences, remembering and repeating them;
- remembering the order of the parts and the dance actions that belong to each part.

The teacher needs to determine the main objectives or learning outcomes to be achieved. For me, in teaching pupils aged 7–8, the chief concern would be to develop their dance actions vocabulary. Hence, I would focus on this aspect alone for these two lessons and undertake a more comprehensive assessment, such as the above, at the stage point (i.e. end of year 2 or 6). An interim assessment of the dance action content explored could take into account each pupil's **physical ability** and his/her **range of actions** explored.

Physical ability
- There is emphasis on developing control and balance in the introduction and section 4 when the children are taking weight on different parts of their feet, spinning and lifting up one leg to look at the boots. The children should show awareness of use of a range of parts of their feet, and use control and balance in demonstrating this range – for example, balancing on toes while looking back to see the heels.
- There is co-ordination demanded in the above and in all the travelling movements, especially in constantly changing moves in section 2 and linking them into the sequence in section 3.

- Elevation is obviously emphasised in sections 2 and 3 so their ability to jump can be assessed.

Range, appropriateness and originality of dance actions explored
- Travelling is an emphasised action in this dance. Children should demonstrate a range of travelling steps including walking, marching, running, skipping, galloping, hopping, jumping, etc.
- Jumping is also an emphasised action. However, in section 2 the children are jumping in the puddles and in section 3 they are leaping over the puddles. They should show the differences and be able to perform a variety of both kinds of jumping action. So, for the jumping into puddles they might use two to two feet jumps, one to two feet jumps, hops, and springs from one foot to the other; for section 3 they should show different kinds of travelling leaps over the puddles – for example, from one to the other foot, or from one to both.

Ways in which the above dance outcome implements the theoretical basis of the midway model

Clearly, the children will be experiencing the art form of dance and will be involved in creating, performing and appreciating the dance outcome. They should report to parents and others who might ask them that they made a dance about dancing in the rain in new wellies. They may also be able to write or talk about the movements they used, in language similar to that with which they discussed each other's work and the video. This will indicate something about how the experience has influenced their aesthetic and artistic development.

Emphasis on the *midway* model through this dance can clearly be exemplified. The following text is presented in order of the table on page 27 in chapter 1.

1. Equal emphasis on process and on product

The dance outcome or product is a qualitative whole in the sense that it is unified with a clear beginning, middle and end, has contrasting sections, progresses logically and contains a variety of expressive content. The processes towards achieving this end should also have been rich experiences. The children will have been engaged in exploring content for the introduction of the dance, for example, by responding spontaneously to the stimulus and to the teacher's structured tasks as illustrated below:

Extract from lesson plan

TASK – improvise freely in response to stimulus.

a. Discussion with children of the idea of having a new pair of wellington boots and playing in the rain.

b. Discussion of the kinds of movements the children might use to examine and admire their boots.
   The teacher should have in mind a range of possibilities and feed them in if necessary, but most children will come up with a full range of responses.

c. Improvise the introduction to the music.
   The teacher could comment on the original ideas and range of ideas observed in order to improve variety and quality in all the pupils' responses. Some demonstrations would also develop their responses.

TASK – with your partner create a sequence of running and leaping over imaginary puddles.

a. Practise running and leaping individually.
   The teacher should remind pupils of the different kinds of leaps they already have in their vocabulary, possibly by asking appropriate questions. The children should select and practise a range of leaps.

b. Practise two ways of working with a partner.
   The teacher should set the task of children working in pairs, one of them the leader, the follower copying the leader's running and leaping action in canon. The children should then select one kind of run and leap and practise performing it side by side in unison.

c. Combine the leading and following sequence, the children taking turns to lead and then performing in unison. The following structure may help:
   A runs and leaps, B follows copying
   B runs and leaps, A follows copying
   Repeat with different leaps
   A and B run and leap together with two different leaps

This is a tightly structured task but it requires the children to select, refine and practise movements in their own ways. In a disciplined way, they are choreographing, making decisions, remembering and repeating the outcome of their exploration.

In the above examples, then, there is equal emphasis on process and on product.

2. Equal emphasis on development of creativity, imagination and individuality, and on acquisition of knowledge of theatre dance

Exploration of content for section 2 of the dance above might progress along the following lines:

TASK – perform the actions of running through, jumping into, kicking and splashing in puddles. A breakdown follows:

a. Set imaginary situation. 'The floor is covered with puddles and you have your new wellington boots on. Show me what you would do.'

b. Either through pupils demonstrating or through the teacher commenting with praise, take some ideas from observation of the children improvising in (a) and ask all the children to practise them – for example, running keeping the feet very close and almost skating over the ground; jumping onto two feet with an emphasis on making a big flat-footed splash; kicking with the inside edges of the feet; performing stamping movements walking in a circle within the confines of a large puddle.

c. Watch the video of Gene Kelly's performance of the solo dance and song in *Singing in the Rain*. Discuss the kinds of movements seen and ask the pupils to keep one idea in mind for their own dance.

d. Improvise to the music for section 2 of the dance.

The above progression, through a task aiming to achieve a richly expressive and varied response to the stimulus, allows for individual imaginative and creative interpretation. At the same time the children are expanding their own repertoire of appropriate responses by observing and learning from each other, the teacher and, importantly in this art of dance model, from a professional 'ready-made' art work. Hence their creativity and imagination is being educated.

Reference to the professional art work enhances rather than directs their responses. The children cannot copy the movements since they do not have the observation skills to be able to reconstruct what they see (an abundance of movement ideas within the dance) into their own action. What they gain is an impression from a qualitative whole; if asked to recall just one movement idea from the video, it is more than likely bound to be reproduced in outline only. However, it is always surprising how much the experience of viewing a professional dance work of this nature inspires the children's own creativity. Somehow, many ideas are triggered off in their imaginations when inspired by originality and excellence in examples on the same or similar themes. Young children are particularly receptive to qualitative examples. They take in much more than they can find words to describe and it is often the case that they find it easier to express such impressions through movement than any other medium. Experienced teachers will note nuances of expression, glimmerings of the content and form of the professional art work in the children's own dances. However, each child is triggered by this inspiration in his or her own particular way. Whatever the strength of the impression made by the art work, the dance outcome is entirely derivative of each child's imaginative and creative interpretation.

In this way, more often than not subconsciously, the children are developing their creativity, imagination and individuality. At the same time, however, they are learning from the public art world what constitutes originality in imagination and creativity in dance choreography. They are also adding to their own repertoire of an expressive dance vocabulary and are possibly noting ways in which movements can be linked in phrases, contrasted and highlighted. Through reference to a professional art work the pupils are learning more about the techniques of dance. Equal emphasis is thereby put on developing creativity, imagination and individuality, and on acquiring knowledge of theatre dance.

3. Equal emphasis on feelings and on training

It should be clear to the reader that if the task outlined above for section 2 of the dance is delivered as indicated, the children's own feelings will certainly enter into the dance outcome. When discussion takes place, when imaginary situations are explored, when children are watching each other's dances and/or the professional example, they will have feelings about what they see. They will laugh and enjoy the part where Gene Kelly 'goes over the top' in splashing, 'splatting' his feet in the water, kicking and spinning with his umbrella out in front of him. They will also laugh and enjoy the moment when the policeman comes by and Kelly gently shakes the water from his feet and pretends to act normally. This engagement with the art work is a feeling response.

The pupils will imaginatively put such feelings into their own performances and choreographic problem-solving, and the process may be regarded as an expression of the child's developing intuition – that is, knowledge absorbed through experience and then emerging in the creative form accompanied by a feeling of 'rightness'. Reid (1983) describes 'illuminated intuition' as that which is fed by direct experience but emerges from the subconscious as inspirational feeling responses to creative tasks.

The marriage of these feeling responses to the acquisition of tech- niques or knowledge of the subject of dance is difficult to achieve, but is nonetheless a necessary objective. Throughout the experiences involved in working on *Dancing in the Rain in New Wellies*, pupils will acquire varied knowledge of dance. From creating dances they will learn what is appropriate vocabulary, how to make phrases, how to colour their actions to express and project the meanings. Rather than accepting anything the children produce, the teacher will need to guide pupils who produce inappropriate responses and help them to discriminate and evaluate what they produce in creative work. Gradually pupils should become aware of criteria of appropriateness and originality, even though they may be unable to understand these terms.

The children should also learn how to improve their perfor- mances. The teacher will need to direct their attention to perfor- mance qualities so that they consciously think about and work on, for example, extra stretch, extra height and extra resilience in jumping actions. A few moments in each lesson directed towards such objectives will gradually increase the children's dance performance skills. Although there should not be an emphasis on technical training and acquisition of practical dance skills at primary level, it is important to keep in mind the fact that children who have some skill can express in a feelingful way better than those without such skills.

Keeping a balance between the subjective feelings, on the one hand, and the knowledge to be learned and/or skills to be practised, on the other, is a necessary aspect of the *midway* art of dance in education model. The above example illustrates how this might occur but, of course, each dance experience varies in the manner in which such an objective is achieved.

4. Equal emphasis on movement principles and on stylised techniques

The dance outcome of *Dancing in the Rain in New Wellies* is almost entirely derived from the movement principles outlined by Laban. The simple basis of these principles is easy to grasp in that every movement we perform in daily life can be described under the four headings of Action, Qualities, Space and Relationship: what the body is doing, how it is doing it in terms of time, energy and continuity, where the body is moving in space and how the movement relates to objects and/or people. The non-specialised terms used to describe movement content make this set of principles accessible to teachers without knowledge of dance. The dance outcome described on page 73 demonstrates how the principles can be used as a framework within which the teacher will set creative tasks.

The difficulty of using general movement principles rather than prescribed vocabulary lies in the lack of criteria to guide the teacher on the range of content appropriate for different age groups within each concept. For example, just what sort of different travelling actions, and how many, is an eight-year-old capable of performing? It is also difficult for the teacher to know what constitutes good dance movement. For example, what does a dance leap look like as opposed to an everyday leap over a puddle?

Lack of a defined vocabulary of dance movements also poses problems in that any progression made has to be determined by the teacher. If, for example, the children have previously explored taking weight onto different parts of the feet in other dance contexts, the teacher would expect some development in their abilities to perform the task in the introduction of the dance described here. They would need less guidance in their exploration and they should produce a greater range of answers to the task because they are applying known vocabulary to a different situation. Of course, each new situation should produce new and different movement outcomes when exploring content, because the idea is different. So although they may have experienced all five of the basic jumps, which answers the task of jumping into imaginary puddles in section 2 of the dance, the qualities and even the look and feel of the jumps will be quite different for this particular dance – jumping *into* concentrates more on the landing than on the flight, uses the arms differently and the focus is perhaps down rather than up.

Later in this chapter on primary dance education, some help is given on the problems of using the somewhat open set of movement principles defined by Laban as content for dance education. For the present, let us now concentrate on positive aspects of the principles as a basis for the dance outcome, *Dancing in the Rain in New Wellies.*

One important benefit of using movement principles rather than set steps to be learned and practised, lies in their flexibility as a means of encouraging creative responses. To set a task of 'taking weight on different parts of the feet' limits the children to a type of movement but allows freedom of choice within the type. For instance, the children will all be answering the task in taking weight on different parts of their feet, but each will be performing individual versions of doing this. At any one moment, a range of different parts of the feet bearing weight – toes, heels, inside edges, flat feet, one ball of foot and one heel successively, etc. – should be evident. The principles therefore constitute a template with which the pupils find their own dance movement vocabulary.

Another benefit of Laban's movement principles for the primary stage in education has to be the fact that the content and terms for dance movement are derived from everyday movement and everyday descriptive words. This makes it possible for everyone to be able to create and perform dances immediately, because we all have an everyday movement repertoire even if physically disabled in some way. We also understand the simple terms used to describe such movements. However, although this may well be a valid starting point for children and adult beginners in dance, there should be a shift away from what can be discerned as everyday action towards that which can be described as the art of dance in the public sense.

The art of dancing, as made clear at the beginning of this chapter, is not a natural activity. There is much to learn in order that the natural everyday actions can be transformed into dance movement. Defined techniques such as ballet and the Graham or Cunningham techniques are means towards this end but none of the classical or contemporary dance techniques is suitable for primary education. So how does the teacher work on an everyday movement vocabulary and make the result look like dance? The answer lies in stylisation and technical refinement of movement. Primary teachers need to learn how to achieve these.

To achieve stylisation, it is often the case that everyday movements are exaggerated. For example, the high knee movements in section 1 of the *Dancing in the Rain in New Wellies* dance will be as high and large as possible, and to emphasise the reason for the movements (to show off boots) the children should be encouraged to emphasise different parts of the leg or foot in focus – for example, knees-high skipping actions with the legs turned out so that the inside of the boots can be seen, or knees-high marches with the toes turned up so that the toes of the wellies can be looked at while marching. Such emphases change everyday skipping or marching movements for the purposes of the dance. Any addition of arm or head movements would elaborate the actions even further. Also taking the movements in directions other than forwards – backwards, round in small circles, or sideways with legs turned out (crossing in front and behind perhaps) – adds an enhanced spatial patterning.

Giving actions a rhythmic pattern also makes the everyday movement into dance. The children's use of the beat and accents in the music should provide a rhythmic structure and gradually they should be able to link movements into phrases appropriately punctuated with pauses and stillness. This means that in section 1 of the dance the high knee movements will change in some way at the beginning of phrases and will be performed rhythmically to the music, thus colouring the movement with accents, pauses and stops. Stylisation, then, can be achieved through exaggeration, elaboration and rhythmic structuring of everyday action. However, it still may not look like dance movement until it has been technically refined.

To achieve technical refinement of all dance movement and to look like a professional dancer takes many years of dedicated practice. At the primary level this aspect of the art of dance model should not be emphasised, yet there are definite merits in striving for sufficient technical competence so that children feel proud and confident in their performances. Without exception the many hundreds of primary children I have taught enjoyed improving their physical skills in dance. Simple exercises to improve their use of feet in skipping, for example, were practised in the playground and in the dance hall before the lesson commenced. These may include:

a. sitting on the floor, legs extended and knees straight, to enable the child to flex and extend the ankles and toes. Greater sensitivity and control can be achieved if the children are able to isolate the movements of the toes and ankles as well as incorporating both parts in full extension. Exercise (a) might be followed by (b), (c) and (d).
b. toes and heels gently touching the floor while in a sitting position with knees bent.

c. standing up, feet alternately pulling out of imaginary treacle on the floor, heels first and toes last.

d. marching, pushing the floor away with each foot lift.

All four of these exercises concentrate attention on the child learning how to extend ankles and toes fully while skipping. Eventually the children will skip with beautifully stretched or pointed feet and this skill can be transferred to other actions such as jumping, leaping and any movements lifting feet from the floor.

There are many ways of improving technical skills in dance actions and generally teachers will learn these from experience or courses. All teachers, however, have the ability to improve the qualities in their children's performances. For example, the lively and energetic qualities needed for section 3 of the dance under scrutiny here can be improved through the use of imagery, through the teacher's encouragement of pupils who show the desired qualities, through use of the video resource and discussion of what makes Gene Kelly's performance lively. There are many ways of improving the qualitative colouring of the children's movements. Also body shape and use of space are easily observed by the teacher. Comments on such spatial aspects which are not necessarily visible to the children will improve their work.

Above all, if children achieve expressive clarity in their dances they will be more likely to master the technical aspects of the movements. For example, a child might choose to perform section 4 of the dance with walking into spinning on toes and rocking back to heels to look at the boots and then sinking while turning into a sitting position. This is quite a complex sequence demanding smooth linking of actions and control in balance. If the child is thoroughly engaged in the expressive intention, however, it is likely that repetition and practice of the sequence to get the meaning across will develop technical competence to enable the child to perform it well. Of course, given the option, it is unlikely that the child will choose movements too difficult to perform, and progressively more difficult demands need to be built into the framework of future tasks so that children do not perform the same movements over and over again in different contexts, never progressing. Teachers should be aware of this danger when using general movement principles and make the tasks progressively more challenging, especially for the most able. Of course, the advantage of movement principles over a set vocabulary of content for dance must lie in the fact that interpretation of tasks (such as that set for section 4 of the dance) can be at different levels according to the ability of individual children.

In this art of dance model for primary schools, then, there should be more emphasis on movement principles but with attention given to stylisation and technical refinement of everyday movement. In this way children will absorb an art of dance vocabulary.

5. Equal emphasis on problem-solving approach and on directed teaching

Although at primary school level there should be more emphasis on the open-ended problem-solving approach than on didactic teaching methods, in this art of dance model there should be some learning directly from the teacher or from professional artists.

The dance outcome *Dancing in the Rain in New Wellies* is almost totally derived from the problem-solving approach in that the pupils have explored and selected movement content for themselves in responding to the tasks. However, there are degrees of freedom for the children when problem-solving: in the introduction, for example, pupils explore movement in response to the idea of having new wellies and admiring them. The discussion serves only as a stimulus for the children's imaginations, and the teacher is not suggesting movement content in any way; one is simply drawing it out from the pupils by talking about the kinds of things they might do in the situation. In this way, the teacher acts as catalyst and guide and the pupils learn from each other as well as discovering for themselves through experimenting with the idea in the creative situation.

An alternative problem-solving approach is used in section 2 of the dance framework. Here, as indicated in the breakdown of the task on page 82, the pupils start with a very open task and then possibly, through practice of specified movements selected by the teacher, through observation and demonstration by one or two pupils and by taking in outline a movement idea from the video, they are directed to expand their own vocabulary with ideas from other sources. The art of dance in education model aims for a constant shift from open to closed tasks, with much of the teaching being *midway* between the two.

Even for 7–8 year old pupils it is possible to discern different degrees of teacher intervention/pupil-directed learning in the dance framework. The introduction, sections 1, 2 and 4 allow for greater degrees of individual interpretation of the task than section 3. The latter section could be tightened up considerably if it is taught in the way described on page 81. Here, the teacher is directing the order of the movement phrases and the pattern of the partner work. This is not totally directed in that the children still choose the travel and leap actions they are going to use, but it limits their input to this choice only.

Most dance lessons should contain some directed teacher input so that pupils are stretched beyond their own capacities some of the time. This directed teacher input can be disguised, though, in that there are several occasions in creative dance lessons where the teacher selects a child to demonstrate a movement idea and then, as indicated above, says, 'Let us all try that movement.' In this way the teacher is requiring all the pupils to experience a way of moving determined by someone other than him or herself. This subtle directed teaching approach may well be used in the context of employing a resource such as *Singing in the Rain* though, in the dance outcome described, it is used for inspiration only. For older children the teacher could have taken a sequence from Gene Kelly's dance and replicated it fairly exactly as a section in the children's dance.

6. Artistic education

a. Understanding what a dance is

The intention of a dance outcome is to convey meaning to an audience, and this immediately puts the experience into an artistic context. Pupils gain further insight into the nature of dances as artefacts, each having unique content and form. At this stage, the teacher will create the structures of most of the dances and these will be simple and conventional with beginnings, middles and ends. These structures are frameworks within which the pupils create their own movement contents. This framework approach provides the teacher with the means of extending the pupils' perceptions of what constitutes a dance by their experience of increasingly complex dance structures. The dance *Dancing in the Rain in New Wellies* is a much more developed form than the *Balloon Dance* (see page 199). The former has an introduction and conclusion with four sections between them and lasts for about two minutes; the latter has beginning, middle and ending phrases and lasts for about a minute. Hence, between the dance experience at five years old to the beginning of year 3, the children's perceptions of what constitutes a dance have developed considerably.

Creating structures for dances is difficult, however, since the process incorporates shaping movement within given confines of time and space. It is therefore strongly recommended that most of the dance outcomes are structured by the teacher, though, sometimes, through discussion with the children, the dance structure can be created during the lesson. Also, occasionally by the end of stage 1 (aged 7) and more often by the end of stage 2 (aged 11), pupils should be able to create simple dance structures for themselves. These are easier for them if they use ready-made forms as templates: poems, music and stories, for example.

The knowledge and understanding put into practice here will have been gained intuitively for the most part in that the children will gain a sense of form from experience of the teacher's 'well made' dance structures. More discussion of this point will follow later but, as with learning from 'ready-mades' in poetry, literature, music and drama, there is much that enters the child's consciousness without a conscious learning of facts or techniques.

b. Skills, knowledge and understanding gained through the processes of performing, creating and appreciating dances
The skills listed on pages 31–33 will all be addressed to some extent in the dance *Dancing in the Rain in New Wellies*.

Performing

Under the heading of 'performing', the children will develop further their physical skills in travelling, jumping, leaping and balancing on, and isolating parts of, their feet. They will practise linking the movements into phrases and how to punctuate these phrases with pauses and stops. They will practise performance of a range of qualities – a slow, quiet beginning and end contrasted with a very energetic leaping climax in section 3. They will share the overall space and show awareness of shaping space as a means of expressing the idea, for example leaping over puddles. They will practise dancing rhythmically to the music and presenting the theme expressively. In the partner sequence they will learn to dance in unison and canon, adapting and fitting in with each other.

Creating

Under the heading of 'creating dances' the children will learn more about exploration and selection of content appropriate to a theme. They will discover new actions coloured in different ways by the rhythmic, qualitative, spatial and relationship features suited to expression of the idea. They will learn more about features in music and the use of them to enhance expression of the idea – for example, the bouncy quality for section 2 of the dance, the energy and phrasing in section 3 which should be matched in the pairs' work of running and leaping movements. They will learn to be discriminating in their choice of content through seeking original outcomes rather than easy answers in their own explorations. Their creative abilities will also be enhanced through taking imaginative leaps in response to watching each other or the video clip. They will gain some understanding of the discipline of creating phrases, remembering them and being able to repeat them. They will add to their growing intuitive understanding of form and they will select movements/stillnesses to show awareness of the beginning, middle and end of the dance and its sections. Finally, in presenting the dance outcome, they should show an awareness of its expressive intention and how this may be communicated to the audience. They should also be able to comment on the difference of genre between their dances and the video example. Gene Kelly's dance is essentially a tap dance and, therefore, some of the movements are derived from a specific tap vocabulary. Nonetheless there are several movements – for example, the on-and-off-the-pavement steps and the cross-over grapevine step – which are universally applicable in Western dance forms. This awareness of style/genre is important in learning how to create dances.

Viewing

Children should observe all the above aspects in their own dance, in the dances of peers and in the video example. They should be able to describe the content using the appropriate terminology (for example, a jump from one foot to two feet) and use some qualitative words to describe the dynamics and expressive aspects in what they see – for example, the indulgent deceleration in Gene Kelly's leap onto and lean from the lamp post. The children will readily ascribe meanings to particular movements but they should listen to what others say and learn that a range of meanings is legitimate in this context.

Pupils should gain experience in evaluating their own dances and those of their peers. When viewing dances, improvisations or phrases, teachers should always give children something to look for and then question them on those specific aspects. If children are asked to criticise what they see, they should learn – through the teacher's example – to be constructive. For instance, in viewing a small group performing section 1, the teacher could ask the pupils to notice any unusual responses and ask them to say why they think the responses are unusual. Children are usually good at doing this and if, for example, a child were picked out for lifting the knees high out sideways and turning the foot up and inwards to view the sole of the wellington boot, the teacher could praise both the viewer and performer for responding well to the task. In this way children learn that guided viewing of a dance is as much a part of the dance education learning process as the physical activities of creating and performing dances.

Appreciation

Through the above processes – performing, creating and viewing the parts and the whole dance – pupils will develop appreciation of artistic aspects of their own and others' work.

7. Aesthetic education

In all the performing, creating and viewing experiences involved in producing the dance outcome *Dancing in the Rain in New Wellies*, the children should be encouraged to perceive the feelings embodied in the movements. They should practise performing to gain a kinesthetic feeling of the sensory qualities: for example, in section 2 of the dance, bounciness denotes expressive qualities of carefree happy enjoyment, a sense of well-being, etc. In most instances talking about their kinesthetic feelings and perceptions of aesthetic sensory and expressive qualities will help children to become more aware of them. It is important, therefore, that the teacher plans for such talk and encourages the children to use analogy and metaphor in describing what they feel – for example, with reference to section 2, 'it feels like being on a trampoline'.

There are a great many opportunities to develop perceptions of sensory, expressive and formal qualities in the dance performed by Gene Kelly. The contrast between the exuberant kicking and jumping into the river of rain followed by his sudden stopping and quietly explaining 'I'm singing and I'm dancing in the rain' to the policemen can be seen as a climax of the dance. There are definite sections in the dance and each phrase has a beginning, middle and end. The introduction and conclusion of the dance are very good examples for discussion and should be compared by the children with their own dances.

Much talk about the video clip will help the children to see more and gain more enjoyment each time they see it. This will gradually heighten the children's sensitivity to the aesthetic qualities of that dance.

8. Cultural education

a. Conceptions of the nature of dance and dances

The idea of a dance symbolically communicating enjoyment of rainy weather (expression) and its structure of it in relation to time (form) derives from the Western tradition of what constitutes a dance. Experience of such dance outcomes will therefore reinforce these concepts. Moreover, the vocabulary derived from an everyday experience of playing in rain has comic undertones in that it is not customary to enjoy the rain in countries that have so much of it! Rain carries a different meaning in hot desert places. Gene Kelly communicates his elation very clearly and the incredulity expressed by others conveys this message even more clearly. Some of the signs and symptoms conveyed in the dance are therefore culturally bound but others have universal meanings – the sense of happiness conveyed through bouncy skipping and jumping actions, for example. However, even though the movements within the dance may have universal meanings, the way that they are abstracted from everyday contexts and exaggerated through extra extension, rhythmical and qualitative patterning is not a universal approach to dance composition. This is essentially a Western approach to choreography.

The video could be compared and contrasted with an African or Aboriginal tribal rain dance which has very different intentions: not to entertain and communicate artistically, but to perform a ritual of prayer for rain or a celebration of it. The children should easily see the differences in the movement and messages conveyed. In the tribal dances the focus is generally inward within the group and not outward to an audience and there is no emphasis on the skill of the dancers as performers. Rather the emphasis is on the strength of the collective need for, or joy in, rain for the growth of crops.

b. Understanding of types of dance (genre) and styles

The dance on video is a mixture of tap and stage musical dancing styles. The children should appreciate this genre as typical of musical films made in the 1950s. They may benefit from seeing other dances from the same film, especially *Make them Laugh*, to see how gymnastics and slapstick entered into a tap dance to make it spectacular and comic. This brief historical glimpse gives some background to the study of the art of dance in the theatre.

Comparison of *Singing in the Rain* dance with their own dances will provide the children with a concept of genre and style in that clearly, their dances cannot be called tap or stage dances. Stylisation is not a main focus in this dance but opportunities should be taken to introduce the concept during stages 1 and 2 so that an understanding of it develops gradually and can be demonstrated by the end of stage 3.

Experience of creating their own dances in a particular style, such as a Chinese dragon dance or African drumming dance, at the same time as studying the real things, will help children appreciate that different cultures produce different dance forms and styles. This is an important aspect of the art of dance in education which should encourage awareness of cultural diversity.

RESOURCE-BASED TEACHING/LEARNING AND CROSS CURRICULAR LINKS

Using *Singing in the Rain* as a resource[1] has proved to be helpful in encouraging the children's enthusiasm, their production of ideas during lessons and their final performance; it is also a means of teaching children to analyse dance styles and their own feeling responses. This resource, therefore, acts as a good exemplar in artistic and aesthetic terms and, as indicated above, it can also be used to inform children about implicit cultural features of dances.

Viewing tasks

In the dance experiences discussed above, however, the resource *Singing in the Rain* is not a central focus. It should affect and guide the variety and quality of the movement content rather than become its source. The teacher would need to decide when and how it should first be introduced but is strongly advised not to show it at the start of the project. The video snippet should be shown first when the

---

[1]This resource is readily accessible and therefore has been retained as an example for the 2nd edition of this book. However, 1999 saw publication of a world-leading multimedia resource pack that was written to fully exploit the theoretical proposals related to resource-based teaching presented in chapter 1 of this book. Example uses of the *Wild Child CD Resource Pack* produced by Bedford Interactive Productions (Smith-Autard and Schofield) are presented in the appendix so that primary teachers become aware of the revolutionary pedagogy that judicious application of technology has inspired.

children are exploring content for section 2 of *Dancing in the Rain in New Wellies*, either at the end of lesson 1 or during lesson 2. It is important that viewing tasks are built into lessons as progressive elements which in some way push the children on in their learning. They are not meant to be entertaining interludes! The task leading up to section 2 of the dance outcome (see page 82), shows that the children's own exploratory improvisations precede their viewing of the video, which is used to extend their own ideas in response to the task.

If this is the very first time the video has been seen the viewing tasks may be structured as follows:

a. view the whole of the dance from the moment Kelly says goodbye to the lady.
   Questions to encourage discussion:
   'Why do you think he dances and sings in the rain?'
   'How do you know he is happy?'
   'Which movements do you remember best?'

b. watch the part of the dance between the sung sections (nearly the whole of it!) and remember some of the movements which you really like – perhaps those which make you laugh.
   Questions to encourage discussion:
   'Which was your favourite movement and why have you chosen it?'
   With one of the children's choices in mind, 'Can we put some words on the board to describe it?' (For example, the flat-footed two to two feet jumps in the large puddle: words or phrases such as splat, splash, hit, smash, making frog-like jumps, large bounces as on a trampoline.)
   'Is this the biggest splashing movement he performs?'
   'Are there some other big movements you remember?'
   'Are there any small or quiet movements?'

Such questions guide and limit the pupils' viewing of the piece but at the same time require them to view, recall and describe particular movements in more detail than in the first viewing task.

Performing tasks

Following the viewing tasks above, the children could be asked to remember a splashing movement they liked in the film and to practise performing it for their own dance. As made clear in chapter

1, it is unlikely that they would be able to copy the movement exactly, nor should this be the aim. Rather, the essence of it should be captured and the teacher should encourage the children to put energy and expression into it, using Gene Kelly as a qualitative example. This kind of referencing in respect of quality and expression in performance could occur about twice in the lessons leading towards the dance outcome. Teachers could concentrate attention on the stretch and resilience in Kelly's movements, on the changes of quality from strong and energetic to soft and small, on the rhythm and phrasing (sentences) in his dance. These are just a few of the qualities which could improve the pupils' performances.

Creating tasks

The above viewing tasks could and should lead into creative tasks. The selection and refinement of their favourite splashing movement from the film for their own dance needs to be thought about in terms of juxtaposition with other movements. The children would need to integrate the action into their own 'sentence' of movement and even if it remains improvisation, there has to be some adjustment of what should precede and follow it.

This may be the closest they get to using actual movements out of the video. The resource will serve creative ends through feeding the children's intuitive grasp of the artistic and aesthetic qualities of the dance. For example, they will gain a sense of expressive variety and form through perceiving the range of movements and expressive ideas in the piece. Its overall structure of beginning, middle and end, each part having contrasts and climaxes, will contribute to a growing sense of form and its artistic purpose. Children will gain this sense through perceiving and feeling the coherence of the piece; it does not have to be pointed out to them. Indeed, these concepts are probably too abstract for this age group to grasp. Nevertheless, as suggested above and in chapter 1 of this book, a good deal of 'rubbing off' may occur and this in turn will enrich the children's creative work in dance.

Cultural/historical tasks

Some discussion of these has already taken place under the heading of artistic education. Clearly the visual/audio resource of the filmed dance helps the children to see what tap dance looks and sounds like. They should also be able to make comment on the time and context of the setting in which the film is set, i.e. a musical set in the 1930s/40s and about Hollywood show business. In addition, it is worth taking the opportunity to discuss the Western attitudes towards rain, and, if the opportunity arises, comparing this film with one about tribal rain dance/s, which can only develop further the pupils' awareness of cultural diversity.

Cross curricular links

Most primary dance experiences are linked into thematic or project teaching schemes, so that the aims for dance extend further than the boundaries of the subject itself.

The medium of dance can enhance and reinforce other forms of knowledge, understanding and skills. For example, meaningful language work can be undertaken by children, such as finding words to describe movements and feelings about them, studying rhymes in the song *Singing in the Rain* and perhaps writing poems about their own dances, and writing stories that relate to their own dance or the video exemplar; there are opportunities to explore musical concepts by looking at the structure of phrases and perceiving the dynamic, expressive and formal qualities of these; and, as we have seen, it is possible to learn about different cultures in various ways.

Conclusion

This chapter on the art of dance in primary schools illustrates how the dance syllabus for stages 1 and 2 of the primary curriculum outlined on pages 55-71 can be addressed through understanding and application of the theoretical basis for the art of dance in education model presented in chapter 1.

The main aim has been to demonstrate the features of the model in detail through scrutiny of one dance outcome and the dance experiences leading up to it. Alternative dance outcomes, experienced at other stages in the primary curriculum, would obviously have been illustrated differently. However, I hope that, having understood the theory behind the practice in this one example, teachers will be able to extend the concepts involved to other examples.

The problem in using a single example only is not so much one of how teachers can relate theory to practice in the context of different dance outcomes, but of how they may translate ideas for dances into qualitative learning experiences. It is one thing to be able to use a theoretical framework to analyse a given dance outcome and its preceding lessons, and quite another to create those outcomes and lesson materials. There is also the problem of making relationships between the different dance experiences when planning a coherent dance curriculum, both within each school year and over the entire primary spectrum.

To these ends, the appendix of this book provides further teacher-created dance frameworks and outlines of content for lessons, including some that use multimedia technology in the context of resource-based teaching and learning. My aim is that teachers will be able to apply the theoretical concepts discussed here and in chapter 1 to the examples of content in the appendix and those in other texts.

3

The Art of Dance in Secondary Schools

Background – towards a consensus view of dance as art

It is perhaps possible to say that there is little evidence of the older modern educational dance approach for dance education in secondary schools today. The shift towards the *midway* model described in chapter 1 has largely taken place because many of the specialist dance teachers entering secondary schools during the past three decades have been trained in this approach and because the GCSE (16+ examination first established as GCE Ordinary level in 1983) and Advanced level examinations (17–18+, first established in 1987) have underpinned and reinforced such changes. Moreover, there has been a much closer liaison between schools and professional dance artists in that the latter have been encouraged to work in education by the Arts Council and Regional Arts Associations. This policy has helped to bridge the gap between dance in schools and dance in the theatre. Visits to the theatre, artists in schools and videos of professional dance work are all important resources for dance programmes in secondary schools today.

In addition to many newly-informed teachers entering the profession, there have been a number of in-service courses for established teachers. Most secondary school dance teachers are, therefore, successfully delivering an art of dance education. However, as indicated in chapter 1 of this book, the changes in practice have pre-empted a thoroughly developed conceptual basis for the art of dance in secondary education. It is important now to identify and examine the rationale and theory behind the practice in order that teachers can be clear about what they are doing in dance education and why they are employing the practices they use most. Knowledge of the theory behind the aims, contents, methodologies and assessment for the art of dance, both within a prescribed National Curriculum and outside it, including the available examination contexts, is a necessity for all teachers of dance if they are to consolidate, develop and extend their practice. The content of this chapter aims to help teachers make theoretical links between chapter 1 of this book and their practice of teaching the art of dance in school.

The dominant model in secondary schools today can be labelled the art of dance in that the three processes of performing, creating and appreciating are employed by most teachers to provide their students with an all-round experience. However, the tried and tested approaches in teaching each strand of the model are in need of development and, above all, of effective integration.

A dance syllabus for secondary schools

The secondary schools which deliver the art of dance model, especially those that lead to GCSE and A level successes, have no choice but to go beyond the syllabus indicated in the physical education National Curriculum for England Order of 2000. Here, as indicated in discussion of this National Curriculum for primary schools, the statements for dance in secondary education also omit any mention of appreciation or evaluation. There are other criticisms that could be made in relation to this newly published curriculum, but there is little point in rehearsing arguments against what has become law, at least for the foreseeable future. In my view, teachers in England offering dance at this level need to acknowledge that the National Curriculum is merely a broad-sweep set of statements that can easily be addressed within their own, or alternative more comprehensively focused, syllabuses. Such syllabuses for secondary schools, I believe, should emerge from a detailed consideration of the recommendations made for content in texts authored by experienced dance educators[1], reports from schools' inspectors[2] or research[3] and the examination board syllabuses for GCSE and A Level stages[4]. A scrutiny of these sources, combined with reflection

---

[1]This book, for example, and others that are listed in the references.

[2]*The Arts Inspected – Good Teaching in Art, Dance, Drama and Music*, Office for Standards in Education, London: Heinemann (1998).

[3]Harland J. et al *Arts Education in Secondary Schools: Effects and Effectiveness*, Berkshire: NFER.

[4]For example, the Northern Examinations and Assessment Board Syllabuses for GCSE, AS and A Level, Manchester: AQA.

on the teacher's own training and experience and informed, perhaps, by in-service training courses (such as those offered by the National Dance Teachers Association in the UK), should result in clear ideas concerning the skills, knowledge and understanding that need to be developed in secondary art of dance experiences.

To assist secondary teachers in this task, the following text presents a syllabus for the two stages of secondary education relating to the 11–16 age group. It is born out of many years' experience and out of my extended interpretations of the content outlined for dance in the 1992 National Curriculum – a more coherent curriculum. These interpretations were featured in the appendix of the first edition of this book. In the second edition, they have been adapted and incorporated into this chapter so that the reader can identify the range of content that is proposed as 'best practice' in delivering a comprehensive art of dance education in secondary schools.

The syllabus below and the syllabuses for the aforementioned dance examinations clearly identify that students should learn how to create[5], perform and appreciate dances. This is evident in the headings used (Dance Composition, Dance Performance and Dance Appreciation) and the assessment items required in the examinations (see pages 150–152). The syllabuses also lay emphasis on students developing knowledge and understanding about the current practices, traditions and conventions of the art form as it exists in the public world.

The reader should note that the content of the GCSE Dance examination (16+) is implicit in the stage 4 syllabus below, and therefore all that is said about the latter is applicable to the examination syllabus. (Further description and analysis of the GCSE, AS and A Level examination syllabuses will be presented towards the end of the chapter.)

A summary chart of the content proposed for students aged 11–16 is followed by a detailed syllabus for each of the two stages: stage 3, for students aged 11–14, and stage 4, for students aged 14–16.

---

[5]Although this term is used throughout this book, the term *compose* is probably more commonly used – especially in relation to older pupils. The syllabuses below use the heading *Dance Composition* and, to confuse you even further, the examination syllabuses label the study as *Choreography* but, to be pedantic, one has to **create** a composition/piece of choregraphy!

SYLLABUS FOR THE ART OF DANCE IN SECONDARY SCHOOLS – YEARS 7–11

STAGE 3: students aged 11–14

Individually, in pairs and in groups, with or without accompaniment and through different DANCES pupils should develop skills, knowledge and understanding in:

A) Dance Composition
develop dance content and use appropriate accompaniments, methods of composition, styles and techniques to communicate meanings and ideas

B) Dance Performance
perform dances, showing an understanding of expression, form and style

C) Dance Appreciation
support their own dance compositions with written and/or oral descriptions of their intentions and outcomes be taught to describe, analyse and interpret dances, recognising different features in composition and performance including style, and commenting on cultural/historical contexts

STAGE 4: students aged 14–16

Individually, in pairs and in groups, with or without accompaniment and through different DANCES pupils should develop skills, knowledge and understanding in:

A) Dance Composition
create dances which successfully communicate the artistic intention, and devise and design aspects of production for their own compositions

B) Dance Performance
perform technically more demanding dances accurately and expressively and dance in a range of styles showing understanding of form and content

C) Dance Appreciation
record the process of composition and describe, interpret and evaluate all aspects of dance including choreography, performance, cultural and historical contexts and production

STAGE 3: students aged 11–14

Syllabus statement
Individually, in pairs and in groups, mostly through structured dance frameworks and tasks, students should:

- *be taught how to develop dance content and use appropriate accompaniments, methods of composition, styles and techniques to communicate meanings and ideas*

Interpretation of the above statement to define: *DANCE COMPOSITION*

LEARNING ACTIVITIES

- develop skills in researching/brainstorming ideas for dances
- learn how to select and treat themes appropriately for dance
- develop skills in selecting and using a range of different stimuli
- use differing accompaniments, including music with different instruments such as human voices; words and poems, etc.
- consider constituent elements of music and styles differentiated through period, place and composer
- explore, select, discard and refine action, quality, spatial and relationship content to communicate meanings
- learn how to abstract and symbolise ideas
- create motifs; develop and vary them
- with increasing autonomy, use composition methods of repetition, contrast and highlight/climax
- extend abilities to create overall form – sections, transitions and unity
- show understanding of relationships between themes of dances and styles

LEARNING OUTCOMES

CREATING – pupils should be led to:

- discover, explore and improvise a range and combination of actions, qualities, spatial and relationship content in response to varied stimuli, including a range of music, to communicate meanings and ideas
- discard, select and refine content from the above exploration and improvisation to create motifs
- repeat content – exactly and through development
- develop motifs and vary them with help from the teacher
- use processes of abstraction to symbolise ideas
- use a variety of ways of orchestrating in time and space for partner and group dances, e.g. use of canon, unison, spatial relationships, group shapes
- structure phrases and sections of dances based on the teacher's framework, and with increasing autonomy plan whole dances
- work on tasks independently, in pairs, and in groups
- stylise movements in relation to the theme

PERFORMING – pupils should be led to:

- remember and perform the dances created and show understanding of the expression and form in the dance
- perform sensitively with others in unison, canon and with spatial clarity
- improve abilities to perform with stylistic coherence and awareness of the accompaniment, if used

APPRECIATING – pupils should be led to:

- describe and comment on their own and others' choreography, including professional choreography in terms of appropriateness of content – actions, qualities, spatial and relationship aspects; form – motifs, developments, contrast, climax, logical sequencing and overall unity and use of music/accompaniment
- interpret meanings and ideas reflected in the choreography
- discuss qualities in performance and ways in which it might be improved to serve the choreography
- describe and comment on stylistic features of dances and accompaniment in relation to themes

Syllabus statement
Individually, in pairs and in groups, students should:

- *be taught to perform dances, showing an understanding of expression, form and style*

Interpretation of the above statement to define: *DANCE PERFORMANCE*

LEARNING ACTIVITIES

- extend range of dance skills through learning set dances and particularly technical studies, i.e. pre-choreographed studies based on physically challenging movement content
- extend vocabulary of dance content (movement principles and stylistically defined dance techniques) through learning their peers' and set dances
- develop ability to dance expressively through performing their own or others' compositions giving attention to the way in which the content expresses the theme (e.g. slow, soft quality to depict calm)
- develop ability to perform dances showing knowledge of form through phrasing, timing and sense of the overall structure
- learn to perform a range of contemporary dances that have been influenced by differing genres or styles, e.g. jazz, ballet, Indian, Capoeira, street dance
- develop knowledge and understanding of stylistic characteristics of dances from different cultures, e.g. African, English folk, etc.
- develop knowledge of factors affecting style – place, time, company, etc.

LEARNING OUTCOMES

CREATING – pupils should be led to:

- extend vocabulary of dance movements, techniques and styles and learn to employ them in their own choreography appropriate to themes (e.g. specific falls or contact work)
- extend knowledge of composition in terms of expression and form through experience of pre-choreographed technical/style studies and through set dances

PERFORMING – pupils should be led to:

- develop and improve abilities to co-ordinate movements of parts of the body – in isolation, simultaneously and in succession
- develop abilities to control and co-ordinate movements of parts of the body in relation to other parts in static or travelling actions
- improve balance, control, poise, mobility and strength of body for dance
- extend range of travelling, jumping, turning, gesturing and balancing while still, and combinations of these in sequences
- extend and improve abilities to show variations of quality in movement, i.e. speed, force and continuity in rhythmic patterns
- extend and improve abilities to pattern actions in space using different and changing levels, directions, size, pathways, shapes
- develop and extend abilities to dance in relationship with other dancers in pairs, in groups varied in time – canon/unison, and space-lines, circles, formations, etc. and in relation to objects, dance space and audience
- learn some specific dance skills and vocabulary of stylistically defined dance techniques, e.g. contemporary (generalised) jazz, African, street
- learn how to stylise dance movement through performing style studies, i.e. studies in the style of specific genres (e.g. ballet, S. Asian) and specific choreographers (e.g. Bruce, Davies, Anderson)
- develop range of vocabulary and style through performing excerpts or whole set dances

APPRECIATING – pupils should be led to:

- demonstrate knowledge and understanding of dance performance through viewing, talking and writing about the expressive, formal and stylistic features that differentiate dances
- demonstrate knowledge and understanding of how the above features are derived through influences of period, place, groups and choreographers
- show increased understanding and knowledge of specific dance techniques

STAGE 3: students aged 11–14

Syllabus statement
Individually, in pairs and in groups, and through discussion, response to worksheets, etc. students should:

- *be taught to support their own dance compositions with written and/or oral descriptions of their intentions and outcomes*
- *be taught to describe, analyse and interpret dances recognising different features in composition and performance including style, and commenting on cultural/historical contexts*

Interpretation of the above statement to define: *DANCE APPRECIATION*

LEARNING ACTIVITIES

- learn how to describe ideas for dances verbally and in written form, and how these have developed from the initial stimulus or starting point
- learn how to describe the content of their own dances, those of their peers, and professional dance works – i.e. actions, qualities, spatial and relationship features – and how these relate to the theme/type of dance
- learn and use the appropriate technical language to describe types and styles of dances and specific technical dance vocabulary
- describe accompaniments and production features of dances, i.e. costume, lighting, design and properties, and comment on their relationship to themes
- interpret meanings of dances using understanding of how moods, feelings and ideas are symbolically presented in dances
- develop awareness of coherence in style and relationship of style to type of dance and techniques employed
- develop abilities to record movement details including floor patterns, rhythm and group shapes, etc. using some form of notation, e.g. motif writing (Labanotation), stick figures or equivalent

- begin to learn about cultural and historical contexts through experience of viewing different styles of dances derived in different periods and places

LEARNING OUTCOMES

CREATING – pupils should be led to:

- support their compositions orally or in writing by describing the stimuli, motivations, processes employed and reasons for choices
- describe and analyse the content (actions, qualities, spatial and relationship features) and interpret meanings they perceive in their own and others' dance compositions
- describe and analyse the form aspects in their own and others' dances
- describe the use of style in relation to the ideas for their own and others' dances

PERFORMING – pupils should be led to:

- perform dances with a greater awareness of all the above features, having described, analysed, interpreted and recorded them

APPRECIATING – pupils should be led to:

- describe and analyse their own, their peers and professional dance outcomes in relation to intentions, content, form, accompaniment and production elements, both verbally and in writing
- interpret possible meanings in relation to the above and discuss these verbally or in writing
- appreciate the relationships between all the above features and begin to comment on attributes such as originality, appropriateness and effect
- make links between idea, type of dance, content, form, style, accompaniment, production elements and historical/cultural contexts

STAGE 4: students aged 14–16+

Syllabus statement
Individually, in pairs and in groups, with increasing autonomy, students should:

- *be given opportunities to create dances which successfully communicate the artistic intention*
- *be guided to devise and design aspects of production for their own compositions. (This is highly unlikely to be extensive in that lighting and staging items are not readily available in schools. It is therefore presented here as an extension to composition rather than an item in its own right)*

Interpretation of the above statement to define: *DANCE COMPOSITION*

LEARNING ACTIVITIES

- extend skills in researching ideas and planning for dance compositions and select increasingly mature ideas, e.g. social and environmental issues
- plan dances individually, in groups and/or with the teacher and class
- communicate intentions for dance compositions with increasing clarity
- employ different starting points – ideas, movement, auditory stimuli, tactile stimuli including clothing, literature, poetry and visual stimuli
- create different types of dances, e.g. comic, dramatic, abstract, pure
- select accompaniments using a range of different types (music, poetry, sound effects, breathing, etc.) in different styles and show understanding of constituents, mood, style of the accompaniment in relation to dances
- select appropriate content to convey expressive intention – actions, qualities, spatial and relationship features including learned specific dance skills if appropriate
- stylise the content appropriately and coherently throughout dances

- employ principles of form – motif, development, repetition, variation, contrast, transition, climax and unity in shaping dances with sections, linked into wholes
- use methods of orchestration of the motifs – numerical variation, group shape, copying, complementing and contrasting, unison, canon, etc.
- consider audience in presentation of all the above – for example, spatial placing, shape, line, focus and projection
- rehearse dancers in appropriate space to improve presentation of dances, showing clarity of intention
- costume and make sets where appropriate, using lighting if available to enhance the intended communication

LEARNING OUTCOMES

CREATING – pupils should be led to:
- select and research appropriate ideas for dances, and plan outcomes individually or as part of a group, demonstrating clarity of intention
- select appropriate type of dance and accompaniment (if any) for ideas, and content/technique and style to convey the ideas
- demonstrate understanding of principles of form and orchestration of dancers to convey the ideas
- develop techniques of rehearsing dancers (especially if standing outside dances in the role of choreographer)
- develop understanding of aspects of production and how they can enhance the dance outcomes

PERFORMING – pupils should be led to:
- perform the above dances conveying the intended expression and with an understanding of form, use of accompaniment, presentation elements, etc.

APPRECIATING – pupils should be led to:
- demonstrate knowledge and understanding of all the above elements

STAGE 4: students aged 14–16+

Syllabus statement
Individually, in pairs and in groups, with increasing autonomy, students should:

- *be taught to perform complex and technically more demanding dances accurately and expressively*
- *be given opportunities to dance in a range of styles showing understanding of form and content*

Interpretation of the above statement to define: *DANCE PERFORMANCE*

LEARNING ACTIVITIES

- further extend skills through learning more complex set dances – technical studies; dances from different sources, e.g. teacher's choreography, peers' dances and snippets from professionally choreographed dance works
- further develop dance vocabulary through the above and style studies, i.e. within a particular style and using vocabulary specific to the style (e.g. a Cunningham study)
- develop abilities to perform accurately and remember dance movements linked into phrases, sections and whole dances showing understanding of expression and form
- extend performance skills such as dynamic variation, focus, extension, line, projection, rhythmic accuracy and musicality
- develop abilities to perform dances alone or as part of a group in a variety of contexts
- extend knowledge of and ability to dance in a range of styles

LEARNING OUTCOMES

CREATING – pupils should be led to:

- learn more about composition of dances through performing a range of well-made dances and studies
- learn more about style through experience of stylistically defined dances and studies

PERFORMING – pupils should be led to:

- develop further their physical skills in co-ordination of body parts and combinations of actions both simultaneously and successively
- increase ability to demonstrate control, balance, poise, mobility, and strength in varieties of dance sequences
- extend range and ways in which actions, qualities and spatial patterning can be performed in isolation and in combination, e.g. different jumps and leaps alone and combined with turns and changes of direction
- extend vocabulary and ability to perform stylistically defined dance techniques, e.g. jazz.
- demonstrate understanding of style through accurate use of body, rhythm, dynamics, weight, etc. For example, jazz dance should show accented isolations particularly of hips and shoulders, syncopated rhythms, downward-stressed grounded movements with sharp changes of direction and focus
- show understanding of expression and form in dances, e.g. qualities of fast lightness emphasised to show liveliness contrasting with a section on slow, heavy and downward action to show sorrow. The ability to change moods and feelings within dances should be developed through such work
- improve performance skills and abilities to dance solo and in groups

APPRECIATING – pupils should be led to:

- increase knowledge and understanding of what constitutes skill in dance
- increase knowledge of vocabulary for dance from experience of movement principles and selected stylistically defined techniques, e.g. Cunningham, jazz, African
- learn more about style and processes of stylisation through performing and viewing dances, including professionally choreographed dance works

STAGE 4: students aged 14–16+

Syllabus statement

Individually, in pairs and in groups, with increasing autonomy, students should:

- *be enabled to record the process of composition*
- *be given opportunities to describe, interpret and evaluate all aspects of dance including choreography, performance, cultural and historical contexts and production*

Interpretation of the above statement to define: *DANCE APPRECIATION*

LEARNING ACTIVITIES

- identify different ways of recording movement, such as writing about it employing correct terminology, drawing figures, floor plans and group positions, etc. and employing simple notation symbols
- learn how to record the processes of composition through journal-keeping or other written forms including the above, to note initial stimulus, research, exploration of movement ideas, reasons for selection, and process of developing and refining motifs, etc. in order to give form to dances
- write and talk about expressive and stylistic features of own dances
- employ frameworks for description of choreography and performance, i.e. movement principles, composition principles, knowledge of types of dances, specified dance styles, performance skills, production features, knowledge of history and cultural contexts of dances
- learn how to employ descriptive language including metaphor to communicate interpretations of dances and to evaluate dances

LEARNING OUTCOMES

CREATING – pupils should be led to:

- record, discuss and write about aspects of choreography listed on pages 31–2 in chapter 1 of this book.
- learn more about choreography from this process of description, analysis, interpretation and evaluation of own dances, those composed by peers and professionally choreographed dances
- use all the above knowledge to improve own choreography

PERFORMING – pupils should be led to:

- record, discuss and write about aspects of performance listed on page 32 in chapter 1 of this book
- learn more about performance from the process of describing, analysing and evaluating own performances (through use of video), performances of peers and professional dancers
- learn more about dances and different interpretations in performance of them by comparing the same dances performed by different people, companies or at different times
- use all the above knowledge to improve own performances

APPRECIATING – pupils should be led to:

- develop abilities to observe, describe, analyse, interpret and evaluate dances
- develop ability to use language to describe content of dances and to convey meanings
- extend range of specialised vocabulary to describe dance movement, techniques and styles
- apply knowledge of dance composition and performance (*see* checklists on pages 31–2) in order to make informed evaluations of dances
- apply knowledge of history and contexts (e.g. Graham style – traditional American contemporary dance; Giselle – romantic ballet, 19th century, Europe)

Perusal of the above syllabus for each of the two stages will point to the integration of the three strands. Under each of the separate lists of learning activities for composition, performance and appreciation, there are learning outcomes for all three strands – creating, performing and appreciating. This presentation is intended because, in my view, teachers need to address all three strands in each and every lesson, albeit giving emphasis to one or two, perhaps. This means, for example, that if students are learning to perform a pre-choreographed dance, they should also learn about composition through becoming aware of its expressive and formal features, and knowledge and understanding of the technique and style of the piece in relation to its time and place origins. This new knowledge constitutes appreciation, of course.

The following text will take aspects from the above syllabus to demonstrate the interrelatedness of the three strands and to show how the theoretical basis for the art of dance in education, described in chapter 1, can be applied to dance for ages 11–16.

Again, as in discussion of the art of dance in the primary sector, it is necessary to start with the dance outcome. It is just as important for secondary students to come to know and understand dance through experiencing dances as it is for primary pupils. Each lesson, or more frequently each series of lessons, should culminate in a dance outcome which can be repeated, performed and discussed as an art work. Increasingly through stages 3 and 4, students will have greater autonomy in defining the intention and structuring the choreography and production. By the end of stage 4 they should be making and performing dances entirely created by themselves. En route, however, they will learn much from the teacher's choreographic, performance and appreciation tasks and from the teacher-created frameworks for compositions which will be employed particularly during years 7 to 9 to help students structure their dances.

A dance outcome

The following description of a dance derived from a teacher-created dance framework (see chapter 2 page 72) for year 9 pupils will provide an imaginary outcome of three lessons. These can be discussed in relation to the selected learning activities from the stage 3 syllabus above, and to ways of assessing the learning outcomes. This outcome and the planned lesson experiences will also be analysed to demonstrate how the theoretical basis in chapter 1 underpins the art of dance in practice for year 9 pupils.

Lesson planning – a teacher's dance framework

Dance title *Pool Idling* (Imaginary setting: outdoor pool on holiday in sunny weather)

Music Introduction of *Shine On You Crazy Diamond* by Pink Floyd from *Fame – A Collection of Great Dance Songs*

Introduction (music, the first section prior to solo flute sound coming in)
A few students at a time enter slowly and dreamily and at random from the edges of the room to their own spot (all facing one direction). They move slowly into different positions (lying, sitting, kneeling, standing) and stare dreamily into space watching imaginary people in the pool, perhaps doodling with hands or feet.

Section 1 (music, the first section up to the first solo guitar lead)
Stretch out into a lying position on backs, arms above heads. From this starting position create a solo sequence of motifs incorporating arching, curling, stretching, rocking and rolling movements, giving an illusion of being in water, floating in it gently and slowly. Keep in contact with the floor most of the time but use one rising and falling action during the sequence.

Section 2 (music, the section up to the accented guitar lead)
Move to partner and perform motifs, including assisted jumps, movements onto and sliding off partner, through, under and around partner, lifting and lowering partner. All of these movements should be performed in slow motion as if playing around in water.

Transition (music, between the above section and the next prior to drum beats)
At clapped hands signal – all run as if through water to form groups of four.

Section 3 (music, the section of music leading up to the words)
In the group of four, choreograph a sequence in unison with one incidence of canon and employing at least one swimming action out of *Waterless Method of Swimming Instruction*. The

sequence should suggest receiving imaginary instructions from the side of the pool to improve swimming strokes.

Conclusion (music, the introductory music repeated)
Move into individual spaces. Repeat and develop some of the solo sequence in section 1 and determine your own conclusion.

Resources used during the lessons include the video recording of *Waterless Method of Swimming Instruction* (1980)[6] by Robert Cohan. The music, like the Pink Floyd piece suggested, should not have much beat or accent. It should be quiet and smooth like the music accompaniment for the video.

Lesson planning – detailed content of lessons leading to the dance outcome above

LEARNING ACTIVITIES
(*Bold text below indicates the processes involved and the aspect of the above syllabus experienced.*)

1. **Exploration** tasks leading to **selection** of the content for the dance:

   a. Stretching, relaxing, arching, curling-in and rolling movements in contact with the floor and standing up, keeping the movement slow, fluid and continuous.
   b. Extending upward movements into controlled falling actions sliding onto the floor on different body parts.
   c. Assisted jumping in pairs – using partner as object to push against without holding, e.g. step into jump from one foot at the same time pressing down on partner's shoulder or back. Partner acting as object assisting flight could be in different positions, e.g. kneeling on all fours for partner to jump off the back thus acting as a take-off platform, but appropriateness to the context of partner work in water should be kept in mind.

[6]This video is no longer available for purchase. However, it can be viewed for reference at the National Resource Centre for Dance (www.surrey.ac.uk/NRCD) and at the Videoplace, The Place, London. Even without access, teachers should be able to visualise how a dance work based on the theme of swimming could be used to support the in-depth dance activities discussed in this chapter. This example has been retained from the first edition because references to the video are easy to imagine.

d. Assisted jumping in pairs with aid from the partner supporting the jumper. Hands around the waist; under upper arm; clasped and receiving one foot; pushing hands against hands; pushing and lifting from behind between the scapuli during a jump – provide a few ideas. Students should find their own answers to this task but should keep in mind the theme of the dance when selecting from their explorations.

e. Movements onto and off partner showing a held moment with one person off the floor. Students should explore lifts, jumps into held positions and different ways of sliding or lowering to the ground to move out of held positions. Ideas might include: one partner jumping upwards to be caught by the other partner surrounding arms to hold close to him or herself, clasping around waist or under buttocks and then allowing the held partner to slide down and touch the floor into a release fall. Alternatively, one partner might lift the other by taking his or her weight on one shoulder or on the back, through the person to be lifted bending over and lying in contact with the body part to be used as a support for the lift. The lift occurs when, in contact, the lifter raises up – causing the lifted person's feet to leave the floor. These are just two examples. There are many ways of achieving lifts and also many ways of moving out of the lift[7]. Students might benefit from imagining the water environment to get the feeling of buoyancy and slow-motion control.

f. **Exploration**, **abstraction** and **development** of motifs from known swimming strokes and exercises. Take aspects of breast stroke, crawl and butterfly, for example, and exaggerate, combine and add movements to them (jumps, for example), make rhythmic phrases out of them, vary and develop them changing level and direction. These are just a few ideas. There are many ways in which motifs can be developed out of realistic action in order to become symbolic. Students should attempt to change the originating strokes as much as possible so that they create abstract symbolic actions that have distinctive rhythmic and stylistic features.

---

[7]Different visual examples of ways of lifting a partner are presented in the *Wild Child CD Resource Pack*, Bedford Interactive Productions (1999) – see references.

2. **Composition** tasks leading to **selection** and **refinement** of content for motifs.

   a. Solo task for introduction of the dance: 'Imagine a hot sunny day and being on holiday. You are going towards the swimming pool and you move slowly, savouring the thought of having a swim. First of all you just watch others in the pool, though, and enjoy the feel of the sun on your body. Select movements to travel from the side of the room into a space and choose a position to show that you are watching people in the pool.'

   b. Solo task for SECTION 1 of the dance: 'From the starting position lying on your backs with arms stretched along the floor and above heads, select movements from 1a and 1b above and link them into phrases to give the illusion of floating and moving gently in water.'   (*32 bars of music*)

   c. Solo task for CONCLUSION of the dance: 'Use some of the motifs you created for section 1, alter the order of them and develop them. This should finish with your own end to the dance (perhaps leaving the poolside or just lying out sunbathing).'   (*16 bars of music*)

   d. Solo task for TRANSITION of the dance: 'Imagine travelling with large running actions across the pool and perform the movements exaggerating the use of legs and arms.'

   e. Duo task for SECTION 2 of the dance: 'Select movements from exploration tasks 1c, 1d and 1e. Link them together into **phrases/motifs** then refine them, paying attention to the qualities of slow motion, fluidity and continuity to give the illusion of playing in water.'   (*48 bars of music*)

   f. Group of four task for SECTION 3 of the dance: 'Each student should contribute movement ideas from 1f above to create a sequence of motifs to symbolise receiving swimming instruction from the poolside. The group should also select one movement idea from the video of *Waterless Method of Swimming Instruction*. Once the movements have been selected, the group should orchestrate them in space (varying the position of each dancer in the group) and in time (using unison and at least one incidence of canon).'   (*48 bars of music*)

3. **Performing** tasks leading to **practice** and improvement of performance.

   a. **Perform** the INTRODUCTION of the dance to improve

expressive qualities and focus in order to symbolically portray the idea. Concentrate on achieving continuity, slowness and gentleness in movements to express tranquility.

b. **Perform** solo task for SECTION 1 of the dance to partner, group or half-class to demonstrate quality in composition and performance – concentrating again on the qualities of slow motion, gentleness, and fluid continuity. Practise and improve qualities, phrasing, musicality and expressiveness.

c. **Perform** solo task for CONCLUSION of the dance. This could be performed for a partner to start with, so that the appropriate qualities are worked on to express the idea. The observing partner needs to be clear on what to look for, so it may be helpful for the pair to have devised and written a checklist prior to performing for one another.

d. **Perform** duo task for SECTION 2 of the dance. This needs much practice to develop the technical skills appropriate for the actions, and on several occasions during the exploration of content for this section, the teacher will need to break down the movement ideas into technical exercises towards improving performance. For example, the assisted jumps with one partner holding the other around the waist while jumping could be broken down as follows:

(i)   practise jumping on your own two feet to two feet, increasing size of jumps and swinging arms forwards and upwards to help elevation. Bend knees on landing and feel weight passing through the feet until both feet are fully in contact with the floor, heels down

(ii) with a partner, practise three bounces and jump high, pushing down onto partner's shoulders while partner – who is lifting by holding around the waist – pushes upwards at the height of the jump and bends with the jumper on landing

(iii) repeat the above but without the jumper pushing down on partner's shoulders. The jumper can increase the height of the jump, perhaps by extending arms from shoulder height up and reaching high during the jump

(iv) repeat the above but travel into it

(v)   repeat but with lifter turning to change the direction of facing for the landing

(vi) repeat but with lifter letting go at the height of the jump and using different forms of jump, e.g. two feet to one foot

In such a progressive way, then, the students improve their technique in performance of assisted jumping skills gaining height, extension and control in landing.

e. **Perform** group motifs for SECTION 3 of the dance to practise timing and group positioning.

f. **Practise** and **perform** parts of the dance combined and the whole dance to work on linking parts and expressive qualities. Performance skills such as extension, projection, focus, alignment and musicality should be observed, discussed and practised to improve the presentation of the dance.

4. **Viewing** tasks contributing to creating and performing tasks and artistic and aesthetic appreciation of the dance.

a. **Viewing** of creative work in progress to make critical comment on appropriateness, originality and quality of own and others' work.

b. **Viewing** of the whole of *Waterless Method of Swimming Instruction* and parts of it in detail to gain ideas for their own compositions and to appreciate principles of abstraction into symbolism. The pupils might benefit from teacher-prepared worksheets in order to guide their viewing of details in the choreography. They could then write about the dance, noting the style of costumes, the historical context of the piece and the Graham style of Cohan's choreography.

c. **Viewing** of performance in performing tasks above to improve own and others' performance of parts and of the whole dance.

LEARNING OUTCOMES

By the end of three lessons students will have:

1. **Created** solo motifs of dance content showing understanding of abstraction and elaboration of movement to symbolise meanings through appropriate choice of actions enriched with rhythmic, qualitative and spatial variation.

2. **Created** a development of the motif/s in section 1 for the conclusion of the dance and a transition.

3. **Created** partner motifs incorporating new skills of working in contact.

4. **Created** group motifs employing previous knowledge of group orchestration of motifs and ideas picked up from the video resource.

5. **Performed** confidently and with technical accuracy the selected content of the dance, showing ability to co-ordinate, control, balance and extend, while performing combinations of actions coloured variously by qualitative and spatial patterning.

6. **Performed** and remembered parts of and the whole dance demonstrating an understanding of its expressive meaning and form.

7. **Performed** the dance showing understanding of performance skills such as projection, focus, group shape, body alignment, timing and musicality.

8. **Appreciated** the appropriateness and originality in their own or others' compositions including the professional dance work, *Waterless Method of Swimming Instruction*.

9. **Appreciated** and critically evaluated their own and others' performances and worked to improve them.

10. **Appreciated** and critically interpreted the artistic/aesthetic aspects of choreography and performance in their own work, that of their peers and in Cohan's dance work.

11. **Appreciated** the cultural and historical context of Cohan's dance work.

Possibilities for assessment and recording of students' progress through the above outcome and in relation to the stage 3 suggested syllabus

A brief discussion of the opportunities for assessment incorporated in the lessons that culminate in the dance, *Pool Idling*, demonstrates how the teacher could use the listed learning outcomes under the headings of creating, performing and appreciating as criteria for assessment.

Dance composition

There are opportunities to assess the students' understanding of methods of composition because for each part of the dance, they are required to create motifs and phrases using abstraction to symbolise the theme and link these motifs and phrases together. They are also required to understand what a transition is and repeat and develop the phrase in section 1 for the conclusion in order to make the dance feel a whole. This kind of work, and the language used to set tasks, develops the students' concepts of form in dance and their ability to employ principles of form in their compositions. They are also extending further their abilities to improvise, select and refine expressive movement content appropriate to the theme of the dance.

Students are given experience of a 'contact improvisation' type of technique in exploring content for section 2 of the dance, and experience of working in and orchestrating a group for the 'instruction' part of the dance, section 3. In all this work students will be led to understand why the content has been selected and how it communicates meanings relating to the theme. In addition to the students' own work, reference to the professional dance work, *Waterless Method of Swimming Instruction*, will reinforce how a choreographer employs the technique of abstracting movement from a realistic context and elaborates it through use of style, rhythm, and exaggeration for the purposes of communicating meaning in dance.

Dance performance

The students will need to adapt and refine their existing skills in seeking and refining movements from their repertoire to answer the task for section 1 of the dance, for example. Similarly, they will base their new learning of partner work for section 2 and the group work in section 3 of the dance upon many previous experiences of working in twos and groups, including concepts such as leading, following, copying, complementing, contrasting and using different spatial relationships to give variety and interest to the work. In section 2 there is emphasis on developing new partner-work skills which involve lifting, pulling away from, supporting, leaning on, sliding off, moving onto, around, through and off your partner. The safety factor is definitely paramount here and sensitive care for each other should be developed in this partner work.

The students will practise and perform parts and the whole of their dance compositions. Having first worked on the techniques required to perform the actions, especially new ones, they should concentrate on linking the actions, and colouring them with contrasting expressive qualities (continuous, slow and gentle in the introduction and more energetic, strong and accented in section 2 of the dance, for example). Each section should be practised to achieve coherence with the music and continuity of expressive intention. Gradually the sections should be performed in succession, ensuring that phrasing is clear and dancers are in the right place at the right time. Attention should be given to performance attributes, such as focus, alignment, posture, extension, projection and musicality in order to develop artistic dance performance skills. In this dance outcome, students are required to reflect the quiet and smooth qualities in the accompaniment in their compositions.

Students should also be encouraged to perform parts of and the whole dance to their peers, and/or to an audience and show sensitivity to the accompaniment while they perform. Use of a video camera and replay facilities will help students to evaluate and improve their own performances.

Memorising the movement content and observing themselves and each other on video, perhaps through use of checklists to identify strengths and weaknesses, will help to improve the quality of the performance. There is little set movement in this dance outcome. However, the students are required to observe and copy accurately at least one action phrase out of *Waterless Method of Swimming Instruction*.

Dance appreciation

During the lessons there is opportunity for the teacher to give the students written tasks. They may be asked to write an account of the movements selected for section 1 and why they selected them. They may well record the group work content for section 3 and describe in detail the action chosen from the video and why it was selected. It would be encumbent upon the teacher to create opportunities for written and oral work during the experiences leading up to the dance outcome.

Work with the resource, *Waterless Method of Swimming Instruction*, could also lead to discussion of the style of the movements, costumes and set – especially in relation to the context of time and place for the theme of the work. The processes of description, analysis and interpretation of the students' own dance work and the work on video will be employed during the lessons culminating in *Pool Idling*.

The **learning outcomes** numbered 1–9 above can be evaluated in relation to the achievements of the class as a whole or, if appropriate, in relation to each individual pupil. A report based on the above three learning outcomes, which are specific to the dance *Pool Idling*, could be used as a means of providing formative assessment feed-back. At the end of the stage (or block of dance experience), this report could be reviewed, along with others that relate to further dance outcomes, to inform evaluation of the students' progress within or at the end of the stage. Here the list of outcomes relating to learning **dance composition**, **dance performance** and **dance appreciation** for the whole stage should be used. These can be found on pages 104–109. Reports collected for each dance outcome (such as *Pool Idling*) should demonstrate the students' progress so that a summary statement can be made relating to achievement under the headings of **dance composition**, **dance performance** and **dance appreciation**.

Ways in which the above dance outcome implements the theoretical basis of the **midway** *model*

The dance outcome *Pool Idling* clearly puts an emphasis on the fact that, in the art of dance model, dance lessons will always culminate in a dance or part of a dance. However, the means towards this end should definitely include all the elements of the *midway* model. So, rather than the teacher creating and teaching the dance to the pupils (professional model), he or she will create a dance framework to ensure that they engage in the processes of creating, performing and viewing. Doing so will assist students' developing understanding, knowledge and skills with regard to choreography, performance and the appreciation of dances.

These creating, performing and viewing processes will be fully integrated although, at any one moment in a lesson, there will be emphasis on one more than another. The content of the lessons leading up to the dance *Pool Idling* illustrates this. Although in the list of lesson content there are clearly-defined composition tasks, performance tasks and viewing tasks, it is very likely that the teacher will require the students to engage in all three processes most of the time. For example, in the task to explore and identify content for section 1 of the dance, the students would no doubt be asked to watch each other and appreciate originality and appropriateness in the responses made. They may then work on improving quality in their own (and perhaps each other's) performing of the movements. Although attention is focused on creating movements for this part of the dance, the processes of performing and viewing are employed to enhance the outcome.

In good practice, then, the integration of these elements will be apparent at many points in any one lesson. Moreover, at this secondary stage, there should be written and/or oral work where students describe, record, analyse, interpret and evaluate dances – their own, their peers' and professional dance works presented in live theatre or on video. Such work may well be supported by reading and research relating to a particular choreographer or dance work, all of which enhances appreciation and leads to further insight upon which students can base future choreographic and performance work.

1. Equal emphasis on process and on product

As in the example discussed at primary level, the dance outcome/ product *Pool Idling* is a qualitative whole having several related sections, a beginning, middle and end with repetitions, develop-ments, contrasts, variety, climaxes, transitions and an overall unity in expressive purpose. It is important that the students in the secondary phase appreciate these formal and structural aspects of the dance outcome and that they start to perceive them in the dances they experience. However, the dance outcome itself is not the sole purpose of dance lessons. It *is* important, but not at the expense of worthwhile processes on the way. Teachers need to balance the achievement of a completed outcome with sufficiently deep and lengthy creating, performing and viewing processes. The time available needs to be carefully planned to ensure that sufficient attention is given to both process and product. The dance *Pool Idling* needs at least four hours of lesson time to complete. If less than this is available over three to four weeks, perhaps a shorter dance outcome is needed.

In developing an appreciation of the product *Pool Idling*, students should also note that the range and variety of expressive content are necessary attributes of a 'good' dance. However, their attention to the needs of the outcome (its expression of the theme, the overall variety and coherence of content) should not outweigh the attention given to the processes leading to the product. In attempting to achieve appropriateness, variety and originality of content, an exploration task with equal emphasis on process and product might proceed in the following manner.

Extract from lesson plan

TASK – imagine you are indulging in the feeling of floating on the surface of a warm swimming pool. Explore and select arching, rolling, stretching, relaxing and curling movements. Start in a stretched lying position on your backs with arms above your head. Keep lying on and in contact with the floor most of the time but include one rising and falling action during your sequence. Keep the movements slow, fluid and continuous.

This is too long to give all at once so it might be split in the following way:

a. Exploration might start with improvisation of the floor movements to the music.
b. Demonstration of some interesting responses, the teacher's feed-back and the suggestion of further images should broaden each student's range of movement ideas.
c. Concentration on linking the movements to make phrases and on variety should guide further the selection process.
d. Motifs could be viewed by peers and discussion take place to improve the selection and performance of the content.
e. Further exploration of the rising and falling actions could be interspersed with viewing some of these actions in the video of *Waterless Method of Swimming Instruction* and/or teacher-led exploration of lifting out of and falling into the floor.
f. The provision of a few ideas should encourage students to explore and find their own ways of performing these actions.
g. Create the sequence of motifs for section 1 of the dance (i.e. the task above).
h. Watch each other's work, comment and appraise. Practise to improve the quality of performance.
i. For homework, write down the content for this section of the dance and explain how the movements chosen convey the idea.

A range of processes could, therefore, take place to arrive at section 1 of the dance. These carefully planned and reasonably lengthy processes are more likely to achieve a rich outcome than taking shortcuts to complete the first section of the dance for the sake of having an end product. If, however, the lesson emphasises processes only and there is scant attention given to creating and performing something which can be repeated, there is little possibility of retaining the range and depth of the exploratory process for the following week.

Equal emphasis on process and product should be aimed at in the art of dance in education.

2. *Equal emphasis on development of creativity, imagination and individuality and an acquisition of knowledge of theatre dance*

The task given above for section 1 can be used to illustrate how a balance between developing the students' own creative responses and learning from the world of theatre dance can be maintained in the art of dance in education model.

The setting (an outdoor pool in sunny holiday weather), which is likely to be in the experience of the pupils, presents them with an imaginary canvas upon which they can place their own content. The starting position, the type of content and the fact that there should only be one incidence of rising and falling within the sequence is pre-determined, but this merely provides a framework or structure within which the students create their own movement ideas. The movements themselves are born out of each student's response to the task. As indicated in chapter 1 of this book, rather than dampen creativity, such limitations give the imagination a start and a secure base from which to travel freely. The range and originality of creative responses will depend on the quality of the exploration and teacher/student feed-back, but opportunity is there in this and all other sections of the dance for individual, creative responses.

The form of section 1 of the dance, with its starting position and one rise-and-fall action in contrast to the series of continuous, slow floor movements, sets a good example of how to create form in a dance. This learning which, at this stage, should be made explicit to the students, feeds their growing understanding of form as it is presented in Western theatre dance works. The knowledge gained here about phrasing, contrast, climax and continuity should be reinforced in creating section 2 of the dance where there is more freedom of choice in both the type and ordering of the content and this can usefully be referenced by study of Cohan's work on the video.

The overall form in *Waterless Method of Swimming Instruction* – its sections and the transitions/contrasts of the dancer manipulating the deckchair, the abstraction of content from swimming itself, from Esther Williams-like swimming films and early twentieth-century approaches in swimming instruction – provides suitable exemplification of the process of abstraction and elaboration of movements to make dance motifs. Moreover, Cohan's constantly changing use of the group in the space can be observed and discussed as an attribute providing variety and interest and the students should be encouraged to learn from this observation to enhance their own compositions. The duo sections can be used as starting points for exploration of content for section 2 of the dance, and the moments of 'swimming' and land-drill form the repertoire from which the students will select and copy a movement idea for section 3 of the dance.

This acquisition of knowledge of theatre dance through use of a video as stimulus and starting point for the students' own creative work provides what Best (1985) terms as 'grasp of the criteria of validity and value' in choreography. Hence pupils learn as much about the discipline through study of professional ready-mades as they do through responding to tasks within the bounds of their own imaginations. Indeed, it is often the case that students produce more creative and original responses when there are certain limitations than if given total freedom. In fact, the latter is more often than not counter-productive in that, unless experienced, students do not have an already built-in range of movement responses to tasks. Like words, movements need to be learned, stored, adapted and used appropriately before they can be said to be a part of the student's vocabulary. Given total freedom, without such a vocabulary, students of this age in particular will freeze and produce nothing.

On the other hand, there has to be a feeling of ownership of the product, too. It is important that there are sufficient creative opportunities included to allow for individual response so that most of the content in the dance seems to have been supplied by the students themselves. Even in the sections where direct reference is made to a resource – for example, section 3 of the dance *Pool Idling*, the students own work should supersede the starting point and take on characteristics of its own. In fact this dance has an abundance of creative opportunity for the students. Their own ideas will develop in the partner and group work (sections 2 and 3), and many of them will derive from their own experiences of playing in pools and of learning to swim.

Of course, the *midway* model for the art of dance in education supports a *midway* approach. The teacher's framework and professional resource create the limits within which the students' imaginations can have free rein. Creativity is nurtured and extended through carefully-structured learning experiences. The discipline and techniques of the art form have to be mastered, but it is not the chicken and egg situation commonly practised in the *professional* model. In the educational context, it is not necessary to master all the techniques first and serve apprenticeship for a long time prior to being able to create one's own dances. This might be perpetuated in professional dance learning circles but, in the art of dance in education, being creative and choreographing dances employing imagination go hand in hand with mastering of the discipline and learning from professional exemplars.

The methods employed to achieve these dual aims are discussed later. Perhaps at this stage, as in the case of the primary example discussed in chapter 2 of this book, if there is to be a leaning one way or the other, there should be rather more emphasis on the pupils' own creative work than on learning about theatre dance.

3. Equal emphasis on feelings and on training

It could be argued that the education of feelings/intuition discussed earlier in this book in the context of year 3 children should be well advanced by the time year 9 is reached. If there has been a consistent dance education between these stages, pupils should have had many opportunities to express and experience feelings in response to dance situations. Each new idea with its implicit range of feelings will have required the pupils to explore and select appropriate movement vocabulary to express it. In this way, their repertoire of movement to communicate feelings will have enlarged and some understanding of associations between movements and feelings will have developed.

By year 9, it is probable that the students have learned that, in dance lessons, you do not express how you are feeling personally but learn how to communicate objective feelings through movements in formed dance compositions. Although the feelings are not real in the same sense as personal feelings, they nonetheless should be felt by the students through *getting inside* the dance idea. This is achieved through imagination – the feelings are imagined and communicated in dance. Hence, the importance of imagery and various stimuli such as music to accompany the dance, in order to inspire and extend the students' identification with feelings. Of course, it is only possible to imagine feelings that you have experienced in some way yourself. So the teacher needs to be sure that the pupils can bring sufficient understanding and knowledge of the feelings that they are attempting to convey in dance in order to be able to re-create them imaginatively.

The more experience of artistically-expressed feelings the choreographer, performer or viewer can bring to the dance situation in hand, the richer it will be. So it becomes a part of the dance teacher's task to provide as many feeling experiences as possible through the processes of creating, performing and viewing dances. In creating and performing dances, a range of ideas/themes, including abstract movement themes such as circularity, will offer the students opportunities to express many different feelings. In viewing dances (their peers' and professionally choreographed and performed dances), students will perhaps gain understanding of new feelings and ideas, thus extending further the boundaries of their imaginations. Study and appreciation of professional dance works are important means of expanding the students' experience and knowledge of life's feelings/meanings. So viewing dances also contributes much to an understanding of feelings and how dance can convey them.

The dance *Pool Idling* provides many opportunities for the students to imagine what it feels like floating in water, playing with a partner in water, learning to swim and so on. These imaginary situations linked to their own experiences conjure up a range of movement ideas to express the theme and the feelings it evokes. Each task outlined for the lesson content provides opportunity for the students' own feelings and imaginings to enter into the expressive form. There is much opportunity too, for the students to develop and utilise their growing sense of form in shaping motifs and phrases to create their dances. This knowledge is more often than not at an intuitive level, in that they tend to make decisions about form because it 'feels right' rather than referring to guiding principles of form. By the end of stage 3 students should have had many experiences of creating dances based upon the teacher's frameworks which, as indicated earlier, should have in-built coherence of expressive form. Through these experiences the students' subconscious knowledge is developed. When this is tapped, as Reid (1983) claimed, the pupils are said to be using intuition. They may not be able to say much about the form they have created, but the decisions made through feeling what is right will indicate their understanding of form at the intuitive level. When the students have more experience, this understanding should become more conscious and objectively applicable to composing tasks.

Clearly then, both kinds of subjective feelings (those related to emotions and those related to intuitions) have important roles to play in the art of dance for secondary pupils. Yet, at the same time, students of this age are demanding more objective ends in that they desperately seek to develop sufficiently good technique in order to be able to perform the movements which capture the essence of those feelings. Secondary students in particular enjoy working the body to improve its facility and enjoy trying out new skills to add to their repertoire. After all, if they have danced from the age of five, they ought to be far beyond refinement of mere everyday movement to create their dance vocabulary. This may be the mainstay of the primary school child's vocabulary, but the secondary student needs to learn specific dance skills and practise dance movements which are far beyond the everyday roots. Hence, their running movements will include stylised extended runs, triple runs, turning waltz runs and the like, all of which emanate from one technique or another and contribute to the Western theatre dance forms' vocabulary of running. Such learning of specific dance vocabulary requires, to varying extents, a trained body in order that the vocabulary can be performed. The process of training to enable students to perform the movements required for a dance should develop hand in hand with new vocabulary. An example will help to clarify this.

In *Pool Idling*, section 1 requires the students to rise up and fall into the ground fluidly and slowly. Falling actions may not have been experienced very much before this dance so the teacher may elect to use this creative task as an impetus for acquisition of some skill and a further extended vocabulary of falling actions. The students' bodies must be properly warmed and prepared before they learn specific falls such as the Graham side fall, forward fall from a tip forward on one leg with the other extended high behind and reaching forward to land on parallel arms, forward fall initiated with slide towards side splits, backward fall rolling through the body to a back lying position and so on. These are just a few stylised and specialised falls the students may be able to add to their vocabulary. They need to learn how to perform them properly and will thus become more skilled in execution of them. Having acquired some skill in the context of specifically-learned techniques of falling, it is likely that the skills required for the students' own ways of falling will be of the same order. Once consolidated, knowledge and skill should be applicable to new and different falls developed as part of the students' creative responses.

A similar set of comments could be made about section 2 of the dance in that here the students need to learn some basic contact improvisation techniques. They need to be able to take each other's weight and lift and put each other down safely and with control to achieve the expressive quality of the dance. Hence preparatory exercise and skills practices need to be built into the lessons before the students can create and perform the dance. This kind of training with clear objectives forms an important part of the students' experience in the art of dance. As well as learning the skills step by step and practising them, the students should be directed to view how the professional dancers perform similar movements in a study of Cohan's *Waterless Method of Swimming Instruction*. Here, analysis of where hands are put in order to lift, where the supporting person's feet are placed during the lift, where the accent is, how the lifted person keeps body tension, etc. will help the students to focus on technical points in order to help their own performance, and on aspects of the skills to observe each other for appraisal purposes[8].

Concentration on one or two technical requirements, such as those above within each dance outcome, will ensure that the teacher is giving sufficient attention to training the students' bodies while they acquire enough dance skills to fulfil the expressive needs of the dance. In this way, the objective ends of the *midway* model are playing a role although, perhaps at this stage, they should not be emphasised. Rather, for lower secondary students, if the balance is uneven, there should be slightly more weight on the subjective feeling kind of education than there is on the objective training kind of education.

4. Equal emphasis on movement principles and on stylised techniques

It should be apparent to the reader that the content of the dance *Pool Idling* is derived from both the Laban-based movement principles and vocabulary based on two contemporary dance techniques – firstly, mainstream contemporary dance with a Graham flavour as exemplified by Cohan in particular, and secondly, something like certain aspects of contact improvisation.

The principles of movement serve both the teacher and the students very well as means towards achieving the expressive outcome. Each section of the dance defines a kind or several different kinds of action to be created and performed. The word 'kind' here to preface actions is important because this explains exactly the role of the principles in forming a framework within which the students

---

[8]There is excellent teaching material on contact improvisation technique and fully interactive touch-button means of controlling it, in the *Wild Child CD Resource Pack* (1999) – see references for details.

choose their own actions in preference to learning and employing a dictated set of steps.

Throughout the dance, there are examples of framework tasks which give scope for exploration and choice. The introduction defines only that the students travel slowly into different resting positions. The sort of steps they take, the combination of them, rhythm of them, direction they take and the ultimate position and how it is arrived at are each student's choice. Section 1 requires the students to explore and make motifs out of a range of actions – arching, curling, stretching, rocking and rolling and to include one rising and falling action. This is very typical of a movement principle approach in that the kind of action is defined, but its detail is left open so that an arching movement can be done with just the head, with the top of the spine, with the whole spine – lying on different parts of the body or sitting, kneeling, standing or even jumping. There are a number of ways in which the concept of arching can be interpreted. Each student has the freedom to explore different ways and to find different answers to the task from those of other students in the group. In addition, each student's use of the dynamic qualities will vary even though the group as a whole is moving slowly and with continuity.

Further differences will be seen in responses to tasks which are somewhat looser than the one above. For instance, section 2 of the dance provides a framework of different possibilities for interpreting the theme of playing in the pool with a partner. Here, students need to be led to explore several different movement principles to interpret the theme of the dance. Partner work concepts (such as assisted jumps and lifting and lowering), spatial relationship concepts (such as through, under, over and round) and the time concept of slow motion are interpreted by the partners in their own ways to express the theme.

Movement principles are, therefore, important sources for the content of each dance outcome but they are not the sole source. As indicated already, in order that students extend beyond their natural everyday movement vocabularies, there is need for reference to specified dance techniques, each with their own range of stylised movement content. Through such references, knowledge of the art form of dance vocabulary as known in the public world is developed. Dance content is not restricted to that derived from each student in response to a task; it also emanates from the professional dance training and theatrical contexts.

A knowledge of some Graham-like falling actions has already been alluded to as a potentially valuable source of content for section 1 of the dance *Pool Idling*. The technique of falling needs to be carefully taught, and if the falls are to capture the essence of the Graham style they need to be stylised with particular attention to its distinctive features. This particular style may be the most appropriate to try to capture in the dance as a whole since, in the exemplar, Cohan also retains a distinctly Graham-based style in his work.

Even though dance vocabulary for section 2 may derive from a contact improvisation technique, the dance can be performed in the more extended and placed Graham-based style rather than the more relaxed on-going fluid style associated with contact work. Adherence to one particular style in a dance is an important factor to consider if the dance is to achieve coherence. *Waterless Method of Swimming Instruction* provides an example of this even in the use of everyday movements which are stylised, rhythmically phrased and exaggerated to achieve a particular Graham look.

The Graham technique, then, can be a source of content not only in terms of movement vocabulary but also in order to capture the essence of a style. Of course, the specific technical vocabulary – if properly performed – defines the truly distinctive Graham style. However, because the technique is very complex and difficult to perform, the possibility of achieving a close resemblance to this style with year 9 pupils is very remote. A sense of the style can be captured and it is encumbent upon the teacher to know how to distil the essences that will colour the movements sufficiently to give the dance a Grahamesque look.

As already acknowledged, known techniques can be used as sources of content for dance in secondary education. In the notes for the dance *Pool Idling*, there is reference to two known techniques for the purposes of extending the students' repertoires of movement. How the vocabulary is learned and made their own is the next topic to be discussed.

5. Equal emphasis on problem-solving and on directed teaching

The dance *Pool Idling* is a teacher's framework composition with very little set movement content included. Indeed, the only set content is determined through the choice made by any group of four for section 3 of the dance (they choose at least one swimming type of action to copy from the video of *Waterless Method of Swimming Instruction*; even this action is not directly taught by the teacher). In all the other work leading to composition of their dances, the pupils are led through creative problem-solving tasks. In my opinion, at this stage in education, the teacher needs to intervene in about eighty per cent of problem-solving occasions in order that the students' responses to tasks progress and develop in range and variety. Otherwise students may become satiated by over-use of the same vocabulary of movement regardless of different themes.

The intervention that occurs, however, needs to be carefully handled so that the students do not feel a loss of ownership of their dance. In the exploration tasks leading to selection of content for the dance (see pages 118–119), the students are given the frameworks – sometimes quite tightly restricted (1a and b), sometimes quite open (1c, d and e). The teacher then acts as a catalyst by making observations or, better still, providing the students with the means (mostly by questioning) of making observations about each other's work. The quality of the questions or teaching points on 'things to look for' determines the quality and depth of subsequent exploration. Sometimes creative learning can be greatly enhanced if the students all try out an idea, either the teacher's or (more often) one of the student's. This may involve a direct teaching approach so that the others absorb the movement by 'getting inside it'. During the processes leading to composition of the dance, however, there should be a strong emphasis on the problem-solving approach where the students are agents in their own learning.

Nevertheless, emphasis on a problem-solving approach does not mean that the directed teaching approach plays a minimal role. At the secondary stage, the students need to learn and practise movements and compositional devices that have been tried and tested and become a part of what constitutes dance in the public world. In performance-oriented work, for example (see 3d on page 121), directed teaching is important in helping students towards efficient and correct use of the body. This task requires students to learn how best to lift each other while jumping and it would be damaging if students were not directed in appropriate distribution of the weight and positioning of the bodies in relationship. A directed teaching approach is also necessary in transmitting how to fall in section 1 of the dance and, if the teacher pays attention to the Graham style of falling, some aspects of this will be transmitted, too. It may be appropriate for the students to learn a style study – pre-choreographed by the teacher in a Graham-based style – to help them stylise their own movements in their compositions.

At times, the students also need to be directed in what to observe in dance works – their own and professional ones – in order to learn facts about dance. This kind of learning (propositional knowledge) about dance is objective and testable and it is easy to use a directive/ instructive teaching approach by setting students to read chapters and to fill in worksheets with answers to questions. Although this method reduces the time taken to transmit knowledge about dance, students who direct their own learning, even in this kind of work, in my view learn more of the facts in the end and are more successful in retaining them. A researching method might be appropriate and this can be labelled pupil-directed learning because the teacher provides the books, journals, pictures, music and video materials and some questions or a task, and the pupils search out the answers for themselves. Project books or work journals to be handed in for assessment can work very well in that pupils can record their own dance choreography and performance work, and knowledge that they gain in viewing dances and researching for information about them.

6. Artistic education

The central purpose with the dance *Pool Idling* is to extend students' knowledge and understanding of what constitutes a dance and their artistic skills in creating and performing dances.

a) Understanding what a dance is:

By year 9, students should have understood what constitutes a dance in that they will have experienced many dances (mostly through the teacher's frameworks) which have formal and expressive features symbolising themes. They will be beginning to perceive principles of form such as variety, logical development and unity as means of achieving coherence in the dances they create and they will have learned ways in which movement in dance becomes symbolic. They should also know something about style and how this characterises dances and dance movement.

The students' learning about the nature of dances is enhanced by watching the professional dance work *Waterless Method of Swimming Instruction*. Concepts of form, expression and style become reinforced through such exemplars and these concepts inform the students' work.

b) Skills, knowledge and understanding gained through the processes of creating, performing and appreciating dances.

Creating

In creating the dance the students will experience a range of tasks – some more open than others – in order to determine the content. The teacher's dance framework will identify the kinds of movements to be included but the students need to explore and select within the categories in the framework. For example, for section 2 of the dance, students will be led to explore and discover a range of assisted jumps, movements onto and sliding off their partner, through, under, and round partner and lifting and lowering movements to give the impression of playing in water. Different partner-assisted movements within this task will be tried and decisions made as to which to keep and which to discard. The students will then need to make decisions on the order and juxtapositioning of the moves to make phrases which complement the music and appropriately express the theme. Linking of the movements with an emphasis on fluidity and smoothness to create the illusion of being in water and to achieve an interesting use of time and space gives plenty of opportunity for the teacher to promote artistic learning.

Temporal variations can be achieved through placing accents in different parts of phrases. A turning-assisted jump might involve a swing-like rhythm where the accent is in the middle of the move-ment. An alternative supported jump would place the accent at the end of the movement if the supporting partner were to catch and hold the elevated partner prior to landing. Variation in the length of phrases is also possible because the music has no distinct phrasing in this section. Rhythmic patterning of the partner movements should be an artistic consideration alongside learning how to use the music as accompaniment. The music selected for the dance is ideal for this section in that it is smooth and ongoing. Accents can be placed anywhere in the movement and phrases can extend over the length of musical phrases or several short dance phrases can be accommodated within one musical phrase. There should, of course, be some matching of accents, phrasing, tempo and rhythm between the music and the movements so that they are complementary.

Spatial interest can be achieved if students are encouraged to attend to the positioning and alignment of their bodies to the perceived 'front' of the dance so that the audience gains the best view. It will also occur if there is variety of spatial relationship in the partner sequence, i.e. the sequence should include movements back to back, side by side, facing, one behind the other, movements round, over, on and off partner and several other variations. This variety helps to make the dance rich in visual patterning.

Repetition and development of content in the final part of the dance requires students to employ the means of development they know – such as changing level, performing with different body parts, adding movements such as turns and travelling, changing the qualities and/or spatial patterning of the original movements. This repetition and development of movements used in the introduction and section 1 of the dance give the dance a unity and completeness in that the beginning parts are re-echoed at the end. Yet it is not exact repetition because the students are asked to develop some of the movements from section 1 in any order and then to determine their own conclusion. Use of such devices to give form to the whole reinforces understanding of the concept and a developing aware-ness of how to structure dances.

Learning how to abstract from everyday and swimming actions in order to create movements which symbolise the idea is an emphasised aspect of artistic learning in this dance outcome. The students will be asked to imagine the movements as if they were actual and then to take the essence of them as bases to retain in their motifs and to elaborate them by adding, adapting and changing them into dance movements.

An example will help to identify the artistic learning that might occur here. If the students are asked to include a breast stroke and diving action into a sequence they will need to select parts of the actions to retain. For example, they could choose the arm action in the breast stroke and the starting position with arms extended and together and a downward action for the dive. These can be made larger and changed to a degree but they should remain recognisable. Further elaboration of the actions by the addition of travelling, jumping, turning or leg gestures and by the variety of qualitative and spatial aspects (except the downward emphasis in the dive) will make the original starting movements into developed stylised dance motifs which symbolise the idea.

Performing

In sections 1 and 2 the selected actions will need much practice to produce the appropriate slow-motion quality that will give the illusion of being in water. This demands control, balance, strength and co-ordination to link actions into fluid phrases. The phrases will, nevertheless, need to be accented in a way which complements the music and it should be clear where the highlights/climaxes occur.

In section 3 of the dance, the relationships with the other dancers in unison or canon will need to be practised and in section 2 the contact work will require much repetition to perfect the interactions which will convey the idea of being in water.

Technical proficiency performing the movements should be developed with helpful comments from the teacher or peers to identify ways in which the movement might be improved. Gradually, with repetition, new skills will become embedded and old skills (e.g. jumps assisted by a partner) will be extended in different co-ordinations when performed in different contexts. The techniques of performing stylised jumping actions are discussed in further depth on page 121 and clearly such a progressive treatment of learning new skills will enhance the students' abilities to perform these and related movements well.

It is often beneficial at this stage in dance education to develop dance skills through a technical study approach. A technical study comprises dance skills choreographed into motifs, phrases and sections to make a formed whole. It can last for about a minute but is usually about three minutes long. As in music, a study concentrates on a limited range of material in order that it is practised as fully as possible. A study, as its name suggests, requires study and challenges the dancer to work towards mastery of its content. A study should ensure that the learners are acquiring new skills to enlarge their vocabularies (which should include different dance styles) or to improve performance qualities.

In the context of *Pool Idling*, there are two sections which could benefit from preliminary learning of a dance study – falling and rising actions for section 1 or contact work in pairs for section 2. The teacher would need to decide which aspect to focus on and create a dance study to another piece of music (if required at all) and teach it to the students in a directed way. The dance study should include a range of content but, more importantly, it should contain the differing technical processes necessary if falling or contact work is to be mastered. It should be used to introduce some ways in which the task in the dance might be answered but it should not exhaust the range of content appropriate to the task. Students should not feel constrained in their creative work by the technical study. Rather, it should act as a stimulating starting point for their own creativity. The main reasons for teaching a dance study – to improve technique and to introduce or develop vocabulary for the dance outcome – should be kept in mind. The dance study (as distinguished from a pure dance) should be treated as a means to the end and not an end in itself.

In terms of performance qualities throughout the dance, students should endeavour to extend their movements, project to an audience, use focus appropriately and express their meanings. Practice of each of these features should greatly improve the performance overall.

Viewing

All of the above features in creating and performing the dance can be viewed by peers, on a video if a camera is available and by the teacher. Description, analysis, interpretation and evaluation of the elements in the dance can take place in order that students learn from others and improve their own work. It is also important to use the professional exemplar of *Waterless Method of Swimming Instruction* as a source of reinforcement of artistic learning. For example, the slow-motion, beautifully extended and controlled movements of the dancers diving from the edges into swim-like actions should provide much to discuss and learn from in order to improve the students' own performance qualities.

Appreciation

All of the learning in the context of creating, performing and viewing *Pool Idling* and *Waterless Method of Swimming Instruction* contributes to a developing appreciation of the constituent elements of a dance as an expressive, stylised and formed whole. Appreciation of the dance includes appreciation of each other's creative responses to the teacher's tasks and of the performance of the dance. Appreciation of *Waterless Method of Swimming Instruction* will also develop, especially if a resource-based teaching approach is used to guide detailed perceptions of its intrinsic qualities. This appreciation will inform and enhance the students' own work.

7. Aesthetic Education

In all the creating, performing and viewing experiences involved in producing the dance *Pool Idling*, the students should be encouraged to develop their aesthetic perceptions both as performers and appreciators.

In performing the dance, the students' awareness of the qualities contained in the movement – the slow, indulgent, luxuriating stretches, arches and curls in section 1, for example – may be felt by the students imagining themselves in a warm pool enjoying a feeling of well-being like a cat on a mat in front of a fire! This imaginary feeling would be triggered by the sensation of the movement itself in its slow, sensuous, indulging stretching and, in turn, the imaginary feeling should produce a more feelingful and therefore qualitative movement outcome. The sensory and expressive qualities should be emphasised in the students' performances and the kinesthetic feeling of these will be aesthetically appreciated during their performances.

In viewing the dance or parts of the dance, the students should have many occasions to appreciate aesthetically the sensory and expressive qualities it contains. Looking at each other's work and guided by the teacher's questions, perhaps, students can be encouraged to find words to describe the sensory qualities of, for example, buoyant, wave-like, swooping, entwining, wooshing upward movements in section 2 of the dance to express free playing in water with a partner – the floating, continuous and slow movements giving an impression of water around the pair. Use of analogy and metaphor feeds each student's imaginary perceptions of the dance and perhaps develops ability to perceive more in an aesthetic way.

The formal qualities of the dance and its parts should also be brought into focus in developing the students' aesthetic perceptions. Here, attention given to the sections and how each part develops logically into a whole provides a sense of unity which can be discussed as a pleasurable completeness when the dance has been viewed. (It may not produce this sensation, of course, especially if there are parts which do not seem to cohere. This, also, would be an aesthetic experience, a negative one.) The repetition and development of motifs and of section 1 at the end of the dance, the linking transitions, the highlights and contrasts, the coherence of style, are formal qualities which contribute to the overall sensation of a meaningful whole dance.

Viewing of the professional exemplar should also help to develop the students' aesthetic perceptions. Here, they are free to interpret the meanings and feelings contained in the dance and should be given opportunities to express their perceptions in discussion and/or writing. Again the use of descriptive words, analogy and metaphor, and sharing them in discussions, may help individual students to open up alternative ways of viewing the work aesthetically. Attempts should be made to promote opportunities for the students to express what they feel about the work and whether they judge it to be good or not. Reasons for their feelings and judgments could be found through use of Osborne's aesthetic template in discussion of the perceived sensory, expressive and formal qualities (see also chapter 1).

Throughout the experiences leading to a final production of *Pool Idling* then, students' perceptions of their own work, their peers' work and of the professional exemplar could be enriched through application of an aesthetic approach to the processes of creating, performing and viewing.

8. Cultural education

Year 9 students will have absorbed many concepts underpinning mainstream choreography and performance in Western contemporary culture. These concepts include the ways in which ideas are translated into symbolic dance motifs, the use of the stage space and manner of presentation to an audience, the duration of a dance work and how the dance is formed to make a whole. Knowledge of expression and form in dances is therefore developing and extending through each dance experience. Yet the kind of expression and form experienced in *Pool Idling*, with its reference to a contemporary dance piece choreographed by Robert Cohan, an American who was strongly influenced by Martha Graham, is very specific, i.e. it can be described as Western contemporary dance. There is much to be learned within this somewhat narrowly focused dance education since contemporary dance, like any other art form, has its own particular 'language' and artistic procedures. If students become conversant with terminology to describe the movements, become experienced in interpreting abstracted symbolic meanings and become able to discern form, they may well develop into informed audiences for contemporary dance (see also 2, page 129) and this is an important part of their cultural education.

Contemporary dance, however, is but one small part of a much larger domain. Dances with roles other than a theatrical one and derived from other genres need to be experienced in addition to those emanating from mainstream Western theatre contemporary dance contexts. This is necessary in order to broaden the students' concepts of the art of dance and dance generally – including folk and social dances, for example.

In the dance discussed here, and especially *Waterless Method of Swimming Instruction*, the theme and the way it has been expressed fall within an historical context. The early twentieth-century approach to swimming instruction and the references to 1930s films provide one stylistic boundary; the Graham-based technique provides another. The students could be led to recognise these aspects as historical characteristics.

Their own dance pieces, however, will contain these elements only to a degree. The reference to the style and technique of contact improvisation which was developed much later than the Graham technique (i.e. 1970s), will give the students' dance a newer look. A conscious attempt to make the students' own pieces reflect today's mainstream dance works rather than the professional exemplar could be advantageous in teaching the students something about style.

A dance artist's workshop and/or study of video material on the use of contact improvisation as a basis for choreography would help the students to discern the essential differences in style. Such learning helps to develop the students' understanding of the history of the art of dance.

RESOURCE-BASED TEACHING/LEARNING

The dance outcome and lessons leading to the final performance of it will have been enhanced and enriched by reference to professional dance exemplars, in particular *Waterless Method of Swimming Instruction* and the dancers' performance of it. It is suggested above that this exemplar is used, for the most part, as a stimulus or as inspirational input in that it provides an extra resource that may indirectly assist the students' own creating and performing activities. In one section of the dance, the resource is used more directly in that the students are asked to copy one of the 'swimming' actions and to include it in their sequence. In these ways, then, resource-based teaching can be seen to play a part in the dance experiences of the year 9 students.

Student-based learning is the distinguishing characteristic of resource-based teaching which at this level and beyond should, in my opinion, feature as an important part of the teaching process. The ideal situation of students working on their own with easy access to video recording and play-back systems[9] and to a library of dance resources may seem a little far-fetched. Yet, in a situation where dance is centred in a studio or room with storerooms close at hand, it should not be a problem. In any event, even if the class has to be taught as one group, students could work from worksheets to find their own answers to tasks and then share these with the rest of the class. If there is just one video playback system, however, the teacher will either have to set group tasks with only one group at a time employing the system, or work through a worksheet with the class as a whole. The disadvantages of the latter are obvious.

[9] Or, better still, CD ROM systems.

Viewing tasks

There are three clear objectives for the use of Cohan's *Waterless Method of Swimming Instruction* as a resource to underwrite the dance experiences culminating in *Pool Idling*.

1. To identify and learn from the ways in which Cohan has abstracted from the starting points of being in water and learning to swim to develop dance motifs.

2. Through analysis of the video, to enhance learning about performance by reference to qualities in the dancing.

3. Through replication of one of the 'swimming' actions, to 'get inside' a part of the dance by performing it and thus experiencing how Cohan abstracts and develops the action, gives it rhythm, style, expression and form.

The teacher could employ a resource-based teaching methodology for each of these objectives, and viewing tasks would feature as necessary starting points within a teaching/learning programme. For example, in identifying the process of abstraction, students could be asked to watch the sequence from the point where the women are hanging from the side of the pool and the men lift them off into performance of two duos, up to these duos performing two lifted jumps where the women touch their toes. Students could be asked to:

a. identify three swimming-type actions and describe what is added and/or taken away from the actions to make them into dance movements;
b. identify other movements which indicate that the dancers are in water;
c. identify recognisable dance movements and name them if possible (e.g. *arabesque* from ballet and contraction and release from contemporary dance);
d. notice the way that the two duos relate in space and in use of unison and canon.

Further viewing tasks should include viewing of the whole work and questions to develop the students' aesthetic perceptions of it. Viewing tasks will also necessarily precede creating and performing tasks deriving from the resource.

Creating tasks

Several of the creating tasks could be supported by use of the resource and a resource-based methodology. A creating task could follow the viewing of *Waterless Method of Swimming Instruction* and might proceed as follows:

- in pairs, with one dancer using the arm actions of a back stroke, find ways of leaning away from your partner (as on the video when using breast stroke in the above described section of the resource) and develop the movement into a phrase including travelling, turning and jumping.

A further task leading to section 3 of the dance might take the following form:

- use the beginning duo and subsequent quartet in the resource, select a swimming type of action to copy;
- note the changes of relationship within the duo and quartet;
- note the use of unison and canon in this section of the dance;
- in fours, create the sequence for section 3 of the dance employing the copied movement from the video and, if you wish, some ideas for orchestration of your motifs.

This task starts using the video in a direct way – copying a movement – and then indirectly as a stimulus or starting point for revision of ways in which relationships can be varied and motifs can be orchestrated in a four.

In such ways, the resource can be used to reinforce artistic learning that has already been undertaken in creating dances and to introduce new learning. The resource should be used more as an impulse for the students' own creative work rather than something to be replicated. Carefully designed tasks will help students towards this kind of resource-based learning while creating their own dances.

Performing tasks

There are many ways in which the performance on video can be used as a teaching/learning tool. The dancers on it demonstrate very well the slow-motion quality to give the illusion of being in water and their extension, control, balance, line, projection, continuity and fluidity in use of their bodies is exemplary. Students may be given tasks to identify some of these qualities and develop knowledge that will improve their own performances. For example, in watching the two men dance their opening duo, they could proceed as follows:

a. watch carefully how the dancers use their knees and feet to convey buoyancy in water while jumping;
b. take note of what the arms are doing to help;
c. also note the degree of tension in the body to help produce the upward lift in the movements even when landing;
d. work in twos, one observing and one performing, to help each other achieve the same buoyancy.

Another task may be focused on continuity and fluidity, and here the performance of the three women in the section following the above duo makes a fine example. The students could practise for themselves:

a. the hands-together snake-like action of arms into the side roll and rise, concentrating on smooth, continuous and fluid action with no jerks or stops;
b. the undulating arms and upper body actions;
c. moving through a) to b) and repeat, keeping the qualities as fluid as in a);
d. now dance your own partner sequences using the same qualities, having discussed where it is appropriate to do so.

Using the video in this way to improve performance brings great benefit in that, once students can see performance attributes as they are pointed out, they know what requires attention in their own work. It is much easier to work from an intellectual understanding of what is to be strived for than to take instruction from the teacher to improve performance. Seeing it in action and conceptualising what it is that makes it good performance abolishes the need for many words and many trial and error practices. The latter without an image can be slow and unproductive. Using a video such as this, with tasks carefully structured to ensure observation of the range of qualities contained in the dancers' performance of each and every movement, can be extremely valuable in promoting an aesthetic response in students which can then be used as inspiration to feed their own endeavours.

Cultural/historical tasks

The kind of knowledge and understanding which can be gained from study of *Waterless Method of Swimming Instruction* as a cultural/historical phenomenon has already been discussed in 8 (page 144). Use of a resource-based teaching/learning methodology, however, will ensure that students develop this knowledge and understanding for themselves.

For example, to study the Grahamesque style of the dance, students could be asked to work from a prepared hand-out which lists principles and characteristics in the Graham technique and then to find incidences of these in a selected section of the work.

Another task requiring written responses might aim to develop the students' understanding of the time and place setting of the theme. Pictures of early twentieth-century cruise ships, costumes, and writings on methods of teaching swimming through land drill exercises, together with programme notes, critics' writings and any other such materials could be used as reference resources in order to complete exercises such as the following:

a. Study this picture (either held on pause or scanned off the video opening tableau if not available from other sources), identify the time and place it indicates and list the features in the picture which helped you to make this decision.
b. Describe the costumes in *Waterless Method of Swimming Instruction* and comment on their authenticity in the context of the time and place setting of the dance.
c. Write a short description of how the choreographer used land drill exercises in the dance and on how other swimming aids indicate the time and place of the dance.

Such work might best be done in introducing the resource to the students rather than at a time when they are getting to know it well. To develop further their understanding of the context of the piece, additional tasks might include viewing snippets of 1930s' to 50s' films of synchronised swimming in order to identify the possible derivation of Cohan's dance ideas.

Resource-based teaching/learning pays dividends in developing the students' knowledge, understanding and skills in viewing, creating and performing dance/s. It can also develop a deeper aesthetic appreciation of a dance work which, in turn, promotes an improved ability to aesthetically perceive other dance/s.

Conclusion

This chapter, on the art of dance in secondary schools, illustrates how understanding and application of the theoretical basis for the art of dance in education (presented in chapter 1) can lead to effective delivery of the content outlined in the syllabus presented on pages 103–115.

As in the chapter on primary dance education, the aim here was to demonstrate in detail how the theoretical basis underpins practice and, again, only one example dance outcome and some of the teaching/learning that led up to its completion was scrutinised to illustrate this theory. This detailed application of theory to practice should help teachers understand what, in my view, constitutes good practice in teaching the art of dance in secondary education. Having applied the theoretical basis for the art of dance to this one practical situation focused on year 9 students, teachers should be able to apply it to different year groups.

THE ART OF DANCE IN EDUCATION AT GCSE, AS AND A LEVEL

To show how the theoretical basis for the art of dance in education is also applicable to the above examination syllabuses, it is perhaps necessary first to outline and describe the contents of the syllabuses.

1. Northern Examinations and Assessment Board – General Certificate of Secondary Education Syllabus for 2001 and 2002 Performing Arts: Dance

(Passages in italics below are directly quoted from this syllabus.)

This syllabus defines clear assessment objectives. It will assess the candidates' ability to:

- *demonstrate the skills of dance performance;*
- *demonstrate the skills of dance composition;*
- *interpret and evaluate dance showing accuracy, imagination and sensitivity;*
- *demonstrate a knowledge and understanding of a dance appreciation including the historical and cultural context.*

The scheme of assessment consists of:

(i) A terminal examination consisting of two papers:
- Paper 1 (20%) – study of a set work. A two-hour paper externally marked. The work set for 2001 is *Swansong* by Christopher Bruce and for 2002 it is *'Still Life' at Penguin Cafe* by David Bintley.
- Paper 2 (20%) – set study internally assessed and moderated by the Board. Performance of a technical study of approximately one minute's duration.

(ii) Coursework:
- Performance of a duo or group dance (10%). *This dance may be the result of work choreographed collaboratively by candidates or by the teacher, or taken from established repertoire. The group is defined as consisting of a maximum of five candidates. The dance may be performed with or without accompaniment and should last for one-and-a-half to two minutes.*
- Composition of a solo or group dance (30%). *The composition should be a length which best allows the candidate to display knowledge, understanding and skills of composition.*
- Assignment (20%). *Based on a study of a named dance work other than the set work, a named choreographer or a named dance genre.*

Northern Examinations and Assessment Board – Advanced Supplementary and Advanced Syllabus for 2001: Dance

The above are two separate examinations, the AS taken after one year of study and the A level taken after two years of study. The AS level requires that students *acquire knowledge and understanding of one chosen dance genre and the culture from which it derives.* The A level requires that students acquire *knowledge and understanding of two chosen dance genres* (not necessarily through performance in both) *and the cultures from which they derive. The genres from which selection may be made are African dance, ballet, modern dance and South Asian dance, manifest in the United Kingdom today.*

The following assessment objectives show that the examinations require students to study dance performance, composition and appreciation. (Passages in italics below are directly quoted from the syllabuses.)

AS LEVEL	A LEVEL
Show the practical skills of dance	*Show the practical skills of dance*
Show the knowledge of skills involved in performance	*Show the knowledge of skills involved in performance*
Show knowledge of the constituent features and form of dances	*Show understanding of notation*
Show knowledge of the cultural and historical context of dances in the genre selected	*Show knowledge of the constituent features and form of dances*
	Show knowledge of the cultural and historical context of dances
Interpret and evaluate dances	*Interpret and evaluate dances*
Scheme of assessment	**Scheme of assessment**
1) Choreography of a group dance in which the candidate does not perform	*1) Choreography of a group dance in which the candidate does not perform*
EITHER	*EITHER*
2A) Choreography and performance of a solo	*2A) Choreography and performance of a solo*
OR	*OR*
2B) Choreography of a solo in which the candidate does not perform	*2B) Choreography of a solo in which the candidate does not perform*
	3) Performance from a notated score
4) Performance of a prescribed solo	*4) Performance of a prescribed solo*

For AS level, candidates have to submit 1) above and choose one other option from 2 or 4. A level candidates are required to present all four items. In addition to the practical papers above which carry 60% and 40% of the marks respectively, candidates for AS level take one written paper worth 40% and candidates for A level take two written papers worth 20% and 40%. The short-answer AS and A level papers cover broad issues relating to the syllabus as a whole. The longer-essay-answer A level paper, Paper 3, tests the candidates' knowledge and understanding of the selected set work. For 2001 the set works are: *Romance… with footnotes* (Jeyasingh, 1993); *The Sleeping Beauty* (Petipa, 1890); *Winter Dreams* (MacMillan, 1991); *Swan Lake* (Bourne, 1995) and *White Man Sleeps* (Davies, 1988).

All three examinations (GCSE, AS and A level) require that students study choreography and performance. To this end, the syllabus content includes all aspects of study detailed in the lists headed 'creating dances' and 'performing dances' on pages 31 and 32 in chapter 1 of this book.

Appreciation also plays a major role in all three syllabuses. Here, theory of choreography and performance is enhanced and extended through a study of the historical and cultural contexts of the genres and dance works studied. Students are required to show knowledge and understanding of the function of dances as determined by changing performance milieu.

Obviously levels of expectation and achievement will differ but there is no doubt that the art of dance model underwrites these examination syllabuses.

Applying the theoretical basis to GCSE, A and AS level examination syllabuses

Clearly, the theory in chapter 1 and range of content and methods which, in this chapter, exemplifies the theory with reference to year 9 students, are all relevant to the teaching of the art of dance at GCSE level. Moreover, although the AS and A level syllabuses appear on the surface to introduce different dance forms, i.e. African, Classical Ballet and Indian, a brief reading of them will show that the conceptual basis underlying the work and the content examined is still that pertaining to the art of dance.

The three processes – creating, performing and appreciating – are central to these syllabuses, though the emphasis is perhaps even more towards the products/outcomes (i.e. choreography, performance and appreciation) of the art of dance than for secondary students in year 9 or below. Nonetheless, the processes involved should be experienced fully too because, as made clear throughout this book, a qualitative process leads, more often than not, to a qualitative product.

In examining a GCSE dance composition, for example, out of 30 marks there is a scale of grading descriptors. The bottom defines a bare minimum (i.e. *the candidate demonstrates a response with a limited movement vocabulary and a minimal use of the group*). The top defines the expected outcome as follows for the 2001/2002 examinations:

> The candidate demonstrates an articulate and highly refined response to the original idea. The dance will show, in relationships, a sophisticated use of rhythmic, dynamic and spatial designs. There is evidence of an extremely effective use of choreographic devices.

Top marks are awarded for performance if the candidates successfully interpret and express the theme, combine technically accurate movements and excellence in body control with sensitive interpretation of the expressive qualities. Furthermore, in the context of the assignment, top marks are awarded if the candidates show:

> ...detailed knowledge and a high level of understanding of the study areas. The work has been completed with accuracy, imagination and sensitivity resulting in an exciting and original assignment.

These descriptions indicate a level of achievement, knowledge and understanding which, in my view, would be difficult to attain without attention given to:

* process *and* product;
* creativity, imagination, individuality *and* acquisition of knowledge of theatre dance;
* feelings/subjectivity of experience *and* training for performance;
* understanding of generally applicable movement principles *and* specific dance styles as sources of content;
* the full range between problem-solving *and* directed approaches in teaching dance.

This points to the fact that, for the above examination syllabuses, teachers should be delivering a *midway* model incorporating a balance of features derived from both the *educational* and *professional* models. The work involved clearly constitutes an artistic education in that the syllabus content lists the skills, knowledge and understanding of the art of dance which students are required to study through the processes of creating, performing and appreciating dances. It is also clear that study of the historical and cultural aspects of the art of dance, particularly in the A and AS level, give the students contexts in which to place their dance experiences.

The broader cultural contexts of the syllabuses are a welcome development in the study of dance in education in a multicultural environment. However, this is not departing from the consensus art of dance model. Rather, it is expanding on the styles of dance that can be included in the model. The African and Indian dance styles are those used in presentation dances (i.e. the performing art form) emanating from these continents. The list of content in both the AS and A level syllabuses requires that these genres, alongside contemporary dance and ballet, be studied as art forms.

The three strands of choreography, performance and appreciation are the organising art of dance concepts in which all the dance experiences within the courses are framed. Hence the *midway* model of the art of dance in education is merely expanded through access to different styles of dance in these syllabuses.

The GCSE level syllabus sets out an impressive set of aims that *indicate the educational purposes of following a course in dance*. These include the aims to:

- develop creative thought and action;
- develop aesthetic and artistic sensibility to dance work and the ability to perceive and express concepts and personal responses.

However, whether or not these aims are achieved remains entirely in the hands of the teacher. The criteria of assessment imply that feeling, imaginative and sensitive presentations will be rewarded with high marks. Yet, how do examiners rate levels of sensitivity? What constitutes imagination, originality and sensitivity at GCSE level as opposed to A level? These and many more questions need answers if it is claimed that dance can contribute to aesthetic education.

Perhaps most teachers would say that aesthetic education is delivered through the appreciation sections of the syllabuses and, certainly, there used to be an element of truth in this premise. Questions such as *What is the mood of this extract? Explain how the following help to create this mood – movement qualities, accompaniment, lighting* (GCSE Paper, 1994) demanded that the candidates interpret the mood which emanates from the dance piece and imagine the feelings/meanings associated with the movement qualities, accompaniment and lighting. This required an aesthetic and subjective feeling response and it also required that students learn to respond in that way with the appropriate language. However, no such question can be found on the papers for the examinations in 2000, for example. Perhaps this is due to difficulties in objectively assessing answers to such questions. In my view, this is a pity since it will lead to a more analytical, fact-giving methodology in relation to preparation for the written papers. Questions such as the following from the A level Paper 3, 2000, reinforce this point.

- Analyse the movement of *White Man Sleeps*, giving examples of progression across the stage, of the use of canon, of partnering and of solo performance.
- Place *White Man Sleeps* in the context of Davies' choreographic career.

- Discuss the relationship in *White Man Sleeps* between the movement, the musical accompaniment and the design.

These questions certainly require students to describe, analyse and make interpretations, but there is no opportunity for them to write about their own feeling responses to the work. The same can be said of all the questions. This would seem to suggest that, although it is now a stated aim at GCSE level at least, there is little evidence to support the case that aesthetic education is a necessary part of these courses. However, if, in addition to developing the students' capacities to perceive details in the movement content, form, design and music constituents of dance works, teachers were to set tasks aiming to develop students' perceptions of aesthetic qualities, their responses to viewing such dance works may be truly deep, rich, imaginative and individual. This might then lead towards achieving the aim identified for GCSE, i.e. *to develop aesthetic and artistic sensibility to dance work and the ability to perceive and express concepts and personal responses* (GCSE Dance syllabus, 2001–2002).

As made clear throughout this book so far, resource-based teaching would seem to be an ideal way of delivering the art of dance in education so that all the facets of the *midway* model, including its contribution to aesthetic education, are covered simultaneously.

Use of the set dance works (and others with which to compare them) as bases for resource-based teaching of the syllabuses, provides the teacher with a means of reinforcing and extending the students' knowledge and understanding of choreography and performance because the students can analyse and learn from the professional exemplars. The use of worksheets to help direct the students' perception of the qualities in the choreography and performance has already been identified as a non-directive way of developing the students' own abilities in choreography and performance. Moreover, if an aesthetic template were to underpin questions on worksheets, students would develop their abilities to appreciate the works aesthetically. This sort of study promotes opportunities for the students to 'get inside' the professional dance works, which surely must improve their ability to write about them in the examination.

In the context of GCSE, A and AS level courses, resource-based teaching/learning is, in my view, an essential methodology to employ in successfully combining the study of professional dance works with study of choreography and performance *per se*. Resource-based teaching/learning is also a means of implementing the theoretical basis of the art of dance in education as expounded in chapter 1 of this book.

It is further contended that comprehensive consideration of all the facets of the theoretical basis for the art of dance in education would enhance and enrich the teaching of dance at GCSE, A and AS level.

Resource-based teaching and the use of technology

In this twenty-first century, it is now fairly obvious that if students in the secondary phase are to describe, analyse, interpret and evaluate professional dance works for the purposes of informing their own composition, performance and appreciation activities, there ought to be technology resources beyond linear video and the few accompanying minimal texts to aid them. It is extremely difficult for teachers to teach, and for students to perceive and learn, for example, how a choreographer has developed and varied a key motif in a dance work, if the only access to visual examination is via linear video. It must be the case that either the teacher has to have defined the numbers and then spent time fast-forwarding and fast-rewinding in order to demonstrate such features, or that hours have been spent editing and re-recording from the original videos (illegally, no doubt) so that such study can take place without the waste of time. How much better it is to have CD-i or CD ROM digital video discs that have been especially authored to allow users to go to any part of the dance work – for example, single motifs even as short as four bars of music, their developments, or variations and contrasting motifs within the same piece, to study aspects of form in detail or even to reconstruct and perform extracts, and all this at the touch of a button or click of the mouse.

Such access to the intricacies of professional dance works extends the students' own practice beyond bounds hitherto witnessed. In the past two years, while promoting it as co-author[10], I have been privileged to use the *Wild Child CD Resource Pack* in demonstration lessons with many classes of boys and girls in year 9, some year 10 and 11 classes and several year 12/13 classes – mostly in the UK, but also in Sweden and Australia. In all cases, teachers have been very surprised as to how quickly students have perceived, understood and been able to apply complex concepts and principles learned from the resource to their own practical or theoretical work. It has been proved over and over again, with groups ranging in dance experience (even

[10]The *Wild Child CD Resource Pack* was authored by Jim Schofield (multimedia) and myself (pedagogy) in 1999 (CD-i) and 2001 (CD ROM). Further details and example worksheets written to extend use of the CD pack for various student groups can be found in the appendix.

beginners) and intellectual ability, that through immediate access to visual examples aided by carefully structured worksheet questions or tasks, students can learn concepts such as abstraction, symbolism, motif, repetition, development, variation, transition, contrast and climax. Moreover, within the, let us say, six lessons that build towards one dance outcome, the focus of study can be changed so that there is comprehensive coverage of, for example, treatment of theme, exploration and selection of dance content, forming it, concentrating on orchestration of the group in time and space and use of music and props integrated into the composition and ways of improving qualities in performance of it. The *Wild Child* resource discs and book are written to promote and deepen all such work and much more.

The design and authoring of the *Wild Child Resource Pack*, and others that are forthcoming, is largely informed by the writing of *Dance Composition* (first published in 1976 but latterly, in its fourth edition, published in 2000) and the first edition of this book. These books presented the theory relating to delivery of the art of dance via qualitative resource-based teaching. The realisation of the theory into practice was made possible through finding and working with an unusually innovative multimedia author, Jim Schofield. Together we found original answers to many pedagogy problems by using multimedia resources coupled to worksheets provided in the old-fashioned way, through text on paper! Problems that we tackled connected with teaching dance composition are discussed in some detail in *Dance Composition* (2000), and several other papers that we have authored jointly outline ways in which we have tackled other problems[11]. Example worksheets that exemplify how this CD resource pack may be used to deepen and extend the students' learning in dance composition, performance and appreciation, can be found in the appendix of this book. There is also an extended example of how the *Wild Child Resource Pack* can be used to improve the students' performance of duo composition that might be presented for GCSE coursework assessment. However, no amount of written material can replace the actual experience of having a fully interactive multimedia resource pack in the dance space with students working on their own or alongside the teacher. This is the future. Hopefully, more such computer-based and perhaps Internet-accessed resources will be available soon so that dance teachers can offer similar access for 'getting inside' professional exemplars to inform their students' own work, as music, drama or literature teachers.

[11]References to these papers can be found at the back of this book.

4

The Art of Dance in Tertiary Education

Background – and differences in approach

Dance in tertiary education, alongside other arts subjects, has been continually challenged to support its claim for academic status. As a subject always under threat, dance has surprisingly achieved much over the past decade or so to establish itself as a worthwhile area of study. However, it has not been able to avoid becoming a victim of recent economic cuts in higher education in particular. There are not as many dance courses as there were in the 1970s and 1980s, but the range and level of content within them is significantly deepened and extended.

It is not intended to discuss the historical development of dance in tertiary education in detail. For the purposes here, this history is only of interest in so far as shifts between what has been labelled in chapter 1 as the *educational* and *professional* models can be discerned. The main concern of this chapter is to study the effects of these shifts of emphasis upon today's practice and to learn how the theory underpinning the *midway* model for the art of dance in education also applies to the tertiary education context.

Balance between theory and practical elements

There have been different emphases and balances between theory and practical elements of the courses. In the late 1970s/early 1980s, in Britain, the swing towards academic study of dance (mostly through relating it to other disciplines, e.g. psychology, sociology, aesthetics, anthropology) became emphasised because of the perceived need to be more accountable and creditable in an academic environment in which all students took degrees and diplomas rather than teachers' certificates (the most common form of dance qualification available). However, the balance has been redressed and, in my experience at present, there seems to have been a shift from theory towards more practical work in undergraduate diploma and degree courses. This may be due to the fact that the validating bodies of the 1980s – most prominently the Council for National Academic Awards – became supportive in valuing practical activity as equivalent to theory. As a result, content, methods and assessment procedures within college and university validated diploma and degree programmes have been developed which can be considered equally as rigorous as those of science-based courses. This is the premise. In practice, dance lecturers still have to 'fight their corner' for equality.

The nature of dance courses in tertiary education

In 1965, when I first started lecturing in a college for specialist physical education teachers, dance was taught in the form of the variously-called Modern Educational Dance/creative dance/movement education, derived by Laban. It had became part of most teacher training courses for primary and for physical education teachers in the period from 1944 until the early 1970s.

Dance specialist teachers were trained at the Laban-based Art of Movement Studio from 1946 until it moved to London to become the Laban Centre for Movement and Dance in 1976. From 1969, dance specialist teachers were also trained at Dartford College of Education (now the University of Greenwich) for a one-year Certificate of Education course for those who had completed a three-year course at the London College of Dance and Drama (a private dance teacher training college which had been established in 1944). Both these courses – and there were others in specialist and general colleges of education – focused almost exclusively on Laban's Modern Educational Dance approach which was considered the most suitable for teaching in schools.

In this *educational* model context, students found themselves exploring Laban's movement principles and creating responses to stimuli in the same ways in which they, in their forthcoming teaching roles (a dominant vocational outcome), would expect their pupils to explore and respond. They sometimes created dances of their own but, more often than not, these were freely-improvised responses to sequences of tasks and there was little concern for compositional structure or principles of form. There was no reference to the *professional* model or to choreographers' works; there were few dance artists who visited educational establishments and those who did were ballet artists; there was no knowledge of contemporary dance techniques or methods of teaching dance composition.

Indeed, it was not until the summer of 1965 that a course in American modern dance was offered for lecturers at Dartington College of Arts. This course (the first of many yearly courses) and the subsequent opening of the London Contemporary Dance School in 1966 injected new approaches into dance courses in tertiary education.

The American modern dance model, with its emphasis on technique and teaching of compositional skills (Graham, Humphrey and Cunningham approaches), caused a swing towards the *professional* model in higher education in the 1970s and 1980s. The extreme of this approach can be likened to the training of dancers in classical ballet at the Royal Ballet School and other such conservatoires. The London Contemporary Dance School has continued along the same lines as a training ground for *professional* dancers and choreographers. Although it has diversified to include degree courses and provides courses for teachers/lecturers and children, the content it delivers is essentially based on the professional training oriented model. Ironically, the Laban Centre for Movement and Dance (now the Laban Centre London) also adopted the American modern dance model when it moved to London and it, too, has developed into a high-level training establishment for dancers and choreographers. Although a study of Laban's work has remained on the curriculum, it is dominated by content best described as a *professional* conservatoire curriculum.

Currently in Britain, students who wish to study dance of this kind in order to become professionals often attend further education colleges that offer A level dance alongside other foundation or pre-vocation courses. As a result they spend more time studying dance than they would in secondary schools. They then have to compete for a place in the privately-funded higher education institutions that are better described as conservatoires. In the growing number of these institutions (including the London Studio Centre, the Royal Academy of Dancing and the Northern Contemporary Dance School), the conservatoire approach in which the *professional* model has been developed and improved, does not constitute what could be called the mainstream art of dance in higher education model. This remains the province of some of the old colleges of education, many of which later became polytechnics and now universities.

Today, dance is taught in the latter higher education institutions in the context of diplomas, bachelor of arts single, double or combined honours degrees and, increasingly, in master's degree courses and above. In most diploma and bachelor degree courses, students select modules in dance such as technique and performance (covering a range of genres and styles), choreography, production, repertoire, notation, history, anatomy and physiology, music, aesthetic and cultural theory related to dance. Courses may also offer modules related to consideration of different functions of dance, e.g. dance in the community, in education, in therapy, in the media of film and television, dance and technology.

Although some teach ballet as a basic technique, the kind of practical dance most frequently found in such institutions can loosely be labelled contemporary dance in that it derives from American modern dance techniques (in America it is called modern dance) created between 1930 and 1960 by Humphrey, Graham, Cunningham, Limon and Hawkins, and those of early European (mostly German) modern dance choreographers such as Jooss, Wigman and Holm. (These are the most influential early American and European modern dance exponents – there are others.) Today, these more traditional contemporary dance forms are replaced by or frequently mixed with current contemporary, post-modern or new dance forms created by choreographers/dance makers such as Brown, Tharp, Gordon, Rainer, Paxton, and Morris (Americans); Kylian, Ek, Bausch, De Keersmaeker and Vandekeybus (Europeans); and Bruce, Davies, Alston, DV8 and several others in Britain.

The list of renowned choreographers above, whose work constitutes an important part of the basis of study for tertiary students, points to the fact that there has been a swing from what is labelled the *educational* model to the *professional* model. However, outside the conservatoires, this swing, though fairly extreme in the 1970s and early 1980s, has somewhat settled towards what I have labelled a *midway* approach to the art of dance in tertiary education.

The art of dance in tertiary education

In order that dance in tertiary education can be analysed, and to determine the validity of my claim that the approach most commonly practised is that which has been described in this book as a *midway* approach, some of the dance modules offered in typical BA Honours courses are outlined below. It is considered that these modules provide suitable examples of current practice. This judgement is not made in isolation. Since the author has been involved as an external examiner and validator of courses in many of the institutions that offer dance in a range of courses, there has been ample opportunity to compare and discern common practices. The 2001 draft benchmark statements for dance that have been produced by the Quality Assurance Agency for Higher Education also endorse this judgement.

Dance study in tertiary education aims towards developing knowledge, understanding and skills that can be applied to a range of vocational outlets such as choreographers, performers, animateurs, community dance workers, dance company administrators, arts management, dance publicity or education officers, dance critics, archivists, dance teachers and the like. Students normally select their courses and modules according to interests, strengths and perceived vocational intentions.

A brief description of modules that may be offered

Dance technique and performance modules at level 1 may take the form of study of a contemporary technique such as the technique devised by Martha Graham. This may be selected as the initial foundation upon which understanding of today's contemporary dance can be built. These students participate in rigorous technical classes to acquire dance skills and Graham-based contemporary vocabulary. The class content – floorwork, centre practice and travelling – culminates in sequences and style studies through which students become acquainted with the style and become able to perform longer pieces in a Graham-based technique. Performance skills such as alignment, focus, projection, rhythm, musicality and expression are practised and improved. The underlying principles and theories of the technique are studied through reading and writing assignments. Assessments may take the form of performance in class work, short style studies, longer dances choreographed to include a range of Graham-based technique, and other such opportunities for the students to demonstrate their performance skills and written work.

Having acquired skills in and knowledge and understanding of a traditional technique such as the Graham technique, level 2 modules might extend the students' abilities and range of vocabulary through study of another contemporary technique such as that devised by Limon, Humphrey or Cunningham. Again, an understanding of the style and content can be developed through practical class work, style studies and longer dances, and principles and concepts underlying the selected technique studied through research, reading and writing assignments. Assessments are more complex and expectations higher at level 2. Students' physical skills should be vastly improved and their contemporary dance vocabulary in these more traditional forms could be well established as a secure base from which to experiment in newer techniques in level 3.

Dance technique and performance modules in level 3 may introduce different techniques which have emerged as a result of recent/post-modern choreography. For example, release techniques, contact improvisation, street dance, jazz and African dance techniques provide varied and different vocabularies of movement which might be more suited to present day choreography.

Choreography modules in level 1 normally engage students in the basic processes involved in choreography – exploration, improvisation, selection and refinement of movement content to create symbolic expression – and require students to demonstrate an understanding of traditional principles of form in choreographing dances. Students may be set tasks and learn from each other in sharing the outcomes. They can also learn from analysis of professional choreographers' works.

Choreography modules in level 2 may well continue to develop students' abilities to choreograph in a conventional way. There is often more emphasis on creating for groups, and much is learned through examination of professional dance works choreographed by established modern dance mainstream practitioners. The module may include choreographic tasks, analysis of videos, presentation of seminars, reading and writing. Assessment is usually focused entirely on choreography of group dances and written work that frequently is presented in the form of log books to describe, analyse and evaluate the processes undertaken and the dance outcome.

Choreography modules in level 3 often include study of various post-modernist approaches. This work opens and broadens the students' concepts of choreography: its themes, content, form, style, environment and its purpose. In order to do this, students may explore the works and processes of artists such as Paxton, Rainer, Brown, Gordon, Childs, Tharp, De Keersmaeker, Vandekeybus, Bausch, Ek, Butcher, Lloyd, McGregor and Anderson. They may be assessed, for example, through presentation of lecture demonstrations based upon research of one of these post-modern/new dance artists and on their own choreography. Their final piece of choreography might combine mainstream and post-modern practices or take either approach in a more purist way. At level 3, the dance produced is usually required to incorporate the production elements of lighting and design and to reflect elements of current practice in professional choreography.

Dance reconstruction modules at all three levels generally aim to develop the students' knowledge and understanding of professional dance works by learning and performing whole works or excerpts from them. This study may take an historical approach to enhance understanding of the history of dance. For example, level 1 students could learn parts out of traditional works such as Fokine's *Petrushka* (1911) and Nijinski's *L'après-midi d'un faune* (1912). Level 2 students might focus on mainstream modern dance works such as Graham's *Appalachian Spring* (1944) and Tudor's *Dark Elegies* (1937) and perform fairly lengthy excerpts from them. Level 3 students may work on current artists such as Bausch to reconstruct and then construct in the style of their works. They may also complete their studies by working with a professional choreographer in order that they perform an entire work based on current dance theatre repertoire. Several institutions take these productions 'on tour' so that students gain experience in all aspects of professional dance presentation.

All of this practical work is, more often than not, supported by research, analysis and interpretation of the works studied and performed through a range of resources including recordings on video or DVD (though not many of the latter are available yet), books, notation, music scores, choreographer's notes (where available), critics' writings, programme notes, pictures and dancers' memoirs.

Theory modules can include a range of study. However, it is generally the case that dance history is taught so that students may gain understanding to support their practical work in performance, reconstruction and choreography by comparing traditions, modern and post-modern developments in dance from the mid-nineteenth century to the present day. Basic aesthetic theory usually features early in the course to consider concepts of dance, art, expression, form, creativity, artistic/aesthetic experience and judgement. Students may then take a critical stance on these aesthetic concepts taking account of Marxist views of art, class, mass audience and consumer culture. Different theoretical approaches may then address semiotic, psychoanalytic, feminist, post-structuralist theories to analyse the political and cultural meanings that can be 'read' in dance 'texts'. For assessment, for example, students may be required to apply semiotic analysis techniques to a performance to decode the meanings produced. Through such study, they learn that meanings are never stable but change and shift through time and in reception by different audiences. Dances can therefore be decoded to discern ideologies and politics relating to sex, gender, class and race as features evident in today's choreographic practice.

As stated earlier, a whole range of modules other than those described above can be offered to include study of anatomy and physiology and health-related dance issues; music and its relationship to dance; dance criticism; dance on film and television; dance and technology; notation; theatre production techniques (lighting and design); politics and policies; administration and management; dance education; community dance; dance movement therapy; and so on. Several of these might include practical as well as theory work. All the modules offer students opportunities to take their study of dance into different directions and, possibly, different careers.

Ways in which the above example of dance practice implements the theoretical basis of the midway *model*

The above example of practice in tertiary education is examined below to substantiate the claim that it amalgamates some of the elements of the *educational* and *professional* models and incorporates many of the new aspects of the *midway* model for the art of dance in education as defined in chapter 1 of this book. It is hoped also that such an analysis of the art of dance in tertiary education will expose elements of good practice which, if fully understood, can be further developed to improve and enhance future practice.

The dance content described above clearly puts emphasis on experience of dances: choreographing, performing, viewing and appreciating them through practical and theoretical study from a range of different perspectives. Although there are modules that obviously focus on each of these strands, there is constant interdependency between them.

In choreography modules, for example, students learn as much from viewing the works of others (their peers and professional choreographers) and performing in each other's dances as they do from choreographing dances themselves. Also, in reconstruction modules, where the emphasis is on performance, it is necessary to view, thoroughly to analyse, understand and appreciate the choreography in order to perform it well.

In both these examples and compared with secondary school practice, there is greater emphasis on study of professional exemplars and developing knowledge and understanding of the practices in professional choreography and performance to inform students' own work. This suggests that on a continuum between the *educational* and *professional* models, the art of dance in tertiary education is located much closer to the *professional* extreme.

Nonetheless, as will become clear below, there is evidence of some of the *educational* model's processes and practices in the art of dance in tertiary education. These should be retained and developed further in order that the *midway* model becomes established and extended as good practice in dance in this sector. This is more desirable than attempting to provide a totally *professional* (conservatoire) course in mainstream tertiary education institutions. Without the full diet of several daily classes and specially-selected students, such an attempt would probably produce second-class results.

1. Equal emphasis on process and on product

In 'good practice' in the *midway* model for the art of dance in tertiary education, there is rather more emphasis on process than it would appear. In all aspects of the modules outlined above, it is important that students become thoroughly knowledgeable about and fully understand the processes involved in creating, performing, viewing, appreciating, describing, analysing, interpreting and evaluating the dance movements and/or dances they experience.

In *technique and performance modules*, for example, students engage in analysis of and come to understand the principles and kinesthetic processes involved in the movement skills that they learn. Consideration of correct posture, placement, balance and anatomical functioning of the body helps students to acquire and improve dance skills. Similarly, understanding of elements of dance movement such as use of breath, accent, weight/gravity, rhythm, line, alignment, extension, tension and relaxation promotes improved performance of dance skills and dances. In determining the processes involved, it is also necessary to study the principles and concepts underlying the particular technique.

In Graham technique, for example, it is imperative that students understand principles of contraction and release which are concepts related to exhalation and inhalation, and the processes involved in attaining the feeling of the movements in somewhere near the way Graham intended. Students should come to understand that there appear to be three corollaries to this central principle: first, that dance movement should originate and be controlled from the centre of the body, which, it is believed, has more emotional impact than peripheral movement; second, that breathing as a basis implies phrasing of movements into 'sentences' rather than a series of skills; and, third, that contraction and release connote introversion and extroversion qualities of movement. There are other important principles to be considered in the study and practice of Graham technique. One is concerned with the opposition of forces, either in the body itself with parts moving in opposition, or in the body in relation to gravity. Another is concerned with space and emphasis of the floor area and low-level movement. Yet another is concerned with rhythm in which the percussive or primitive beating quality is distinctive. Knowledge and understanding of all four principles, through feeling them in the moving body, viewing others employing them in performance, reading and writing about them and applying this knowledge in acquiring and improving Graham-based skills, constitute an important part of the process of learning Graham-based technique and performing Graham-based studies and dances. This kind of teaching/ learning puts an emphasis on coming to know the processes in the movements themselves and, at the same time, engaging in the process of learning how to perform them successfully.

A very different approach is often adopted in a more professionally-oriented training. Here, the movements are prescribed by the teacher (expert), directly taught and repeatedly practised by students (apprentices). Corrections are given, of course, but these are often accompanied by demonstration so that students have a visual (as well as a cognitive) model of what is to be achieved. If movements are broken down they are usually practised as separate parts which are gradually put together into the whole again. For example, a turning step pattern with accompanying arm and body co-ordinations might well be split into just the steps, then the arm and body movements, then these amalgamated and the turn added later. Such an approach is common in dance classes in tertiary education where the emphasis is on acquisition of the skills to be practised as products of the dance classes. Certainly, students need to acquire skills and abilities in order to combine and perform them as products of technique and performance classes. Moreover, it is not helpful to students aiming for performance assessments if too much emphasis is put on developing an understanding of the processes. No matter how well the processes are understood theoretically, the practical realisation of this understanding resides in a quality product – the skilled performance. What is needed, of course, is a balance between the two approaches with an equal emphasis on process and product.

In *choreography modules*, process is definitely as important as product. Throughout the modules outlined above, students are encouraged to explore, improvise, research for themselves and experiment with new procedures in order to inform their choreographic endeavours. These processes require individual imaginative flair (to be discussed below), and this cannot be produced to order. Students need to work on choreographic projects in their own time to become immersed in the processes of creative production. After research and experimentation there needs to be a time for reflection and imaginative thinking centred on the particular choreographic problem. The processes of selection, development and refinement of content then take place. During this time the students develop feelings towards the evolving choreography. They can hate it and discard it or feel good and excited about it and continue, even if they know that it needs a lot of work to get it right. There is rarely an indifference about it. These personal feelings are essential in creative work. This engagement – an interaction between the evolving choreography and the creator – is an aspect of the art of dance model which is missing from primary and secondary dance education (except perhaps for examination students). Tertiary education students have the luxury of time outside of lectures to enjoy such processes.

Choreography lecture time, then, is not necessarily focused on personal creative responses. Rather, in my view, the lecturer might best consider this an opportunity to introduce or consolidate knowledge of principles and practices in choreography. For example, in a study of orchestration of motifs for a large group in a mainstream contemporary dance, students may be guided to view Jiri Kylian's *Symphony of Psalms* (1978) – the epitome of brilliance in this respect. Then, having identified some ways of orchestrating a motif, the students can practise this for themselves. Lecture time is also an important feedback and sharing time. In the context of viewing each other's choreographic products, students can learn not only about the choreography as an outcome that shows, for example, clarity of intention, originality in interpretation of the theme and treatment of content, depth in development of the motifs and richness in orchestration, but also about the processes that led to this product. Here, perhaps in the form of a written log, discussion and introspective thought on the processes involved helps the students to understand more about them.

If the 'journey' is as important as the 'arrival', understanding the nature of both is relevant in a *midway* model.

Further discussion can clarify how process plays a role in other modules, e.g. reconstruction modules where 'getting inside' the work to be performed requires students to attempt to understand the motivations behind the work and the procedures employed in creating the work, in so far as these can be discerned by analysis of the work itself or other sources. Such analysis can be likened to analysis of literary texts to appreciate the author's uses of language in transmitting the ideas and images.

Suffice it to say that learning about and through qualitative processes, even in essay writing, will surely provide the possibility of qualitative products.

2. Equal emphasis on development of creativity, imagination and individuality, and an acquisition of knowledge of theatre dance

It has already been suggested above that students in tertiary education have the time, opportunity and capacities to develop their potential to be creative and imaginative in responding to choreography assignments. By this stage in their dance education, they do not need the security of a teacher's framework within which to choreograph their own movements (except perhaps at the beginning of the first year). Rather, they need a carefully-designed exposure to principles and practices in choreography and tasks which are sufficiently structured but allow freedom of interpretation and choice in response to them. For example, level 1 students, near the beginning of the module, may be required to complete the task on page 178 in my book *Dance Composition* (2000). This is based on analysis of the beginning of Bruce's *Intimate Pages* (1984) to discern the richness in use of relationship possibilities for two bodies and the use of time to express feelings between the two dancers. Here, the students are required to choose one of the titles – an argument – forbidden love – despondence or a related idea of their own and use music selected for them. The limits of the task above provide sufficient security in that a title is offered and there are numerous relationship possibilities open to them through analysis of the video snippet. Yet there is much freedom to interpret the title in their own way, to select from the video any three duo relationships and create as many of their own as they like, to use time aspects to express in their own ways and above all to select actions, spatial and dynamic content without restrictions. The best outcomes will show imagination, creativity and individuality and at the same time will show what they have learned about principles and practices in choreography in, let us say, the first four weeks of the module. They will have:

- devised original motifs, abstracting from non-verbal communication and symbolising in dance terms;
- repeated, developed and varied them;
- designed at least one contrast in the duo;
- created an overall unity of form;

- used a full range of duo relationship possibilities;
- used qualities of time to give expression to their movements;
- used the music in many different ways (a lecture could have been devoted to this);
- interpreted the theme imaginatively;
- communicated the expression clearly.

This list of attributes would more than fulfil the criteria in respect of showing knowledge of principles and practices in theatre dance choreography. The best outcomes would achieve high marks. However, duos with few signs of imagination, creativity and individuality would score average marks even if there were evidence of all the above listed criteria. They may lack originality, freshness, distinctiveness, excitement, aesthetic interest – they would be more predictable and 'academically sound'.

Through discussion, it is possible to educate the students to distinguish the original and creative from the sound and 'safe' responses to tasks.

Choreography experiences in tertiary education are an obvious context in which the duality discussed here should occur. However, as all dancers, actors and musicians would endorse, there is as much creativity, imagination and individuality required in interpretation of a role/text/score as there is in creating one. In each excerpt performed by the students in reconstruction contexts, there is room for them to be creative, imaginative and individual in applying the understanding they have gained through theoretical study of the dance work and analysis of it in video performances. Critical study of the piece will develop an in-depth appreciation of it and, if the students' performance is based on this without limitations on interpretation being imposed by the lecturer, there is ample opportunity for creativity, imagination and individuality to play important roles in making decisions on how to express and perform the content of the reconstructed excerpt.

This implies a less didactic approach to teaching reconstruction than would be expected, perhaps. A more detailed discussion of methods of teaching that encourage a freer interpretive response from students is presented in (5) below. It is perhaps sufficient to say here that students should be given room for such freedom in the use of their imagination and creativity, especially as they progress from level 1 to level 3.

Learning about theatre dance is, of course, an essential aim for students in tertiary education. In all the above modules, there will be constant reference to theatre dance exemplars. Not only is this the case in choreography and reconstruction modules, it is also extremely important in study of theoretical aspects of the course. In such modules, examples of historical era, style, expression, form, symbolism, semiotics, etc. need to be drawn from theatre dance traditions/conventions and current practices. Video resources have become essential means, but artists-in-residence/workshops and frequent theatre visits are also vital if students are to develop knowledge and understanding of the art of dance in contemporary culture.

Again, 'good practice' in the art of dance provides an even diet of both opportunity to allow the students' creativity, imagination and individuality to develop and opportunity to gain a great deal of knowledge from theatre dance. The former ensures that the limitations do not restrict individuality and originality and that the 'rules' are broken, changed or abandoned and replaced with new ones as the students progress through their art of dance experiences. The latter ensures that the students grasp the criteria of validity and value in dance and set their own originality and imagination against a background of the traditions and limitations of the art form itself. (See Best's 1985 quotation on page 9.)

3. Equal emphasis on feelings and on training

It is important to ensure that the students' feelings can enter into and play an essential role in successful learning in the art of dance. This is particularly the case in choreography, of course, where students create dances based on their own ideas, working through the processes from conception to realisation. Given a task such as the following level 2 assignment, students have the opportunity to work on themes about which they feel strongly:

> *Compose a group dance for 4–5 dancers. The dance should be based on a current cultural issue.*

In this instance, students would be encouraged to start from their own feelings and explore ways in which these feelings can be expressed in dance movement. However, they will learn, if they do not know already, that their own strong feelings alone are insufficient bases upon which to build a dance.

There is no one way to proceed, but it is certain that if the feelings are to be communicated through the medium of dance, knowledge of public conventions and shared meanings must also shape the outcome. Students need to research the topic and make decisions on how it should be treated. In doing this, they might make reference to ways in which professional choreographers have treated the same or similar topics and employ a few strategies gleaned from such sources. However, in order that their own feelings enter the work, it is important that they are not too strongly influenced by such references.

Students will have learned how to strip down an idea and symbolise its essence, how to stylise movements, and how to create form; and they may also have studied various choreographers' procedures, e.g. Cunningham's chance strategies. All of this knowledge is brought into the creative process but it is to be hoped that by the end of the second year, this knowledge will have been absorbed and become a part of students' intuition.

When can a student choreograph without consciously thinking about principles and methods? There should be a time within the tertiary education experience of choreography when the student feels confident that, in starting from feeling and strong motivation to create, the dance will evolve and develop almost entirely through intuition. Of course, intuition in this context refers to knowledge gained and absorbed into the subconscious without conscious thinking-processes being involved. (See chapter 1 page 13.)

When a dance has been composed, there may well be an objective evaluation of it when knowledge is employed almost as a checklist (criteria of assessment can be used at this juncture) in order to make refinements. There should be a fairly flexible shift between feeling/ subjectivity and knowledge/objectivity during the choreographic processes.

In technique and performance modules where clear objective ends are pre-determined, there may appear to be less room for feelings and subjectivity to be involved in learning how to dance. However, as made clear in (1) above, if students do not inject feeling into their dance performance, it will remain mechanical and uninspiring to watch.

The feeling discussed here, however, is not the same as life feelings, e.g. sadness or anger, nor is it the same as those related to a theme for choreography as above, e.g. feelings evoked by the topic of marital rape. Rather, it is feeling intrinsic to the movements themselves, such as the feeling of openness, giving, indulgence and freedom in an upwards extending release, or the feeling of exhilaration in fast travelling and leaping actions, or the soft quiet closing of the body in hugging knees slowly in a sitting position. These sensory qualities need to be felt. The movements should have life and light and shade.

This sort of feeling can only enter the movements by means of the students' subjective commitment. This has erroneously been labelled 'sincerity', but, in my view, it is an attribute which can be achieved once the students are comfortable with the skills or dance sequences, provided that they are encouraged to enter into the feeling of the sensations intrinsic to the movements.

Hence, in a technique class, once the skills themselves are mastered, there should be a shift towards developing the ability of students to project the feelings in the movements when they perform them.

In reconstruction, both the feeling sensations in the movements and the expressive meanings they evoke need to be felt by the student performing the excerpt. If there is no feeling, the student has little chance of conveying the idea of the dance. Again, then, once the skills have been mastered and the student understands the choreography – phrasing, rhythm, timing, spatial and dynamic aspects, focus, expressive intentions and so on – 'getting inside' the choreography requires that students enter into the feelings it contains and express them when performing the piece.

Even in more academic situations, such as seminars in aesthetic theory related to dance, students should be encouraged to express what they feel about a topic and back it up from their own experiences. This may be stretching the point but, all too often, lectures are treated as information-giving events and seminars as smaller versions of the same thing. In any context, students will learn more if they become subjectively involved. Having received lectures and read about the concepts of classicism and romanticism, for example, students could view and analyse a dance work such as *Swan Lake* and then discuss ways in which it reflects these concepts. Here, students' own interpretations can be extended by listening to the views of others and the lecturer's input may well become the richer through discussion of alternative ideas which had not been thought of in preparation of the topic.

In conclusion, then, it would appear that in the art of dance in tertiary education, there should be emphasis on feelings – subjectivity of experience and on objective ends. However, the module content will dictate the balance. Equal emphasis should be strived for in choreography and ultimately in performance contexts, too. Moreover, in interpretation of dances viewed in the theatre or on video there should always be a feeling response, preferably before detailed analysis takes place. The latter can sometimes hamper the former.

In summary, it may be fruitful to keep in mind the following proverb:

Tell me and I will forget,
Show me and I may remember,
Involve me and I will surely learn.

4. Equal emphasis on movement principles and on stylised techniques

In tertiary education there is a good deal more time to devote to the learning of defined dance techniques than there is in secondary education. As stated in chapter 1 of this book, a comprehensive art of dance education will include study of a range of dance techniques so that the students have extended repertoires of content from which to select for choreographic and performance purposes. A range of different styles opens up expressive possibilities far beyond the restrictions of one style. This view is endorsed by Challis (1999) when she states that:

> ...technique is not a system of training, but a system of education through which a dancer acquires not only bodily shape and facility but also learns the traditions, conventions and values which underpin the concept of dance being taught: the artistic body is thus skilful, intelligent and expressive of that form. (1999: 145)

This specificity of each technique is the reason for selection of different contemporary styles in the technique and performance modules above. Each style has its own expressive boundaries and its particular vocabulary. Put them together, and the student has an extended vocabulary. However, learning just one technique and achieving a degree of expertise in performing it takes time. Learning three or four techniques over three years permits perhaps only a superficial knowledge and modicum of skill in each of them. Yet, as stated above, students need a more extended vocabulary than one technique allows, even if studied in depth. So, what is the answer to this problem?

The teaching of defined dance techniques in the conventional and conservatoire manner for a period of two hours (numerous exercises which carefully build co-ordination, strength, mobility, balance, extension, elevation and so on) has little relevance in the tertiary education contexts, unless there is provision for daily classes in technique and further classes in performance. Some institutions do provide daily classes within the modular system but others have to cover both technique and performance in modules with one or two lectures per week. However, even in latter contexts, students can and do reach high standards in technique and performance. The route is merely a different one.

Certainly, techniques need to be taught through the careful build-up of appropriate dance exercises and sequences devised for teaching the skills. In a Graham class, for example, students will learn some of the floor exercises, centre practice, travelling movements and falls. However, each class, in my view, should contain a long sequence, style study or dance that combines movements into phrases and contrasting sections in the style of the technique. A technical or style study lasting about three minutes reduces much of the repeating and perfecting of exercises before such dance sequences are taught, the procedure practised in a conservatoire training. There is no time for this approach in other tertiary education institutions.

Teaching stylistically-defined techniques through dance studies permits technique and performance to be taught simultaneously. A good study will challenge the most able and be within the reach of the least able (the most complex parts can be simplified). It will include a variety of technical skills and emphasise the style of the technique. It will require the students to focus on performance skills such as dynamic variation, rhythm, projection, focus, alignment, spatial accuracy and expression. The study should be a formed, coherent whole and the students should learn how to dance it showing awareness of phrases, sections, transitions, contrasts and climaxes.

This approach in the teaching of technique through pre-choreographed studies/dances provides students with vocabularies of individual dance skills (for example, different travelling steps across the room from the corner) and, at the same time, demonstrates ways in which movements can be put together into stylised phrases and dances. Students are therefore learning to dance through dances.

This is also the case if they take reconstruction modules in which they also learn a range of dance movements within styles – the style of the technique used by the choreographer and the style of the choreographer. For instance, in learning excerpts from *Dark Elegies* (1937), students would be learning some modern ballet technique in the style of Anthony Tudor. In addition, students often have opportunities to extend their own technical dance skill and stylistic vocabularies through performing in other students' dances. First year students, for example, can gain much from dancing in third-year pieces. Often there are individual students with particular expertise who, if given the opportunity to choreograph or teach open classes, can extend the students' experiences even further. For example, an input of street jazz and lindy hop can be contrasted with experience of Alexander technique, South Asian dance and Chinese dance to name but a few. The opportunities outlined above are limited to practical experience. It is possible, of course, through study of historical developments and changes in dance works to become acquainted with other stylistically-defined dance techniques (e.g. classical ballet) through viewing and learning about them theoretically.

There is a range of opportunities for students to gain knowledge, understanding and a fair degree of skill in a variety of stylistically-defined dance techniques. It is important that students become familiar with a range of publicly-defined dance techniques. Since this is the 'language' of the art form, they need to know at least a part of it and should become skilful in using its specific terminology and concepts.

Students in tertiary education also need to know and understand movement principles such as those defined by Laban. As indicated throughout the book so far, this descriptive analysis of movement is invaluable as a flexible and comprehensive framework which can be used in both practical and theoretical contexts.

It remains an essential tool for choreography. It can be used to define tasks, to explore movement ideas, to describe and discuss movement, to guide observations of movement, and to frame checklists for evaluation of movement.

In defining tasks, the movement principles themselves can be explored. For example, the concept of flow or continuity can be explored to discern the range of sensory and expressive qualities involved in moving freely and continuously, hesitantly, in a held-back manner, with sudden stops, with staccato quality, going and stopping and so on. If every aspect of the analysis were to be used as a starting point for such explorations of dance content, students would be exposed to a far wider range of expressive possibilities than would be the case if their dance experiences were limited to learning prescribed techniques.

In exploring movement ideas for choreography, students could identify the type of movement – for example, high-extended jumps – and then try out variations by adjusting body shapes through positioning of the limbs, etc. The movement principles provide different possibilities within each movement concept. Once motifs have been created, knowledge of the movement principles provides a framework within which students can try in different ways to develop or vary the content of the motif, through change of level, direction, quality of movement, addition of action, etc. (See *Dance Composition*, 2000.)

Laban's framework also provides a checklist for use in observation, description, analysis and evaluation of dance content. Students can be guided to observe and discuss the actions: qualities of time, force and continuity; spatial aspects such as size, level, direction, pathway; and relationship features – dancers relating to others, to objects, to the audience. These movement principles together with knowledge of stylistically-defined dance techniques provide students with an extensive and comprehensive repertoire of concepts and terminology for use in observing, describing, analysing and evaluating dance content.

In the *midway* art of dance model, tertiary education students should gain knowledge and understanding and acquire dance skills through experience of both a range of prescribed dance techniques and a set of movement principles, such as that defined by Laban. The former needs to be more emphasised here than in secondary education, but not to the detriment of limiting the students to the very specific boundaries of content that each dance technique prescribes. The latter should act as a frame of reference for the full range of dance content both within and beyond the defined techniques. It constitutes a generalised vocabulary of movement and language within which the specific technical content can be embraced.

5. Equal emphasis on problem-solving and on directed teaching

In most discipline areas, students at this level certainly have to become more autonomous in their learning. In the performing arts, however, there is still the strongly-held view that students require more rather than less practical contact time with lecturers. With continual cuts in contact time, it has become a major battle to retain the additional hours required for practical modules. Arguments for favourable treatment in terms of hours and staff–student ratios have to be strongly supported with educational reasons if they are to be acknowledged by managers of timetables and funding. Perhaps there needs to be some re-thinking about the balance between student-based and lecturer-based teaching/learning.

In my view, all of the above-named modules except *technique and performance modules* emphasise the problem-solving, student-based learning approach. In *choreography modules*, for example, the weighting of directed lecturer input is minimal in comparison to problem-solving tasks. In the majority of choreography contexts the lecturer acts as catalyst while the students are agents in their own learning. This is not surprising, of course, because students are the creators and have to be active rather than passive learners.

Reconstruction workshops are different in that the lecturer, especially at level 1, teaches the students the content of the excerpts. Nevertheless, this direct teaching of movement content is only a first step in students coming to know, understand and gain skill in performance of the excerpt. The students have to 'make it their own' through research, reading, discussion, many viewings of professional performances of the excerpts and practice of its content. All of this work to 'get inside' the excerpts can be student-based. Practice should always take place outside the lecture time so that lectures are used for input of additional content, for sharing information gained from students' research and for monitoring and evaluating performances in progress. In this context, too, weighting is towards student-centred learning.

Theoretical modules, like other subjects in degree courses, require students to put in at least twice the allotted lecture time for their own thinking, researching, reading and writing work. In dance, most theoretical modules require students to view work on video/DVD or in live theatre contexts and to spend time after the performance reflecting on and writing notes or reviews to support their learning. Here again, there is more time spent in student-centred learning than in lectures but, even in the latter, there is tendency to provide frameworks, principles and ideas which are then discussed by the students in lectures and seminars. It is through these opportunities in lecture time that students test the knowledge they have gained through research/reading/viewing tasks against that of their peers and the lecturer. Hence, lectures sometimes, and seminars always, need to be student rather than lecturer-centred.

Technique and performance modules remain the only ones which would appear to require a lecturer-centred approach. Certainly, in the *professional* model it is still a dominant practice to have the instructor in front of the students, often demonstrating the movements before teaching them. The class members are often positioned in formal lines and the instructor dictates what they should do, when they should do it, where and with whom it should take place. There is nothing wrong with this method especially if the teacher is an expert. It can be a very rewarding experience and it is a means of students experiencing the discipline needed to acquire skilled dance performance. However, such classes will not achieve all of the objectives for modules where the focus is on performance as well as technique.

While there needs to be some emphasis on process, there must also be emphasis on feelings and subjectivity if the students' performances are to be given life. These qualities cannot be imposed; they need to be gained by the students through their own efforts. Moreover, if the students learn stylistically-defined techniques through technical/style studies, they may benefit from the approach outlined above for the learning of excerpts in reconstruction lectures. The difference, of course, lies in the fact that it is likely that the lecturer will have choreographed the studies and therefore can and should take the role of expert more frequently while the students perfect it.

Students in tertiary education should progressively develop into independent, autonomous learners. They need in-depth information from lecturers some of the time, but need them mostly to guide, inspire and provide feedback for their own learning.

6. Artistic education

All of the content discussed above constitutes artistic learning in that, through every experience in every module, students will learn more about the art form of dance, mostly through the study of dances, creating, performing, viewing and appreciating them.

Current practice in the art of dance for university students makes constant cross-reference between the students' own work and the public world of dance. Within all the *theoretical and practical modules*, the range of dance works studied, from the conventional classical ballet to the experimental post-modern, exposes students to a plethora of dance movement, approaches to choreography, styles, themes, design aspects, accompaniments and approaches to audiences.

Concepts of what a dance is will be extended, challenged and changed. Experience of many dance works emanating from different eras, in different styles and performed in different contexts for different purposes, will provide examples of changes in principles, practices and conventions underpinning the art form of dance. Students will learn that concepts are never static and that, in common with all art forms, dance and dances are constantly changing.

Rather than reiterate the above text with a different emphasis, it seems sensible to redraw the essential content of artistic education for students in tertiary education in an extended form of the list in chapter 1.

Artistic learning through:

Choreographing dances

- understanding and interpretation of themes/ideas, especially those relating to contemporary issues
- translation of the themes/ideas in dance terms, i.e. into symbolic action employing a range of different strategies and conventions – traditional approaches, e.g. abstraction into symbolism, formalism; post-modern approaches, e.g. chance, minimalism, deconstruction, use of pedestrian movement
- making decisions about the type of dance, e.g. dramatic, pure, comic, abstract; and the style, e.g. mainstream/traditional contemporary, post-modern or new dance in style, balletic, jazzy, street-dance flavoured, social or ethnic dance styles – pure or mixed
- exploring movement ideas discovering actions, qualities, rhythmic and spatial features to express the theme into the type and style of dance planned: knowledge of stylistically-defined dance techniques balanced with knowledge of a set of movement principles should be employed in the search for new content
- exploring and making decisions about the numbers of dancers, gender, and the relationship possibilities between them to express the idea, e.g. positioning, group shapes, orchestration, contact/ non-contact, etc.
- understanding of how the music or accompaniment can be used: students in tertiary education should experience making their own music/sound tracks at least once
- selecting and linking of movements to make motifs and phrases
- stylising of content appropriately considering the choreographic conventions/approaches, type of dance and overall style
- deciding on the order of the movements and refining motifs and phrases, again considering the above
- structuring the motifs and phrases in time, space and the relationship between the dancers
- developing the phrases, perhaps repeating them in time, space and relationship configurations
- understanding and use of formal devices: repetition, development, variation, contrast, transition, climax, logical progression, unity or alternative construction processes such as chance
- creating sections/parts of the dance and relating them to make whole dances
- considering and planning staging aspects of dances: lighting,

design, costume, make-up, use of accompanying visual/audio materials, etc.
- rehearsing of dancers to achieve the expression
- presenting dances in conventional/alternative spaces with consideration of the role of the audience (programme notes, etc.)

Performing dances
- acquiring of appropriate physical skills: actions combined with dynamic, rhythmic and spatial patterning or stylistically-defined skills from specific techniques
- performing the above with co-ordination, accuracy, fluency, control, balance, poise and authority
- practising of the co-ordinations that link movements into phrases, sections and dances
- performing the content concentrating on qualitative expression through variation of dynamic, spatial and relationship features
- performing dances and parts of dances with understanding of the formal qualities, e.g. pauses, highlights, contrasts
- presentation of the theme through dancing with appropriate expressive intention
- practising to music or other forms of accompaniment alone or with others in unison and canon
- developing performance qualities such as extension, projection and focus to express meaning
- concentration on line, body shape, clarity of design, positioning
- clarity and unity of style

Viewing dances
- all the above aspects involved in creating and performing dances should be observed, described, analysed, interpreted and evaluated by students viewing their own and professional choreography throughout their dance education

These three processes – creating, performing and viewing dances – will culminate in the development of ability to appreciate artistic features of dances.

Appreciation of artistic aspects of dances
- students will learn to discern with increasing accuracy and sensitivity a range of qualities in choreography and performance. From their own experiences in choreography and performance, and through learning how to employ description, analysis,

interpretation and evaluation, they will be able to perceive distinctive artistic features: style, form, expression, techniques and production

- in order to further appreciation, students will learn to employ a range of resources to discover background information and specific details about dances, choreographers, performers, designers, musicians, etc.
- students will gradually adopt a number of theoretical perspectives to view artistic content, devices and meaning and performance, e.g. history, semiotics, aesthetics, cultural theory

7. Aesthetic education

Aesthetic education through dance occurs in a number of different ways in choreographing, performing and appreciating dances. All of the discussion in chapter 3 relating to aesthetic education of secondary pupils through dance experiences pertains here. However, students in tertiary education know and understand in a distinctly different way what may constitute the aesthetic in a dance and the nature of aesthetic experiences.

In studying the art of dance in tertiary education, it is essential that students gain knowledge of aesthetic theory relating to dance. This area of study as a branch of philosophy is essentially discursive. There are no right or wrong answers, rather there are concepts, and arguments supporting or negating those concepts. Students need to consider various writers' views in order to determine their own on the following concepts:

- the nature of art, the art of dance, a dance as an art object, intentions and expectations
- expression in art – imagination, creativity and individuation in art – art and artistic traditions
- form in art
- concepts of beauty, meaning and truth in art
- aesthetic experience, aesthetic qualities in art and outside art, aesthetic criteria and judgements
- aesthetic criticism, interpretation and evaluation

Having studied such aesthetic concepts, students may well become more open to and able to perceive the aesthetic dimensions of dance works, their own, those of their peers and those professionally choreographed and performed. Their discussion as to why they liked or disliked a dance should become much more informed in that they can point out the excellence or otherwise, using aesthetic criteria and terminology.

For example, students can employ the aesthetic framework discussed in chapter 1 and defined by Osborne (1970) referring to the sensory, expressive and formal qualities in the dance/object perceived; or, having studied alternatives, they may prefer to employ, for example, Beardsley's framework (1958) of general canons which can be used in making aesthetic judgements in art. Beardsley suggests that merits or demerits can be ascribed to works of art in relation to the canons of unity, complexity and intensity. The canon of unity is employed when an art work is described as well organised (or poorly organised), formally perfect (or flawed), or having (or lacking) a logical pattern, coherence of style and structure. The canon of complexity relates to statements such as: the work is well developed, rich in contrasts and variety (or lacks variety and is dull); it articulates the theme in depth and with subtlety (or it is banal and crude). The canon of intensity relates to the 'human regional qualities' or feelings contained in the piece, i.e. the dramatic, vital, forceful, tender, tragic, delicate, comic qualities (as opposed to objects lacking expressiveness which could be labelled insipid or pale). Moreover, Beardsley suggests that experience of viewing an art work possessing these qualities would afford the perceiver an experience which can be qualified as aesthetic in that it is unified, complex (deep) and intense (absorbing and feelingful).

Students with this knowledge and understanding have invaluable devices for making and understanding the different kinds of judgements that can be made about art works and the types of reasons given to support the judgements. They can also set this aesthetic discussion about dance and dances against other theoretical approaches used to discuss, interpret and evaluate art. (Some of these approaches are described under the heading of 'cultural education' below.)

The difficulty of ensuring that the students' dance education contributes to their aesthetic education lies in the fact that different lecturers teach them different aspects of the course. Hence, tutors who deliver *technique and performance modules*, for instance, may not be conversant with the aesthetic concept of the sensory, expressive and formal qualities contained in the movements and may, therefore, not be able to help students perceive the qualities kinesthetically in their own movements or visually in others' performances. It is encumbent upon the students themselves to make such links, though, in ideal circumstances, the theory and practice should merge if references are made to both by the two sets of tutors. Similar comments could be made about the students' work in choreography and in reconstruction where aesthetic perception of the dances as art works is imperative if the students' dance experiences are to be labelled study of the art of dance.

Every experience of choreographing, performing and viewing dances should have potential for developing the students' aesthetic experience and appreciation. Theatre visits and work with dance artists are particularly advantageous in this respect except that, as yet, it is often difficult for students to gain aesthetic insight into the artists' work because the artists do not have the concepts or language with which they can share such insights.

This constitutes a gap in the theory of dance practice *per se* and has much to do with the distance between the two worlds of dance – the *educational* and *professional* worlds. Perhaps the growing popularity of resource-based teaching (see below) in the *midway* art of dance in education will force the two worlds to liaise and to learn from each other. Educationists are already learning from professional exemplars. It is the other way round that needs to be addressed so that the work of professional artists is appropriately focused to enhance artistic and aesthetic education.

Students in tertiary education, then, should both experience the aesthetic in dance and dances for themselves and come to know and understand the theory behind the practice. In this way, they could be described as aesthetically educated in both the subjective and objective senses.

8. Cultural education

The discussion in chapter 3 under the heading of cultural education is relevant here in so far as the students' experiences of creating, performing and viewing dances develops their understanding of concepts and practices underpinning the art of dance in Western culture. In tertiary education, however, such understanding could be endorsed and extended through application of new theoretical areas of study.

In the above-described content for dance in tertiary education, developing an understanding of the art of dance as part of the contemporary culture in which students live is of paramount importance.

To this end, students study semiotics, the theory of signs. This is also described as structuralism in that the approach is based on analysis of dance works as texts which are organised like language with their own specific grammar and which can be read to reveal underlying deep structural significances. The signs within dance encode both general and dance-specific cultural meanings. This theoretical approach requires that students consider dances to be culturally-produced phenomena which can reveal psychological perspectives of the author/choreographer, ideologies, social values, sexual politics, and views pertaining to class, race and so on.

Cultural education must include consideration of dance works as reflecting the culture from which they derive and in which they are performed. (The latter requirement refers to works choreographed long ago, because they will probably reflect something of the culture from which they emerged and much of the culture in which they are being interpreted and recreated for performance.)

In study of dance from a cultural perspective, however, students should also come to realise that culture itself is a constantly shifting and changing social process in which all meanings relate to the various social systems that exert influence on its products. Hence, this kind of study is forever on shifting sands.

Moreover, it tends not to consider the art work itself because it focuses outwards on the social conditions of production. This theoretical approach offers students an antithesis or opposing argument to the concept of the art of dance having aesthetic purpose. Of course, students could argue against cultural theoretical perspectives and be in favour of applying aesthetic and artistic criteria in discussion of art. Clearly, they should understand and be conversant with these differing points of view.

History is a further essential theoretical study of the art of dance. Concepts such as classicism, neo-classicism, romanticism, modernism and post-modernism need to be understood in both their historical and cultural contexts. Study of dance history provides a theoretical framework within which students come to understand traditions, conventions and changes in practices of choreography and performance.

Through the study of dance as a cultural/historical phenomenon, students learn that there is no such thing as constant aesthetic meaning in art works. In this climate of changing meanings, students come to understand that concepts of expression and form in art are also open to challenge and that post-modern artists or those described as avant garde, will continue to experiment with these concepts to produce new and shifting boundaries. What counts as art is therefore ever changing.

The aim in this kind of cultural education is to ensure that students leave university with an open mind and a readiness to discuss and challenge constraining or restricting views of the art of dance. Students with an open mind in these respects are more likely to promote shifts and changes in their future practices in the art form of dance.

In the *midway* model, cultural, historical and aesthetic theoretical perspectives provide conceptual bases for study of dance in tertiary education in that all of the theory develops greater knowledge and understanding of the art of dance itself and its works as cultural, historical and aesthetic phenomena. This is different from the approach in the early 1970s, when discipline areas loosely related to dance were studied for purposes of making dance a respectable degree study. There was very little reference and application to dance but today, theory is always supported by and applied to dance; theory informs practice and practice informs theory. Without the use of video or CD resources and theatre visits this would be very difficult. References create the links between theory and practice. Dance works, and choreography and performance practices, in the professional public dance world merge with educational concepts and practices to create what can be called a *midway* art of dance model in tertiary education. On a continuum between the *professional* and *educational* models for dance in education, the model for further and higher education would probably be placed much closer to the professional end in terms of content but close to the educational end for methodology. The result is perhaps more *midway* than might be expected.

RESOURCE-BASED TEACHING/LEARNING

Resources in the form of dance works on video, CD-i, CD ROM, DVD or better still through live performances are central in study of the art of dance in tertiary education. The content in each section of this book headed 'resource-based teaching/learning' can be applied to further and higher education in that there is constant use of resources to support students' work in choreography, performance and appreciation: artistic, aesthetic, cultural and historical. However, there is a difference between using such resources as references or stimuli for practical and/or theoretical dance study and resource-based teaching/learning through resource packs. Surprisingly, in 2001 as in 1994, it is still the case that the latter is not a developed feature of dance courses in tertiary education.

In specialist dance teacher training courses, the practice of devising resource packs for teaching GCSE/AS/A level students has been in place for some years. In these school or further education college-based courses, however, dance teachers are usually responsible for the whole course and time is allocated to dance overall rather than to specific dance activities: technique and performance, choreography, etc. This might make it easier to teach through a resource pack which, according to the rationale given in chapter 1, should address all three strands: creating, performing and appreciating dances (the latter including historical and contextual study). In universities, however, courses are frequently taught by several different lecturers and content is split into separately-assessed modules. So what role can resource packs take in tertiary education?

Resource packs are certainly needed for dance at this level. The students might then be able to advance their own learning in a truly student-centred manner. Perhaps this 'open university' approach will catch on in the event of even further cuts in time, lengths of academic year and degree courses overall. However, even if time allocation remains the same, there are distinct advantages in making resource packs available to students.

Resource packs[1] for further and higher education – a prescription for future practice

Resource packs can be based on any aspect of dance study. It would be most advantageous, for example, if the lecturer concerned with history could direct the students to use a resource pack on, say, romantic ballet. The pack could contain a video or, better still, an interactive CD ROM disc[2] on which snippets of romantic ballet works would be interspersed with text on screen, voice-overs or reference to readings in books or within the pack booklet itself. Pictures, photo-graphs, programmes and posters, etc. and questions based on the reading and viewing tasks given in the carefully-sequenced programme of learning could also be contained in the pack. (A CD ROM could offer the student a number of different levels and routes through the content which has a distinct advantage over the linear

---

[1]See chapter 1 pages 46–47 for a description of what a resource pack might contain.
[2]Interactive video is computer-controlled video. The video images are pressed onto a disc which is digitally read by means of a computer. It is possible to jump from place to place on the disc at a touch of a button or mouse, to have more than one image on screen and to overlay the picture with simultaneous moving graphics, text and voice-overs.

approach necessarily taken in VHS video production.) In effect, the resource pack can replace lecture preparation. The lecturer need no longer spend endless hours sorting and editing appropriate video snippets (if available) and photographing slides from books in order to deliver information on romantic ballet. How much better it would be to have a really good resource bank of such learning materials on a single disc and spend the lecturer's time with the students in deep debate on the topic after they have gained the essential information and understood the concepts through use of the pack.

For the teaching of all the modules described above, especially *practical modules*, resource packs devised to structure students' learning could be extremely advantageous. Each pack would be the equivalent of several brilliantly-delivered lectures but students would use them on a one-to-one basis and could go back over bits of information, play some of the video snippets again to capture the detail, listen to the music accompanying the dance work under scrutiny, read passages again and relate them to the viewing tasks, and so on. Students could even learn short excerpts of the work/s to exemplify a particular point. This would certainly be beneficial in *choreography, technique and performance modules*, while in *reconstruction modules* it is of central concern.

All of these instances attempt to demonstrate the benefits of resource packs in student-centred learning. Resource packs take students much further than reading books or listening to lectures. Of course, this is due to the fact that the student-based learning involved in using the packs requires a student's active response to the practical, viewing, reading, listening and discussing tasks as he or she progresses through the pack. (See the example outline for a resource pack based on a video in the appendix. In addition, see examples of the detailed worksheets that accompany the *Wild Child CD Resource Pack* to demonstrate ways in which technology can greatly extend study of choreography. These also can be found in the appendix.)

A resource pack for teaching dance technique and performance would seem to negate the claim above that it remains the single area of dance study which requires more rather than less lecturer input. However, rather than replace the lecturer in this context, a resource pack could speed up and enhance the students' learning of technique and performance. If such resource packs were available for teaching, say, Graham technique, students could advance their learning by leaps and bounds in that it would be like having master classes at one's fingertips on numerous occasions.

Imagine, for instance, having superbly-performed floor work exercises on screen during lectures. This immediately frees the lecturer to observe and comment on the students' attempts. Then imagine that students have use of the CD ROM between lectures in order to perfect their skills through access to a detailed and slow-motion breakdown of the actions involved. The disc would provide notation, anatomical or kinesiological input if required, audio teaching points, information about the co-ordinations, dynamics, rhythm, spatial patterning, use of breath involved in the movements, and so on. This kind of resource would surely improve skill acquisition in the same or similar ways employed in individual tutorials. Furthermore, additional content on the CD ROM might go on to develop the students' performance abilities through over-lay graphics, notation, voice-overs, shots of the movements from different angles, slow motion, freeze frame options, etc. to focus on qualitative features such as variation of dynamics, fluency, line, focus, projection, expression and a sense of form in performing the piece.

Through publication of packs such as those outlined above, and perhaps numerous other packs on choreography through which students could study particular choreographic procedures, individual choreographers or groups of choreographers, resource-based teaching/learning will become an important method for the art of dance in tertiary education in the future.

This view was expressed in the first edition of this book and, as stated previously, it is somewhat surprising and very disappointing that since 1994, only two CD resource packs have been published. The first, *Wild Child – A CD-i Resource Pack for Dance Education* was published by the author and her multimedia partner, Jim Schofield in 1999[3]. As indicated in chapter 1, this pack contains two CD-i discs, one audio disc and a 272-page *Resource Book* with hundreds of tasks that, via an interactive digital video player (CD-i machine) linked up to a television, can be used for delivery of all aspects of the *midway* model for the full range of students – primary through to tertiary. In 2001 the *Wild Child* pack was published in the CD ROM format for use on computers.

This pack is exemplary in promoting the resource-based teaching/ learning dance education discussed above. Indeed, through a recently delivered module BA Hons. level 1 dance students successfully

---

[3]Published by Bedford Interactive Productions Ltd. For further information see references. Also see *Dance Composition* (2000) for a detailed description of ways in which the pack can be used to teach composition.

employed the above CD resource pack to interrelate theoretical study of conceptual and analysis bases for dance with practical choreography work. This course demonstrated that through visual exemplification of analysis tools, students learn at a faster rate and can apply the principles and concepts learned from the multimedia pack to aid their own practical creative work and their theoretical analysis of other dance works. The latter work was assessed and staff noted a vast improvement in acquisition and consolidation of concepts and principles studied at this initial stage of the degree. Some sample worksheets and descriptions on how they might be used at this level are included in the appendix.

Testimony to this pack and to the embedded resource-based teaching/learning approach is provided below in a review written by a lecturer working with both physical education and dance specialist post-graduate students in a university's teacher training courses:

> Working in higher education, the resource pack has made a valuable contribution to every module I have taught this year. Indeed, having begun to explore its possibilities I have become increasingly aware of how much more it has to offer. Students learn to use the CD-i very quickly, hence it has contributed to teaching/learning in both lectures and directed study time.
>
> To date, worksheets on dance content and dance form have proved particularly valuable in helping students to understand these aspects of composition. As a result they have been able, in directed study time, to compose their own dances in response to tasks selected from the appropriate worksheets.
>
> Some understanding of a resource-based approach to teaching dance as art in education is a prerequisite for successful interaction with the resource pack. Knowledge of the conceptual framework upon which the pack is based enables the user to plan a route through the contents appropriate for delivery of desired learning outcomes.
>
> At present the *Wild Child CD-i Resource Pack* is the only one of its kind. This is a pity since a library of such resources is much needed. However the resource pack offers such breadth and depth and is so versatile that it provides an almost inexhaustible resource to which students can be referred... the *Wild Child Resource Pack* provides a template for the study of other dance-as-art resources, and as such makes a significant contribution to the world of dance in education.
>
> Killingbeck (2000: 225)

This review acknowledges that technology can and should be employed to enhance dance education resources and points to the current lack of new multimedia resources. It also endorses the approach taken by the authors of *Wild Child* in that the pedagogy clearly dictates the range of multimedia techniques employed, and that ease and flexibility of use is prioritised over 'clever tricks' technology.

The second product to have emerged is the *William Forsythe Improvisation Technologies* (1999) CD ROM with a booklet. This is very different and much more limited in its use than the *Wild Child* resource, in that it features the choreographer's personal approach to improvisation rather than a full dance work. The breakdown of principles behind William Forsythe's improvisation techniques may provide very useful starting points for dance students' own explorations of movement content. The analysis certainly gives an in-depth insight into the sources of his style of choreographic movement and so, as a resource to support research of William Forsythe's distinctive approaches to choreography, the students have a wonderful text. It is a pity, however, that the booklet has nothing in it to aid the teacher or student in how the CD ROM disc could be used to support practical dance creating and performing activities.

To be fair, it has only recently become possible to present video at its real-time speed and in nearly full-screen images on CD ROM discs. This is why the *Wild Child* video footage (56 minutes long) was put onto a video-based technology (CD-i) in the first instance. However, the demise of the latter and, as yet, the lack of interactivity in its successor DVD technology, has forced us to shift to a computer based technology – CD ROM. It is predicted that in the next few years, the necessary digital video requirements in terms of speed and quantity will be addressed so that CD ROMs and downloading of resource materials over the Internet becomes the norm rather than the exception.

The above text has focused on video-based resource packs featuring the work of professional choreographers and performers. There are, of course, websites that can be accessed as important information banks for lecturers and students in tertiary education. These are certainly useful endorsements or extensions of materials that might be found in books or on linear video. Students are becoming very used to searching for information on choreographers, etc. to inform their essays or lecture demonstrations, for example. However, to date, access to quality video demonstrations of their work over the Internet is limited.

Alternative dance and technology experiments, both in live performance spaces and via the Internet, have proliferated in the past decade or so. Most of these experiments result in the use of technology to add to or change the dancers' bodies, the space, sound, time or 'real' aspects of a performance. Certainly, study of and perhaps experimenting with choreographers' uses of technology to shift and change our perceptions from the real to the virtual, or to add animations or filmic features that extend/alter meanings in choreography, should feature in the students' courses if they are to be able to embrace new works that challenge the concept of dance. As in all such marriages between forms, some dance and technology merges may be nominated as examples of a 'new' art form. Students in higher education should be led to confront and discuss such views.

In addition to experiments in the use of technology in choreography and performance, some researchers have attempted to create resources that provide users with animated figures or video clips of real people so that they can choreograph on the computer. *Life Forms* published by Credo Interactive Corporation is a well-known CD ROM-based resource that fits the former description. Sita Popat's web-based *Hands On Project* 1999–2000[4] fits the latter description. This project, through carefully-planned frameworks created by the author, aims to engage any interested participants in an interactive dance-making process. This website is the most advanced of its kind so it must be taken account of in the context of serious application of technology in teaching/learning dance composition.

Resource-based teaching/learning in tertiary dance education then, to some extent, has employed advances in technology. However, the creation of resources that expose the intricacies in the dance works of professional choreographers for the benefit of students' learning lags behind. It is hoped that the next few years will redress this gap in provision of resources for dance at all levels of education.

Conclusion

Throughout this book the *midway* art of dance model has promoted a multi-dimensional approach in that it is strongly contended that all three strands (creating, performing and appreciating) are

[4]http://www.satorimedia.com/hands_on/

experienced as interdependent. Higher education is no exception. Even though the content is split into separate modules with an emphasis on performance rather than choreography, it all builds towards an in-depth appreciation of the art of dance. Creating, performing and appreciating dances permeate the modular programme described in this chapter.

The model described can justifiably be claimed as a *midway* model in that there is evidence of elements of both the *professional* and *educational* models, albeit much altered through time. There is also evidence to support the view that the art of dance in tertiary education contributes towards artistic, aesthetic and cultural education and employs a modified form of resource-based teaching.

Conclusion

Chapters 2, 3 and 4 have demonstrated the inextricable relationship between current good practice and the theory expounded in chapter 1 for the *midway* model of the art of dance in education.

The distinctive features of this model are important in dance experiences in all sectors – primary, secondary and tertiary education. These are:

a. the three processes of creating, performing and appreciating;
b. emphasis on dances;
c. the education that these lead to – artistic, aesthetic and cultural.

This book has defined the distinctiveness of the *midway* model in the above terms and in terms of a combination of aspects from two opposing models to warrant the title of *midway* model for the art of dance in education. The degrees to which each sector employs these aspects might be illustrated as in the table on page 196.

This is an attempt to show the different emphases put on the retained aspects of the *educational* and *professional* models by primary, secondary and tertiary education practitioners respectively. It therefore identifies differences in interpretation of the *midway* model in the varying educational contexts.

The feature not listed above, but which has been discussed in all three contexts as an essential means of delivering qualitative learning experiences in the art of dance in education, is resource-based teaching/learning. While access to live dance performances must remain at the top of the priority list in the art of dance in education, the essential back-up resources, especially video and new technology CD or DVD recordings, are very sparse indeed.

It is surely time that dance teachers, in common with other arts teachers – music, art, drama and poetry, for example – could

Features retained from the educational *and* professional *models*

EDUCATIONAL MODEL	PROFESSIONAL MODEL
Emphasis on the process	Emphasis on the product
Emphasis on development of creativity, imagination and individuality	Emphasis on knowledge of theatre dance as the model towards which to aspire
Emphasis on feelings – subjectivity of experience	Emphasis on objective ends, e.g. trained bodies for performance of dances
Emphasis on a set of principles as a source of content	Emphasis on stylistically-defined dance techniques as content
Emphasis on a problem-solving approach to teaching: teacher as a guide, pupil as agent in own learning	Emphasis on directed teaching: teacher as expert, pupil as apprentice

THE ART OF DANCE IN EDUCATION MIDWAY MODEL

←——— PRIMARY ————————————————→
←——————————— SECONDARY ———————→
←——————————————————— TERTIARY ———→

purchase such resources and accompanying materials to support the content of lessons/lectures. It is salutary to note that since the first edition of this book (1994) there has been little improvement in the number and availability of quality resources. In the UK, the National Resource Centre for Dance has developed a short list of resource packs for sale, and some dance companies have produced packs based on their dance works included in examination syllabuses. However, as stated earlier in the book, all of these packs are based on the old linear videos and accompanying texts that can frequently be described as information leaflets about the choreographer/s and the company. Hence, there is a lack of teaching material presented in the accompanying books and so there is little interaction between the video and the texts.

Consequently and alarmingly in 2001, it is still relevant to note that:

...these packs do not yet contain the comprehensiveness, level or depth of treatment of topics needed, especially for A level courses and beyond. Moreover, packs that contain a linear video combined with notes, books, slides, literature, pictures, worksheets, etc. are becoming outmoded now that interactive video is on the market.

Smith-Autard (1994: 152)

To take us forward from 1994, chapter 1 in this new edition established the rationale and need for interactive CD resource packs and described the new CD-i/CD ROM *Wild Child Resource Pack* (1999)[1] for dance education in all sectors. Subsequent chapters made reference to this pack as exemplary in employing a resource-based teaching and learning approach in the context of the art of dance *midway* model.

In 2001, however, the pack – written by the author with Jim Schofield – is still the first and only pack of its type in the world. Perhaps it is not surprising that other packs of this nature have not yet been produced. In a constantly-changing technology environment (from laser vision to CD-i to CD ROM), it is certainly difficult to maintain the quality of touch-button controlled video presentation at the real-time rate (25 frames per second minimum) and near to full-screen images for video footage of reasonable lengths of time packed with other materials such as text, voice-overs, drawings and animations. These features are essential if teachers are to have flexible, user-friendly resources to support and enhance the teaching and learning of dance. Unfortunately, to date, it takes a great deal of expertise, funding and time to author such resources. There is no one piece of software or easy recipe to combine programs so that dance teachers with a little computer knowledge could write resource packs. However, new pieces of software incorporating new multimedia techniques and new capacities for downloading video onto and from the Internet are all under development, so hopefully, processes will become easier, much cheaper and within the capabilities of dance teacher authors of the future.

This future has to be on the horizon into the new millennium and so the *midway* model of the art of dance in education will become further established as access to such resource materials improves.

---

[1] See the Resources List at the end of the book for more details and/or go to www.dance-interactive.web.com

Appendix

Content of this appendix

The intention here is to offer primary and secondary teachers alternative dance frameworks and to show the relationship of the content in each of these frameworks to the syllabuses presented in chapter 2 or 3.

Teachers will also find some example charts and worksheets from the *Wild Child CD Resource Pack*, not only to demonstrate the value of such a resource to achieve depth in teaching and learning through use of a professional dance work, but also to show teachers how they might write their own worksheets to support teaching and learning through use of video/CD resources.

Alternative dance frameworks and learning activities appropriate for the delivery of the syllabus for Stages 1–2

1. *Balloon Dance* YEAR 1

DANCE FRAMEWORK

Section 1: grow and shrink into different body shapes (balloon shapes) three times moving slowly, stopping and going to indicate blowing up

Section 2: float and burst with a jump to fall

LEARNING ACTIVITIES

DANCE CONTENT – ACTIONS: whole body actions – stretch and curl

DANCE CONTENT – QUALITIES: slow and interrupted

DANCE CONTENT – ACTIONS: travel, jump and fall

DANCE CONTENT – QUALITIES: soft, gentle travel and jumps free and up in space into strong, quick jump and relaxed fall

DANCE THEMES AND STIMULI: create image of balloons through the above

DANCE FORM – MAKING DANCES: create improvised responses to tasks; perform whole dance

Accompaniment: sound effect of blowing balloon up slowly three times. Light , soft continuous music for travel and bang on drum or children shouting BANG at the end.

2. *Journey on a Strange Planet* YEAR 2

DANCE FRAMEWORK

Emphasis on use of feet:

Introduction: from sleep stillness get up as though sleep walking

Sections 1–4: use feet and knees on spot and travelling to suggest changing surfaces – bouncy (trampoline), sandy, sticky (treacle) and hot

Conclusion: spin into bed place and wake up from a dream!

LEARNING ACTIVITIES

DANCE CONTENT – ACTIONS: use of whole body – stretch into use of parts of the feet – full variety

DANCE CONTENT – QUALITIES/ SPACE: quick, slow, light, continuous, stopping in different directions

DANCE THEMES AND STIMULI: respond to changing stimuli with varied expression

DANCE FORM – MAKING DANCES: improvise within structured tasks; perform whole dance

Accompaniment: bouncy music (electronic, perhaps) which also has changes in it for sandy and sticky parts. The 'hot section' music could be played at double speed to achieve the effect in movement.

3. *Clown Dance* YEAR 4

DANCE FRAMEWORK

Section 1: Travel with 'funny' runs – around 'ring' – variety

Section 2: create balances on different body parts – funny

Section 3: 'funny' walks taking weight on parts of feet – variety

Section 4: partner work – over, under, through, around, on, off – create sequence

Section 5: repeat section 1, falling over to finish

LEARNING ACTIVITIES

DANCE CONTENT – ACTIONS: discover different runs and gestures, combine balancing/still body shapes; discover different ways of walking

DANCE CONTENT – QUALITIES/ SPACE: use combinations of speed, force, continuity and aspects of space to vary

THEMES AND STIMULI: use music effectively; express 'funny' character appropriately

DANCE FORM – MAKING DANCES: improvise sections 1, 3, 5; create motifs for 2 and 4; perform whole dance

Accompaniment: any lively circus music with a strong beat and clear phrasing.

Alternative dance framework and learning activities appropriate for the delivery of the syllabus for Stage 3

1. *Storm Dance* YEAR 7

DANCE FRAMEWORK

Whole class dance – solo in group

Section 1: from Karate position move across space with acceleration, increasing size of steps. Repeat three times, end in space

Section 2: perform taught motif

Section 3: rush to one side and perform three lightning actions; repeat to other side in unison

Section 4: rush to space and perform percussive solo storm

Section 5: rush in circle; jump with claps of parts touching in air, e.g. hands to knees; spin and fall to end

LEARNING ACTIVITIES

DANCE COMPOSITION: select from exploration to make martial arts motif into travel plus slow arm swirling

DANCE PERFORMANCE: learn motif concentrating on qualities

DANCE COMPOSITION: select from exploration of striking actions using appropriate qualities – abstracting from forking, striking, sheet, cracks and rumbles of thunder, pelting rain, etc.; improvise variety of percussive actions – thunder, lightning, rain, wind mixed to form repeated motifs; use music phrasing and dynamic qualities to help dance expression

DANCE PERFORMANCE: perform solo within the group

DANCE APPRECIATION: a range of viewing, describing and interpreting tasks in lessons including written work

Accompaniment: the above framework was created to fit Elgar's *Enigma Variations –* (*Troyte*).

A dance framework, learning activities and lesson planning appropriate for the delivery of the syllabus for late in Stage 2 or early in Stage 3 and employing Wild Child CD Resource Pack *as an example of resource-based teaching*

The dance framework below is based upon a section from the scene entitled 'Play' in the Ludus Dance Company's performance of *Wild Child*. In relation to the dance narrative, this is the part in which the 'Wild Child' has gained confidence and performs an initial solo dance. Gradually the other three dancers join in and then they all dance together in canon and unison.

An example DANCE FRAMEWORK

DANCE OUTCOME: 'Joining in'   **Music: Track 4** – *Wild Child*

SECTION A: the accumulation in canon of four dancers performing an eight movement sequence twice through.

Dancer 1 starts	**Motif**
Dancer 2 finds an appropriate place to join in with dancer 1	**Repetition**
Dancer 3 finds an appropriate place to join in with dancers 1 and 2	**Repetition**
Dancer 4 finds an appropriate place to join in with dancers 1, 2 and 3	**Repetition**

SECTION B: repeat the sequence in unison once through   **Repetition**

SECTION C: pairs in canon perform own motif developed out of the above:

Pair A performs	**Development 1**
Pair B performs	**Development 2**
Pair B performs again	**Repetition**
Pair A performs again	**Repetition**

ENDING: find a finishing position to show that you are friends in a group   **Climax**

In order to use the resource effectively, the teacher should create an appreciation worksheet such as the following to guide the students' viewing. Obviously, the relevance of the questions is best appreciated with 'hands on' access to the resource. Nevertheless, the questions can be used as examples to guide teachers in writing their own in relation to the resources they use.

TEACHER'S *Appreciation Worksheet to study aspects of* **DANCE CONTENT** *and of* **DANCE FORM** *in the section entitled 'ADD-IN' from* **Wild Child**

Watch the whole excerpt as many times as required to <u>discuss answers to the following questions</u>:

1. What sort of actions are the dancers using? Why do these actions suit the character of the 'Wild Child'?

2. What kind of jump did you see? How are the rolls and slides performed?

3. Describe the qualities of speed and continuity.

4. The 'Wild Child' starts the action by challenging the others to copy him. How does he do this? Who is the first to add-in? When does this happen in relation to the 'Wild Child's repetition of motifs, and what does the dancer do to start the sequence?

5. Describe how dancers 3 and 4 'add-in'.

6. Canon accumulation is the term used to describe the way in which the dancers join 'add-in'. What does this mean?

7. What happens towards the end to show that they all have joined the game? What is the dance term to describe this?

The above lesson materials can now be employed in formulating the following two lesson plans.

MAIN OUTCOME: *A dance for four based on 'Add-in' in* Play

Learning outcomes Performance	Learning outcomes Composition	Learning outcomes Appreciation
Actions: jumps, rolls, turns, slides Linking actions into sequence Qualities: continuous, with energy and fast Spacing in group Relating in unison and canon	Composing a motif Repeating exactly Simple developments of the initial motif/ sequence Organising 4 dancers in space and time Canon accumulation in 4 Canon 2 + 2	Perceiving all listed under performance and composition in 'Add-in' resource and interpreting meanings Perceiving and commenting on these elements in own and others' dances

Delivery of Lesson Material using the
Wild Child CD Resource Pack

LESSON 1

Appreciation

- Set the context of this excerpt of *Wild Child*. View 'Add-in' all the way through. Then watch the 'Wild Child's solo motif'.

- Appreciation Worksheet questions 1 and 2.

Performance and Composition – using music

- Warm-up: travel fast on feet anywhere in space and perform a quick turn when teacher calls out 'turn'.

> Teaching Points: Travel with the music and turn without stopping moving feet fast. Like the 'Wild Child', lean your body into the turning movement to keep it continuous. Practise to improve.

- Explore rolling actions in a space by yourself.

> Teaching Points: Look for the tucked side roll as performed by the 'Wild Child', a stretched out log side roll, a forward roll, backward roll and the sort of roll the 'Wild Child' performs from a sitting position onto hands and feet and back again. Encourage this range by observing pupils who perform the movements or suggesting them while they explore.

- Now explore jumping actions.

> Teaching Points: Try a straight 2–2 jump, a turning jump, a travelling leap. Bend knees on take-off and landing and stretch in the air during the jump.

- Next explore jumping actions into slides.

> Teaching Points: Try different slides – on sides, in sitting positions travelling backwards. Land from jumps, bend knees into slides taking care to look where they are going. Link the 2 movements smoothly.

- Working in twos, both doing the same movements in unison, make a sequence using the 4 actions of **jump**, **slide**, **roll** and **turn** onto feet at the end in this order.

- Practise the sequence with the music, linking all actions to make them continuous.

- Now link with another pair and teach each other the two sequences. You now have 8 movements – **jump**, **slide**, **roll** and **turn** (pair 1) and **jump**, **slide**, **roll** and **turn** (pair 2).

Appreciation

- Set the resource disc to play from just before the unison section at the end and ask the pupils to watch this section, noting how well the dancers perform together and the energy and continuity in their movements. (Question 7 on the Appreciation Worksheet.)

Performance and Composition – using music

- Practise the unison Section B of the dance with the music (this is virtually the same all the way through so it does not matter where you start).

> Teaching Points: Make sure the pupils are evenly spaced. Concentrate their attention on rhythm and timing to ensure that they keep together.

Appreciation

Half the class watch and appraise the other half considering both composition and performance.

LESSON 2

Appreciation

- Recall the 'Add-in' dance and watch it again, but this time ask the pupils to note the order in which the dancers join in with the 'Wild Child'.

- Appreciation Worksheet questions 3, 4 and 5.

Performance and Composition – using music

- Warm-up as in Lesson 1 then practise Section B of the dance to recall it.

- Work on Section A in the dance and plan the use of space carefully as each dancer joins in.

> Teaching Points: Dancer 1 performs the whole sequence twice through. Dancer 2 joins in at an appropriate point, let us say with the first roll and so on until they are all dancing. There is plenty of time since there are 16 movements overall. So dancer 4 need not come in until movement 12. The spacing organisation is difficult unless they keep to the same pattern established for the unison motif in Section B. This would be easier. Also make sure that those waiting to come in are on the periphery of the space.

- Perform Section A followed by Section B.

- Divide up into the original pairs. Each pair should discuss how their own original sequence of 4 movements can be developed.

> Teaching Points: Change direction, change the speed, add arm movements (to the jump, for example), do two turns rather than one, add a turn to the slide. These are a few ideas. The pupils should make sure that they are keeping the original movements virtually the same but simply making them a little richer or more elaborate.

- Organise and perform Section C in the dance.

> Teaching Points: Make it a kind of game of 'we can do that too'. The couple waiting to dance should watch the pair dancing with interest.

- Create an ending to show that all are friends (like in the resource).

- Practise and perform the whole dance with the music, concentrating on the expression.

- Video and/or watch each other perform the dance.

> Teaching Points: Look for and comment on the composition and performance – the teacher using the learning outcomes as a checklist.

Composing a phrase motif using initiating and supporting contact work in twos derived from analysis of the content in the 'Love Duo' of the **Wild Child CD Resource Pack.** *This work is appropriate for the delivery of the syllabus at Stage 3 or Stage 4*

The following worksheet (taken from the *Wild Child* pack's Resource Book) demonstrates how students can copy specific movements from the resource in order to explore the concepts or principles behind them and then to explore these ideas in their own creative work. This is one way of extending vocabulary and creating from a given to find original dance content.

PRACTICAL WORKSHEET: 'Love Duo' – *initiating and supporting contacts*

Appreciation leading to exploration and composition

1. Study the five examples of initiating and supporting actions on the disc to categorise them into initiating or supporting contact movements or both.

2. With a partner, perform each of the five contact actions to identify its defining characteristics. (For example, the head in hand support is very lightly supportive of a body part in contact with the supporter's body part.) Write a list of the defining characteristics.

3. Take each of these defining characteristics and explore them to find at least three other ways of performing such initiating/supporting contact actions.

4. Concentrate on the rhythmic content of each of your contact actions, identifying the use of impulse, impact and swing to create momentum.

5. Link and mix these together to create phrase motifs symbolising a soft, caring relationship.

6. Watch the sub-section contact duo in the 'Love Duo' on Disc 1 to note how extensively the couple travels and try to use as much floor space as possible while you perform your contact actions travelling from place to place.

Extract from Worksheet 1 – Dance Content Section 2:C:1 *Wild Child Resource Book* Page 3.

Once the phrase motif is composed, the students could be required to turn their attention to improvement of their performance of it by using the resource for reference. The *Wild Child Resource* Disc 2 has a section that is specifically geared to this process. The worksheet below may help teachers to utilise professional performances in a similar manner in order to improve the students' qualitative performance.

PRACTICAL WORKSHEET: contact work – sequences

Study of the sequence from the 'Love Duo' is presented to inform your own performance of contact work sequences that require continuity and fluency. This worksheet aims to reinforce and extend the teaching material on the disc.

Sequence 1: whole phrase – text on the video itself provides teaching points as follows:

Continuity, accents and living pauses

1. Watch the whole phrase through to identify the above three qualities. The following questions may help you to discuss the qualities.

- Where are the accents and what is their function?

- What is meant by 'living pauses' and how many do you perceive?

- What do the dancers have to do to achieve continuity?

2. Now study the sequence by viewing the breakdown. Pay attention to the text descriptions, noting particular words that describe the qualities contributing to a fluent, continuous sequence.

Breakdown: text on screen preceding the video and cues on the video itself provide teaching points as follows:

a. The travel into jump, fall and roll use acceleration to gain momentum.
   CUE: ACCELERATE TO GAIN MOMENTUM

b. The slide, roll and pull-up link seamlessly to end in a pause
CUE: LINK SEAMLESSLY

c. The tip leads into the fall into arms and smooth turn and rise.
CUE: TIP FALL SMOOTH

d. Hand pushes give impetus to the turning partner.
CUE: HAND PUSH IMPETUS

e. A simultaneous lean and spring produces the lift into recovery-moves away.
CUE: LEAN LIFT RECOVER

3. Notice how some words have implicit expressive and rhythmic features – for example, lean, fall and lift. Now formulate a sentence that describes your own phrase and break the phrase into parts, finding words that will bring out the qualities, the pauses and continuity (fluent linking of 'words', commas and full stops) to present the appropriate expression.

Extract from Practical Worksheet 1 – Performance: Technique Section 2:C:2
Wild Child Resource Book Page 9.

Appreciating the 'macro' form of the 'School' section in the **Wild Child CD Resource Pack** *and then using the concepts discovered to develop and vary the students' own motifs. This work is appropriate for study of composition in delivery of the syllabus at Stage 3 or Stage 4*

FORM TIME CHART for 'School' – A PE Lesson

Sections
Step Dance & Learning

A1	A2	B1	A3	B2	A4	A5	B3
Motif	Rep.	Trans.	Rep.	Trans.	Dev.	Rep.	Trans.
8 bars	8	4	8	4	8	4	8

Joins Step Dance

A6	B4	A7	A8	A9	B5
Rep.		Dev.	Dev.	Rep.	Trans.
8	2	6	8	4	4

Change of Game

C1	C2	C3	B6
Motif contrast	Dev.	Dev.	Trans.
6	6	8	6

Repeats to Trial

A10	A11	A12
Var. Cli.	Rep. Var. Cli.	Rep. Var.
6	8	4

The chart above represents the key motif (A), the transitions (B), the contrasting motif (C) and the developments and variations of this content. The use of such a 'storyboard' helps students to perceive form. While they are viewing they could be directed to learn from the choreography by answering the following questions. Also, they could apply what is learned to their own compositions. For example, the students could note ways in which motif A is developed and then use the same methods to develop their motif A.

FORM – RELATED DANCE TASKS WORKSHEET
for 'School'

Appreciation – group discussion or individual tasks to develop perception of form

1. Look at Motif A and describe how the repeats maintain interest though the movements stay the same.

2. Look at and note down how the motif is developed in A4, A7 and A8.

3. What makes A10–12 variations rather than developments?

4. Why do you think there are so many repetitions of Motif A in *School*?

5. Look at all the transition elements labelled B and identify the functions that they have and the similarities and differences between them. Do you agree that they are correctly labelled as transitions?

6. How far do you agree that A10 and A11 constitute the climax of the piece? If you do not agree, give an opinion as to where the climax/es might be.

7. Describe how the interrelationship between the sections labelled A, B and C creates unity of form.

8. To what extent does the form of *School*, including the floor and group patterning, contribute to the theme of this scene in *Wild Child*?

Appreciation and performance building to composition work based on a piece of repertoire (for example, a set technical study for GCSE or A Level) used as a resource in delivery of the syllabus at Stage 4 and above

Performance

1. Learn and perform a technical study set from a previous year's examination (GCSE/AS/A level) and which is available on video (and in notation) or a section of repertoire. (The *Wild Child Resource Pack* contains two such pieces with many multimedia features to aid teaching and learning.)

Appreciation

2. Description and analysis of content:

   a. describe and analyse the main actions in all the contrasting sections of the study
   b. notate or record some key motifs in some way
   c. discuss with a partner whether or not the actions create the contrast in the different sections
   d. describe the qualities of the actions – speed, force, continuity and their role in making the contrast in the sections
   e. notate and/or find words to describe the qualities, using several rather than one word where possible
   f. describe the use of levels, direction and size of movement to make the above sections contrasting

Performance

3. Practise and perform the study in sections, emphasising the contrast in actions, qualities and spatial features.

4. Video your performance and compare it with the professional example – analyse and evaluate:

   a. your accuracy in performance of actions
   b. your ability to link actions into phrases with 'commas' and 'full stops'
   c. your ability to show qualitative contrasts
   d. your use of space (e.g. clear changes of direction, overall coverage of the floor)

Appreciation into performance

5. Describe and analyse the overall form of the study – motifs, phrases, sections, transitions, contrasts, climaxes and repetition of sections. Practise performing the study giving attention to these features of form.

6. Work in twos to identify key movements/short motifs which occur throughout the piece.

   a. choose three of the above and identify:
      - exact repetitions
      - developments of them and how they are developed
      - number of times each is used
   b. identify the movements leading into and out of each of the repeats of the three key movements/motifs
   c. practise performing the movements/motifs, making the differences clear

7. Identify the style of the study:

   a. list the features which create the style
   b. practise the sections of the study in which the features you listed are emphasised
   c. video your performance and evaluate the style of your movements
   d. practise to improve the style

8. Describe the music – its type, its style, its expression, its form – and discuss how it relates to these elements of the dance:

   a. listen to the music with your eyes closed and visualise the movements of the study
   b. select the section of the dance you find most difficult and listen several times to the music, then dance it without the music thinking it in your head
   c. perform the section with the music (it should be improved if you have internalised the rhythm and phrasing)

9. Describe the use of space in the room:
   a. draw the floor pattern of a section containing mostly travelling actions

b. walk the pattern in the space ensuring that the full amount of space is used

c. perform the movements using all the space

d. dance the whole study concentrating on patterning in the stage space

10. View the video performance of the professional dancer and analyse his or her performance skills – focus, alignment, line, projection to an audience, expression, light and shade, sense of form, use of music:

a. use this checklist to evaluate your own performance

b. practise the aspects least good until they are improved

The above activities should help the student understand the extent of work that is involved in 'getting inside' a piece so that it is fully mastered. It is more likely that a successful performance will materialise if the student has thoroughly internalised the complexity of the choreography than if it is taught and learned by rote.

Composition

1. Select the motif you like best in the study or piece of repertoire and use it as a basis for your own choreography:

a. as a solo:
   - through development and variation of the content, actions, spatial features
   - through changing the qualities of time, force and continuity
   - using a different piece of music
   - giving it a different style

b. as a duo or trio:
   - through developing the content for one body and performing the original simultaneously with the development to make the relationship complementary
   - through orchestrating both the original and the development using canon and unison, changing spatial relationships and direction
   - taking the choreography further as determined by the group, possibly using different music and in a different style

   c. create a dance in the style of the technical study/piece of
      repertoire

Composition tasks based on a technical study or section of
professional repertoire from time to time will help students to
become familiar with a vocabulary of movement which is new and
different from their own. In most composition situations, the source
of content is dependent on the student's own limited repertoire.
Employing a piece which they have learned for performance as a
basis for choreography makes them use new movements or a new
style in their own way. These then become a part of their repertoire.

Appreciation, performance and composition work using a resource pack to deliver study of a set work (for example, Siobhan Davies' White Man Sleeps (1988) – an option for the AS/A level syllabus in 2001) combined with the students' own practical dance study

A good resource pack does not only focus on the study required for an examination paper. Rather it permits flexibility of use in that it offers several routes through the contents and different levels of learning. In the art of dance, the headings of composition, performance and appreciation might be a convenient way of organising the content.

Where to begin is the first decision to make in using a resource pack. If, for example, worksheets contain tasks that are progressive, the teacher could decide to take the students through the first tasks only on each worksheet to introduce the topic of the resource pack. Alternatively, students might benefit more if they were to undertake study of the appreciation section first. This should require them to contextualise the topic both historically and culturally. Whatever is decided about the starting point, a good resource pack will promote developmental and progressive threads through each aspect of the topic building towards an overall understanding.

Just as there are different routes through a resource pack, there are many different ways that could be employed in creating a resource pack. The example below is just one – there are many other ways of dealing with the same topic.

Example Resource Pack on Siobhan Davies

(It is important that any work with a resource pack is linked to at least one visit to see the Siobhan Davies Dance Company in live performance.)

The textbook *White Man Sleeps* (1999) is a good resource to assist in analysis of Siobhan Davies' *White Man Sleeps* (1988), more specifically the chapter by Sarah Whatley. This chapter guides students in undertaking analyses of the work to enable them to answer questions that typically arise on Advanced level examination papers. The text below takes a different perspective in that the attempt here is to outline the range of content and activities that might be included in a resource pack consisting of a video or, better still, a CD ROM; of the work or excerpts from it; and an audio disc of the music/sound, texts (books, journal articles, reviews), pictures, programme notes and reference to any relevant websites. (The current website address for the Siobhan Davies Dance Company is www.sddc.org.uk.)

To achieve flexibility of use and an integrated study involving appreciation, performance and composition, the pack might include:

Aims and objectives of the pack and possible routes through it identified.

Appreciation

Study of Siobhan Davies' artistic development (history) and a survey of her works through:

- Background information on Siobhan Davies, for example from books such as Sanjoy Roy (ed) (1999) *White Man Sleeps*, Stephanie Jordan (1992) *Striding Out*, Gill Clarke, 'In conversation with Siobhan Davies' in *Dance Makers Portfolio* (1998 Butterworth, J. and Clarke, G. eds.) and from the website.
- Notes on some of Davies' works in chronological order. These are obtainable from the National Resource Centre for Dance (UK).
- Source materials made up from a series of critics' or authors' statements, reviews and programme notes.
- Essay or discussion questions based on the above readings.

Appreciation

Tasks related to one or more of Siobhan Davies' works to consider:

- treatment of the theme
- aspects of dance content – actions, qualities of movement, use of space and relationships of the dancers to each other, objects and/or the set
- elements of form and orchestration of the dancers in time, space and number
- stylistic features
- characteristics in and use of the music and how the dance relates to it
- the costumes and set in relation to all the above
- sensory and expressive and formal aesthetic qualities

Composition

Based on selected excerpts from the dance work. For example, students could be led to focus on a duo to:

- copy three actions where the dancers are in contact, e.g. balance, counter balance, lean, turn, lift
- employ the qualities listed in the above to link the actions into a motif
- set the duo in spatial relationship with another duo
- video the result
- discuss how far it contains the essence of a Davies style

Performance

Learn and perform a pre-choreographed solo style study based on a solo within a Siobhan Davies work (in the pack recorded in notation and on video). Work on improving performance through:

- considering the meaning and feeling in the words used to describe the movements. For example, relax, drop, fluidly sway, light, continuous, controlled, sustained, throw-away, smooth, sudden, lyrical, soft, giving
- study of the video and the students' performances in some of the ways listed above for the study/repertoire
- using answers to questions on a worksheet to aid writing of an essay on the features of the study that need to be worked on in order to capture Davies' choreographic style

Appreciation

Comparative study of two or three works could help the students to discern changes and developments in Davies' choreography. At the end of about half a term of work with the pack, the students will have developed in-depth knowledge about and appreciation of Davies, her choreographic style, her works and the Company. They will also have extended their own choreographic and performance abilities.

Further Resources

Smith-Autard, J.M. *Dance Composition* – **Fourth Edition (2000)**

There are many ideas for lessons on composition and performance in the above book which are suitable for Stages 3, 4 and above. They include resource-based teaching/learning methods and should be most beneficial for students working towards GCSE, AS and A level standard examinations in the UK or equivalent in other parts of the world.

BBC2 1998 *Sportsbank Special: Dance*

A very useful video containing five 30-minute programmes for Stages 3 and 4 secondary dance education first shown between February 23 and March 23 1998. The five programmes, which contain many demonstrations by professional choreographers and dancers, are entitled:

Teaching today – four teachers teaching dance composition, performance and appreciation.
Programme 1: *Dance Athletes*
Programme 2: *Street Dance*
Programme 3: *Dance Rhythms*
Programme 4: *Dance Partners*

Smith-Autard, J.M. 1998 *Sportsbank Special: Dance*

Teachers' Notes for the above BBC2 *Dance* series – the video material in each programme is used as a basis for further content for teaching dance composition, performance and appreciation.

National Dance Teachers' Association 1998 *Teaching Dance in the Primary School*

A very useful video that shows a range of primary teachers with children aged 4–11. The booklet that accompanies the video gives details of the lesson planning including three dance frameworks, and demonstrates how the teaching meets learning objectives for Stages 1 and 2. (The latter section was written by the author of this book.)

Bibliography
and Further Reading

Abbs, P. (ed) 1987 *Living Powers: the Arts in Education,* London: The Falmer Press
Abbs, P. 1988 *A is for Aesthetic: Essays on Creative and Aesthetic Education* London: The Falmer Press
Abbs, P. (ed) 1989 *The Symbolic Order: a Contemporary Reader for the Arts Debate* London: The Falmer Press
Arts Council 1993 *Dance in Schools* London: Arts Council of Great Britain
Beardsley, M. 1958 Reasons in Aesthetic Judgments in Hospers, J. (ed) *Introductory Readings in Aesthetics* New York: The Free Press, 1969
Best, D. 1985 *Feeling and Reason in the Arts* London: Allen & Unwin
Best, D. 1992 *The Rationality of Feeling* London: The Falmer Press
Brinson, P. 1991 *Dance as Education* London: The Falmer Press
Broudy, H. 1972 *Enlightened Cherishing* Illinois: University of Illinois
Butterworth, J. and Clarke, G. (eds) 1998, *Dance Makers Portfolio – conversations with choreographers* Wakefield: Centre for Dance and Theatre Studies, Bretton Hall
Calouste Gulbenkian Foundation 1980 *Dance Education and Training in Britain* London: Calouste Gulbenkian
Challis, C. 1999, Dancing Bodies: Can the Art of Dance be Restored to Dance Studies? in McFee, G. *Dance, Education and Philosophy* Oxford: Meyer and Meyer Sport, 1999
De Mille, A. 1960 *To a Young Dancer* London: Putnam
Department for Education and Employment 1999, *All our Futures – Creativity, Culture and Education* London: DfEE Publications
Department of National Heritage 1996, *Setting the Scene – The Arts and Young People* London: DNH
Foster, R. 1976 *Knowing in my Bones* London: A & C Black
Foster, J. 1977 *The Influences of Rudolf Laban* London: Lepus Books
Gibson, R. 1982 'The Education of Feeling' in Abbs, P. (ed) 1989 *The Symbolic Order: a Contemporary Reader for The Arts Debate* London: Falmer Press
Glasstone, R. 1986 'Selection and its influence on the training of dancers' in *The Growing Child in Competitive Sport* London: Hodder and Stoughton
Graham, M. 1935 quoted in *Martha Graham* Armitage M. (ed), NY: Dance Horizons
Gough, M. 1993 *In Touch with Dance* Lancaster: Whitehorn Books
Harlow, M. and Rolfe, L. 1992 *Let's Dance: a Handbook for Teachers* London: BBC Education

Harrison, K. and Auty, J. 1991 *Dance Ideas for Teachers, Students and Children* London: Hodder and Stoughton

Haynes, A. 1987 'Changing Perspectives in Dance Education' in Abbs, P. *Living Powers* London: Falmer Press

Jobbins, V. 2000 'Dance in Curriculum 2000' in *Dance Matters* National Dance Teachers' Association Spring Edition, 2000

Jordan, S. 1992 *Striding Out* London: Dance Books

Killingbeck, M. 2000 'Wild Child Resource Pack' in *Research in Dance Education Vol. 1 No. 2* London: Carfax Publishing, Taylor Francis

Laban, R. 1948 *Modern Educational Dance* London: Macdonald and Evans

Langer, S. 1953 *Feeling and Form* NY: Routledge and Kegan Paul

McFee, G. 1999 *Dance, Education and Philosophy* Oxford: Meyer and Meyer Sport

National Dance Teachers' Association 1993 *Dance Matters* Winter Term NDTA

Northern Examinations and Assessment Board, General Certificate of Education, *Dance* AS and A Level Syllabus for 2001

Northern Examinations and Assessment Board, General Certificate of Education, *Performing Arts: Dance* GCSE Syllabus for 2001 and 2002

Office for Standards in Education 1998 *The Arts Inspected* London: Heinemann

Osborne, H. 1970 *The Art of Appreciation* Oxford: Oxford University Press

Pring, R. 1976 *Knowledge and Schooling* London: Open Books Publishing Ltd

Redfern, H.B. 1972 'Dance as Art, Dance as Education' in *Collected Conference Papers in Dance* (1973) ATCDE

    1973 *Concepts in Modern Educational Dance* London: Henry Kimpton Publishers

    1986 *Questions in Aesthetic Education* London: Allen and Unwin

Reid, L.A. 1969 *Meaning in the Arts* London: Allen & Unwin

    1981 'Knowledge, Knowing and Becoming Educated' in *Journal of Curriculum Studies* Vol. 13 No.2

    1983 'Aesthetic Knowing' in Ross, M. *The Arts – a Way of Knowing* Oxford: Pergamon Press

    1986 *Ways of Understanding and Education* London: Heinemann Educational Books

Robertson, A. and Hutera, D. 1988 *The Dance Handbook* London: Longman

Rolfe, L. and Harlow. M. 1997 *Let's Look at Dance* London: David Fulton Publishers

Russell, J. 1974 'Dance in Education – Artefact or Expression' in *Laban Art of Movement Guild Magazine* No.52

Smith-Autard, J.M. 2000 *Dance Composition* (4th edition) London: A & C Black

    1994 'Expression and Form in the Art of Dance in Education' 6th *DaCi Conference Proceedings* Sydney, Australia: Macquarie University

    1995 'Dance at Key Stages 1 and 2' *Teaching Physical Education at Key Stages 1 and 2* London: PEAUK

    1997 Four lecture/demonstration papers – 'Resource-based Teaching and Learning'; 'Multimedia and Resource-based Teaching'; 'Design of a Multimedia Title'; 'Video Capture and Video Edit' in *Proceedings of The Workshop in Multimedia and Dance Pedagogy – Developing Expertise* University of Limerick, Ireland

    1999 'New Technologies applied to New Approaches in Dance Teaching' in *Conference Preceedings: Dancing with the Mouse – Format for the Future* S. Carolina: Winthrop University Press, USA

Smith-Autard, J.M. & Schofield, J.

    1995 'Resource-based teaching and Interactive Video' *Proceedings of the Conference – Border Tensions* Guildford: University of Surrey

1995 'Technology or Pedagogy – Multimedia and Dance' *Proceedings of 2nd International Congress on Dance and Research* Brussels: Vrije Uni

1995 'Developments in Dance Pedagogy through Application of Multimedia in Interactive Video' *Proceedings of Dance '95 – Move into the Future* Wakefield, Yorkshire: Bretton Hall College

2001 'New Technologies Partnering New Approaches in Teaching Dance' in *CADE 2001, Glasgow – Proceedings* Glasgow: School of Art Press

Smith, J.M. 1976 *Dance Composition: a Practical Guide for Teachers* (1st edition) London: Lepus

1982 'Technique and Style as aspects of Expression in Dance' in *Conference Papers in Dance* Vol. 3 NATFHE and British Society of Aesthetics

1987 'New Directions in Dance Education' in *The British Journal of Physical Education* Vol. 18 No.3

1988 'Dance as Art Education: New Directions' in Young People Dancing 4th International Conference – *Dance and the Child International* Vol. 1

1990 'Dance Perspective on the National Curriculum' in *Towards the Future: Dance Education in the 90s* DaCi and NDTA

1991 'Teaching Dance Performance in Secondary Education' in *The British Journal of Physical Education* Vol. 22 No.4

Spurgeon, D. 1991 *Dance Moves – from improvisation to dance* Sydney: HBJ Publishers

Stevens, S. 1992 'Dance in the National Curriculum' in Armstrong, N. (ed) *New Directions in Physical Education* Illinois: Human Kinetics Books

Teacher Training Agency 1999 *Using Information and Communications Technology to meet Teaching Objectives in Physical Education – initial teacher training* London: TTA

Witkin, R. 1974 *The Intelligence of Feeling* London: Heinemann Educational Books

Dance works on video employed as resources in the text:

Cohan, R. 1988 *Waterless Method of Swimming Instruction*

Kelly, G. 1952 *Singing in the Rain* (MGM Film)

Video-based resource packs:

BBC 2 1998 *Sportsbank Special: Dance* (video containing five 30-minute programmes for secondary dance education first shown between February 23 and March 23 1998)

Smith-Autard, J.M. 1998 Teachers' Notes for the above BBC2 *Dance* series

National Dance Teachers' Association 1998 Video – *Teaching Dance in the Primary School* published by the National Dance Teachers' Association

CD resource packs:

Bedford Interactive Productions Ltd 1999 *Wild Child – A CD-i Resource Pack for Dance Education* Dewsbury: BIP (see website: www.dance-interactive.web.com)

Bedford Interactive Productions Ltd 2001 *Wild Child – A CD-ROM Resource Pack for Dance Education* Dewsbury: BIP (see website: www.dance-interactive.web.com)

Forsythe, W. 1999 CD ROM *William Forsythe Improvisation Technologies* Frankfurt: ZKM

Index